Last One Out Turn Off the Lights

Is This the Future of American and Canadian Libraries?

Edited by
Susan E. Cleyle
Louise M. McGillis

THE SCARECROW PRESS, INC.
Lanham, Maryland • *Toronto* • *Oxford*
2005

SCARECROW PRESS, INC.

Published in the United States of America
by Scarecrow Press, Inc.
A wholly owned subsidiary of
The Rowman & Littlefield Publishing Group, Inc.
4501 Forbes Boulevard, Suite 200, Lanham, Maryland 20706
www.scarecrowpress.com

PO Box 317
Oxford
OX2 9RU, UK

British Library Cataloguing in Publication Information Available

Library of Congress Cataloging-in-Publication Data

Last one out turn off the lights : is this the future of American and Canadian
libraries? / edited by Susan E. Cleyle, Louise M. McGillis.
    p. cm.
  Includes bibliographical references.
  ISBN 0-8108-5192-X (pbk. : alk. paper)
  1. Internet in library reference services—United States. 2. Internet in library
reference services—Canada. 3. Reference services (Libraries)—Forecasting.
4. Internet searching—United States. 5. Internet searching—Canada. I.
Cleyle, Susan E., 1965– II. McGillis, Louise M., 1963–

Z711.47.L37 2005
025.5'2—dc22
                                                            2004020419

∞™ The paper used in this publication meets the minimum requirements of
American National Standard for Information Sciences—Permanence of Paper
for Printed Library Materials, ANSI/NISO Z39.48-1992.
Manufactured in the United States of America.

To

Sarah, Thea, Jane, and Maren,
library users of tomorrow

Contents

Contents

Preface

Roch Carrier

The other day I met a learned scientist whose research is very special-ized. I asked him about the libraries he uses to help him find the infor-mation he needs to carry out his work. "It's not the library that I use," he replied. "My colleagues and I use the information linked to the hu-man genome project. We use that network to communicate and to share information." This encounter made me wonder, not for the first time, about the future of libraries. Just a few weeks earlier, I had spo-ken with a prominent lawyer, on his way to plead an important case, who told me that he did not need libraries at all to do his research. I also meet many kids who find everything they need on the Internet and for whom a library is an ugly room at school filled with old books.

Am I exaggerating?

Wondering about libraries was not a preoccupation of my youth. Growing up, I did not have many books close at hand. There was no library in either the school or the community. Later I came to know li-braries as I studied, wrote, researched, and taught. Most recently, since my appointment as national librarian of Canada in 1999, I have come to haunt libraries—seeking to understand what they do now and imag-ining what they might do in the future.

My travels across Canada have included many visits to libraries; meetings with librarians; readings to kids; and discussions with teach-ers, readers, and researchers. I have learned about summer reading clubs, cataloging-in-publication data, and virtual reference service.

Many a patient practitioner has explained metadata to me. I have come to know about the preservation needs of newspapers, for example, and the challenges facing the print disabled. And I have been troubled and moved by the twin problems of low literacy among young people and inadequate school libraries.

I have welcomed all these encounters, many of which have been enlightening and encouraging. Today's libraries are innovative enterprises, connecting with their communities in ways that would have been unimaginable to earlier generations. Yet, while programs may have changed, and the means of delivering them would astound our predecessors, the values of libraries remain constant. The threads that tie the first reading rooms in this country to today's digital libraries are values, and very Canadian values at that.

In response to a growing sense of awareness and pride in Canadian creativity and ingenuity, as evidenced by our publishing, and through the concerted and tireless efforts of a lobby of librarians, scholars, and concerned Canadians, Parliament created the National Library of Canada as a federal cultural institution in 1953. The National Library was founded on the values of pride in our culture and of equal access to information for all Canadians.

When national archivist Ian E. Wilson and I began to talk about the future of the National Archives and the National Library of Canada, we knew we had to make changes if we were to be relevant to Canadians. Our collections are incomparable, but for many they are also invisible and impenetrable. School kids, for example, want information in every format, and they want to find it easily. The competition is everywhere, especially on the Internet. If we are going to compete, if we are going to be relevant, if we are going to help Canadians, then we are going to have to change.

The first direction for our change is as follows: a new kind of knowledge institution with a more proactive role in serving Canadians. We must find new ways of serving the users. To do so, we need to determine what the "competition" is doing. Many are going for monetary profit in the "business of information." Libraries must be more innovative than the competition. A young and experienced CEO of one of these businesses told me, "Today, if it's not easy and fun, people have no interest." While I don't necessarily agree, after a while I came to realize that librarians must pay attention to this comment.

The other directions for change include a truly national institution with increased presence, services, and impact throughout the country;

Preface xi

one national collection based on partnerships and networks; a prime learning destination; and a lead institution in knowledge and information management. Acting on these directions will follow tried and true library practices: consulting with partners; understanding the communities we are serving; adapting innovative technology to library service; taking risks; and working with others, in networks, to serve Canadians better. Virtual Reference Canada is an example of a good partnership.

Fifty years after the founding of the National Library of Canada, a new institution—Library and Archives Canada—is taking shape. Library and Archives Canada will embrace and reflect this country's diversity of voices and experience in its collections, its staff, and its partners. It will welcome and accommodate information seekers of all kinds. It will reach out to communities and share with them the collection it holds on their behalf. It will offer equality of service to all and respect both intellectual freedom and the rights of creators and consumers of information. Moreover, through its programs and international initiatives it will project these Canadian values abroad.

The future of Library and Archives Canada will be built through partnership with archives and libraries and other partners across this country. Our future, the future of libraries, will be built on Canadian values. This twenty-first century will be the steward of our documentary heritage and will be a source of enduring knowledge accessible to all. Libraries are about preserving the past to create the present and prepare the future.

Note: Since this preface was written, Carrier's vision has become a reality with the formation of Libraries and Archives Canada. Carrier served as national librarian from October 1999 until his retirement in June 2004. In September 2004, Ian Wilson was officially appointed to the newly created position, librarian and archivist of Canada.

Acknowledgments

In the course of putting this book together we received the support of a number of individuals and institutions. We would like to thank Memorial University of Newfoundland and Sir Wilfred Grenfell College in Corner Brook. For their support and belief in the project, we would like to thank Susan Easun and Norman Horrocks. Thanks to Ian Galloway and Jessica McCleary of Scarecrow Press for seeing the book through to press. For her advice, ideas, and honesty, we would like to thank Elizabeth Behrens. We would also like to thank John Holmes for his help with the cover photo. Finally, a very special thanks goes to Don Duffie and David Peddle, our husbands, whose unconditional support made it possible for us to realize this project.

Introduction

Change the Lightbulb or Flip the Switch—Our Choice!

Susan E. Cleyle and Louise M. McGillis

Feeling good about being a librarian in the twenty-first century? Think you have a handle on the technology and the many different information choices available today? Let's face it, libraries and librarians are perfectly situated to shine in the information age; after all, our business is the acquisition, organization, and dissemination of information. If we are feeling so confident about the future, why is the literature filled with articles trying to find a place for us to fit, and why are we in a state of collective amazement that we may not be the information resource of choice for many of the technologically savvy users of today? We are no longer in the forefront—we are losing users, and as a result, librarians are being challenged to shape up or be permanently relegated to the sidelines.

If we are losing users today, what will become of us tomorrow? We have toddler-age children whose toy cash registers came with debit cards and to whom the mouse is like a sixth finger. In addition to feeling confident using technology, these new users are growing up in a culture of immediate gratification. They want the information and they want it now! They also want their information experiences to be fun and entertaining. How will we serve and communicate with these new users? It is clear we need to move from the traditional "come to us" service to a new and innovative "get the service to you" model. How do we achieve this? How do we get back in the game and preserve what is good, while at the same time move forward and do new things in very different ways?

We need to get up and get out from behind our reference, cataloging, or collections desks and meet users "where they're at." This is a tough sell for many of us who know the information business and have long-held beliefs about what libraries need to be and what we think users need. How do we make change happen? We need administrators who will make tough decisions and who are willing to look beyond the traditional for solutions. We need new, energetic frontline workers who will listen, implement, and change. Finally we need those who cannot make the leap to find places where they can contribute without impeding innovation.

This book looks at the future and speculates about the role of librarians in it. Will librarians even be around, or should we call it a day, turn off the lights, and leave the information business to webmasters, vendors, and users themselves? Contributors were asked to view their topics from new perspectives and to think about the future outside the box of traditional librarianship. The result is a thought-provoking read that dares the reader and ultimately the profession to take action. The five parts encompass a variety of writers from both the United States and Canada. Our experiences, achievements, and circumstances are similar, and as a result, the challenges to the profession on both sides of the border are parallel.

The chapters in the first part address the challenges facing librarians by examining the tug of war between libraries and the web. Irene McDermott tackles this topic head on, arguing that if librarians want to be relevant to this new user group, they need to tap into the technology and investigate 24/7 reference, live chat, and cell phone reference. As McDermott notes, "We must become as easy to use as microwave ovens, as ubiquitous as Google." Stephen Good reminds readers that librarians must achieve a balance by seeking out both the best of the innovative (that sexy new technology) and the traditional (those solid library values). Amanda Etches-Johnson also focuses on technology by looking at "blogs," demonstrating how they can be used to build community and information links with our technically advanced users. Like many contributors, she talks about the need for librarians to step out of the comfort zone and embrace XML.

Libraries are being tested by bookstores such as Chapters and Barnes & Noble. Some argue they are the libraries of the future, with their inviting children's areas, coffee shops, and well-stocked magazine sections. Librarians see the popularity of these places as a clear indication of a need for the "library as place." Should librarians shrink print collections to make space for teaching facilities, reading and viewing rooms, information commons, and coffee shops? Is this a desperate measure to keep our buildings alive or a recognition that the library serves a different role because it is the heart of a different kind of community? Users of today want their library visits to be as interesting, entertaining, and relevant as their other life experiences.

The chapters in the second part address the topic of "library as place." Ruth E. Kifer presents a look into the academic library of the future. She argues that with its food court, neon lights, and focus on access over print, the Johnson Center Library is providing a new kind of research environment. Paul Whitney discusses how the Carnegie Library evolved from a traditional grandiose library to a sanctuary for Vancouver's most needy citizens. According to the author, "Although social workers are sometimes more prevalent than library workers, the provision of books and information along with the promotion of literacy and Internet skills remain central to the service provided by present-day Carnegie staff." Patricia Jobb provides insights into how the space of public and school libraries can work together to provide students with new and innovative library services. While these articles focus directly on the topic "library as place," this concept weaves a thread throughout the book. John Teskey notes the growth of the information commons in academic libraries, while Stephen Good defends the need for "comfy furniture, chess sets, peace and quiet, and of course, story time."

Resources hold our future in the balance. What about paper? Are books a thing of the past? Electronic journals have certainly changed the way librarians do business, shifting the focus from ownership to access. Will the future of librarianship be reduced to acting as a link between the user and the vendor, or will the future involve building truly user-friendly gateways (with the complexities residing on the back end) to the multitude of information sources available?

The chapters in the third part of the book look at the consequence of "pushing to the desktop" and reflect whether it is indeed "the end of the world as we know it." All authors agree, while it means "death" for some things, it also means the beginning of new opportunities for librarians. Roy Tennant suggests it is the end of the age of MARC and AACR2 but the beginning of a new age in which librarians can provide focused access through the development of federated searching. He argues that while librarians missed the boat in the first wave of the Internet, it is not too late to catch the second wave. If we incorporate the web more fully and offer the best collection of information resources possible, the web can help us redefine ourselves. John Teskey reviews the first phase of electronic access and some of the collaborative ventures to provide access. While he does not think librarians have taken full advantage of the opportunities presented to them (e.g., library instruction), he outlines some areas where opportunities remain for librarians to make their mark. Melody Burton argues that the rise of electronic access will continue to transform reference services into a "dynamic learning environment" and that we need to make access more intuitive, where we can imagine "a library website with the option 'I'm Feeling Lucky' when faced with a menu of indexes and databases."

If libraries are being changed in an attempt to preserve their existence in a future information world, then so are the people who work in them. What qualifications will the librarian need to work in the library of the future? Will librarians need business, computing, or marketing degrees in addition to or in place of a library degree?

The chapters in the fourth part tackle the controversial topic of certification. Ernie Ingles and Allison Sivak state that "the only constant of our workplaces will be that of continued, rapid change." They advocate in favor of certification and formalized programs in management and suggest the need for functional specialists. This "post-hiring" schooling would give libraries flexibility in their hiring and would result in the socialization of library values and practices. Barbara K. Stripling also favors certification, focusing her article on ALA-APA's certification program and how it will result in a better-prepared profession based on competencies and knowledge. Taking the other side of the debate, Alison Nussbaumer advocates against certification, arguing that formalized programs will not help librarians improve their status, salary, or working conditions, goals she sees as achievable through changes to library school curriculums and the pursuit of professional development tailored to the individual librarian. The need for new kinds of library workers is also noted by Ruth E. Kifer, who points out that in addition to creating a new physical space, librarians need to think about the people working in these spaces. She states, "Perhaps we should begin to look to the retail environment for our recruits and not be afraid to create marketing positions within our organizations."

Association work outside of the library has always been an integral part of our professional fabric. While just about all librarians belong to a library association sometime during their careers, the length and depth of this involvement vary, along with perceptions of its value. Are library associations doing their job? If they are failing today, how can they succeed tomorrow?

The chapters in the fifth and final part look at the value of associations and reflect on how they can position themselves to serve a very different profession and professional. Helen H. Spalding and Mary Ellen K. Davis from the Association of College and Research Libraries present a challenging piece about the impact a changing social fabric has on the profession and, in turn, the association that services that profession. Barry Bishop reviews the success of the Texas Library Association, attributing much of it to the fact that TLA is responsive to its membership. Madeleine Lefebvre and Don Butcher from the Canadian Library Association examine the generation gap between new professionals and retiring librarians and argue the need for a national association that focuses on lobbying, advocacy, and building a community of shared values. Finally Gillian Byrne, a new professional, provides an honest and direct discussion about why associations don't speak to her. She feels she is not being allowed to participate and indicates that library associations have shut her out. She offers suggestions and solutions and provides a warning: "Let me play or I will not pay."

This entire book has a common theme: The ground underneath libraries is shifting. A new generation of users is before us, and they want a library that reflects their needs and wishes. Are we up to the task of resoling our comfortable shoes and going where users want to take us? Not changing will prove disastrous. If we are not willing to respond to the technological and societal shifts, we might as well call it a day, turn off the library lights, go home to our computers, and "do a Google" search just like our users. We need to act and we need to act now. We still have a great deal to offer, but we must stand up, move out from behind our desks, and prove it.

Enjoy!

Part 1

THE TUG OF WAR BETWEEN LIBRARIES AND THE WEB: WHO WILL END UP IN THE DIRT?

In the end, the web will not defeat us. We will use it to pull ourselves out of the dirt, to wipe off our sensible shoes, and to triumph.

—Irene E. McDermott

Teachers use computers; computers don't replace teachers. Ditto librarians.

—Stephen Good

Many libraries have come to the realization that developing their collections and waiting for patrons to come to the library is short sighted and irresponsible.

—Amanda Etches-Johnson

1

The Microwave of the Reference World

Irene E. McDermott

In the year 2000, I bought a new microwave oven. My old microwave dated from about 1978. It still worked, albeit sluggishly. However, I had heard that the new models could do amazing things. So, in spite of my compulsively skinflint nature, I decided to invest in the latest technology—a floor model that, due to a scratch in its paint, was marked down by 30 percent. Wow, was I glad I did. My new microwave uses sensor technology; that is, it detects steam coming off hot food. I toss in a frozen dinner, touch the Frozen Dinner button on the control pad, and my "Healthy Choice" comes out just right. I push the Rice button, and the machine heats my rice to perfection: no burning, no crunchy morsels. I select the Sensor Reheat tab, and last night's lasagna comes out perfectly piping hot.

Now, the questions arise: Does the availability of this new technology signal the end of cooking as we know it? Have broiling, searing, and reducing become mere memories? The popularity of the Food Network and such magazines as *Gourmet* and *Bon Appétit* suggests this is not true. I am not, and will never be, a "foodie," a person who delights in preparing fabulous repasts. Still, I am fortunate to have foodie friends who invite me over for the most elaborate and delightful meals. Here's the funny thing: These cooking experts use the best ovens, pots, and pans. Yet, they too own and use microwave ovens. It is one of the gadgets in their cooking toolbox.

Microwave ovens do some tasks very well. Ask a microwave to re-heat something that has been cooked before, and you will usually have success. Heat that coffee; warm that soup. They excel at popping corn, but don't ask them to bake bread or brown meat. Even vegetables are better steamed on the stovetop than shriveled by too many electro-magnetic pulses. Of course, that doesn't stop me from using my mi-crowave for cooking that would be better done over a fire. The dang thing is so convenient. Often, I don't care if my food is soggy or pale, as long as it is warm.

As it is with chefs and microwaves, so it is with librarians and the World Wide Web. The Internet is so convenient to use—I can even get it on my cell phone. It fulfills many kinds of information needs easily and well. But it can't do everything. It is just another gadget in the li-brarian's toolbox. You know that and I know that because we are trained experts, but our public often thinks the web will solve *all* their information needs. Even if they do realize that the Internet can't com-pletely answer their questions, they often don't care. They go for the quick and easy answer. Is this wrong? Guess what. It doesn't matter be-cause it's going to happen anyway.

HUMAN INFORMATION-SEEKING BEHAVIOR

The two most important things I learned in library school were not about book preservation or cutter numbers. They were laws of human behavior, and when I heard them, I knew they were true. I wrote them down and committed them to my heart and mind: Humans tend to be (a) lazy and (b) irrational. They tend to "satisfice," settling for the "good enough" answer. Unfortunately, these tendencies are directly antithet-ical to a librarian's raison d'être. We exist to facilitate access to infor-mation by instilling order on an intrinsically chaotic world. Yes, it's a lit-tle bit obsessive compulsive, but it is work that is important to civilized society. We are guides to high-quality, thorough answers to almost all questions in life. Unfortunately, our public doesn't understand this—they don't know what we do or even who we are.

My own mother, a lifetime library user, said to me just the other day, "We have the nicest new librarian at my branch."

I said, "Mom, did he check out your books for you?"

"Yes. And he was very nice."

"Mom . . . that was a *clerk*!"

If my mother prefers to talk to the friendly clerk instead of the reference librarian, indeed if she thinks that the clerk *is* the reference librarian, then we as a profession have an image that is already in the dirt, with or without the web.

OUR CHANGING ROLE

A 2003 survey from the University of California at Los Angeles Center for Communication Policy shows that the Internet is the first thing in fifty years that has attracted the young away from the tube: "Almost one third of children now watch less television than before they started using the Internet at home—up from 23 percent in 2001."[1] Not only that, the same study says that "the Internet is viewed as an important source of information by the vast majority of people who go online; in 2002, 60.5 percent of all users considered the Internet to be a very important or extremely important source of information,"[2] more important than their libraries, their librarians, or even their library clerks. Ouch. That really hurts.

LIBRARIAN AVENGERS

Being a librarian means being misunderstood, and this can make us angry. Erica Olsen[3] explains why our public should fall to their knees and worship librarians. An example from her blog: "Overheard at library: 'PubMed? That's the bar you go to when you visit ClubMed.'" Erica understands our pain. Thanks, gal (see figure 1.1).

So, if our public turns to the web instead of the library for answers, does that mean our profession is obsolete? To answer, let me ask you the following: How often have you helped those patrons who stumble up to your reference desk all red-eyed exclaiming they have been looking for something on the web for hours if not *days?* You ask them to describe what they seek, you type it into a search engine, and the perfect site appears within seconds.

I'm telling you, our patrons seriously lack searching skills. When they try to search on the web, they use meaninglessly generic search terms. They seem to have no sense of unique key words. For example, in a recent e-mail titled "Thank you, Thank you, Thank you!" my sister, a computer goddess in her own right, lauded me for helping her find the text

Librarian Avengers

Look it up.

LOOK IT UP!

©1999 Terry Moore

Why you should fall to your Knees and worship a librarian...

Ok, sure. We've all got our little preconceived notions about what librarians are and what they do. Many people think of them as diminutive civil servants, scuttling about "Sssh-ing" people and stamping things. Well, think again buster.

Librarians have degrees. They go to graduate school for Information Science and become masters of data systems and human/computer interaction. Librarians can catalog anything from an onion to a dog's ear. They could catalog you. Librarians wield unfathomable power. With a flip of the wrist they can hide your dissertation behind piles of old Field and Stream magazines. They can find data for your term paper that you never knew existed. They may even point you toward new and appropriate subject headings.

People become librarians because they know too much. Their knowledge extends beyond mere categories. They cannot be confined to disciplines. Librarians are all-knowing and all-seeing. They bring order to chaos. They bring wisdom and culture to the masses. They preserve every aspect of human knowledge. Librarians rule. And they will kick the crap out of anyone who says otherwise.

Figure 1.1.

of a poem on the web using Google. "I just typed in my title and found the poem immediately," she writes. "You are fabulous! Is there anything you *can't* do?" I got high praise for merely suggesting the use of a phrase search. My sense is that she had tried to locate the text of this particular poem by typing *poetry* into the Google search box.

And don't get me started on our patrons' general want of critical thinking skills. My friends, in the digital age, we have an increasingly important role to play in society, if not in the preservation of civilization! "Hey, if it is on the web, it must be *true*, right?" Wrong! We must help our people distinguish between solid information and pure rotting rubbishy talk, psychotic ramblings, and even the dreaded "low-value speech."

Still, our role changes from intermediaries, to gatekeepers of knowledge, to that of teachers and salespeople. When people feel sick, they go to a professional, their doctors. But our patrons don't even know they *have* serious information deficits much less realize they have "information insurance" (i.e., *us*, prepaid by their tax dollars) at their disposal. Somehow we need to make our patrons understand that we can help them find *quality* information over the Internet.

WEB REFERENCE RESOURCES: GOOGLE AND BEYOND

Given that our patrons want to search the web to answer their questions, what tools can we offer to help them? In November 2002, at the Internet Librarian conference in Palm Springs, California, Danny Sullivan, creator of Search Engine Watch,[4] began his keynote speech by simply saying, "Google has won. We can all go home." Google,[5] as we all know, is the uncannily precise search engine that librarians use for almost everything, including spell checking and finding quotes. Dang, it's good. But, like the microwave, even Google has its limitations, even for professional searchers.

For one thing, its precision comes at the cost of recall. Its PageRank system points toward the popular, not the most complete information. And it has some serious quirks that all librarians should be aware of, tendencies that Steven Johnson calls "Googleholes."[6] For one thing, according to Johnson, Google results skew heavily toward online stores and away from general information. "Search for 'flowers,' and more than 90 percent of the top results are online florists," he reports.

Also, it tends to skew synonyms toward those that are most often used by the online community. Hence, a search for the word *apple* pulls up information about Macintosh computers, not fruit. Finally, Google tends to rank articles written in PDF format quite highly, while ignoring closed databases such as the *New York Times*. That is why these databases with exclusive front ends are known as the "invisible web." Google just can't see them. So, most amateur searchers who use Google exclusively won't know that any information exists apart from that they find on the open web.

Johnson is quick to point out that these blind spots are really not Google's fault, per se. Google is not, and never has been, an encyclopedia, a pure reference source. "It's closer to a collectively authored op-ed page, filled with bias, polemics, and a skewed sense of proportion," writes Johnson. "[It is] a perfect condensation of the Web's wider anarchy. Just don't call it an oracle."[7]

The Invisible Web

Google is good, but it is not the end of a hearty web subject search. For more complete information, we can point our patrons toward the "invisible web." The term *invisible web* sounds so intriguing—it evokes images of ghosts, smoke, and magic. Maybe we should call it the "haunted web" or the "web of mystery and imagination." Too bad the real meaning of the term is so prosaic. The invisible, or deep, web refers mainly to databases with information that is available for free over the web but that can only be searched through their particular web search page, or "front end." Search engines can't search or index these databases because the data in them are not stored in HTML. As an example, a particular article about health care published by Health Canada[8] cannot be found using Yahoo! We can find it only by searching via its home page.

The invisible web turns out to be more about common sense than about magic, as far as librarians are concerned. We usually intrinsically understand the character of the secluded database as opposed to the rangy, wide open web. Yet, most amateur searchers do not. These databases can be tremendously valuable for in-depth and current subject information, and without us our patrons would know nothing about them.

How do *we* locate these hidden gold mines of information? Fortunately, there are information professionals out there who have crafted handpicked, annotated directories—virtual searchable maps—to these valuable sites, just for us!

Invisible Web: Searchable Databases and Specialized Search Engines

The subtitle says it all. Chris Sherman, associate editor of searchengine watch.com, and reference librarian Gary Price offer this database of databases[9] as a companion site to their book *The Invisible Web: Uncovering Hidden Internet Resources Search Engines Can't See.*[10] Click on one of the eighteen major subject categories in the directory to "drill-down through the database" into subcategories; these open up into pages that link to search portals for otherwise invisible information.

Figure 1.2.

Librarians' Index to the Internet

When librarians need the best web resources on a subject they know little about, they point their browsers directly to the Librarians' Index to the Internet (LII),[11] which was founded by librarian Carole Leita at the Berkeley Public Library. Browse by category or search by keyword to find quality subject portals and databases (see figure 1.2).

Infomine

Infomine[12] is a virtual library of databases and directories aimed at those doing university-level research. Visit Infomine to find electronic journals, electronic books, mailing lists, online library card catalogs, and other scholarly resources that cannot be detected by search engines.

Academic Info

Former law librarian Mike Madin developed and maintains Academic Info, a commercially sponsored educational subject directory.[13]

Although a portion of his portal lists sponsored links to online degree programs and test preparation pages, the majority of his site is a categorized listing of otherwise "invisible" digital collections from libraries, museums, and academic organizations. Madin tries to add between 250 and 500 new resources monthly.

The Virtual Reference Library

Toronto Public Library, Ontario's largest, has commissioned librarians to select valuable subject sites and portals to databases with an eye toward those especially valuable to Canadians. Browse by subject through the Virtual Reference Library,[14] as this collection is called, or search it with keywords (see figure 1.3).

Live Librarians on the Line

If our patrons realize we can save them time and frustration by assisting their web searches, they are going to be frustrated if we are only available to them during regular library hours. More and more li-

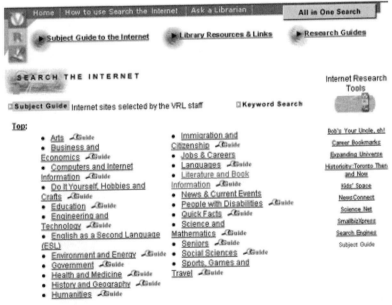

Figure 1.3.

braries are trying to ameliorate this problem by getting into the business of answering reference questions in real time over the web using chat software. This service is meant to be available all day, every day so patrons can have their reference questions answered whenever the need for information strikes. This is obviously a big project for a single library to accomplish on its own. For all day, every day coverage, it is best that we band together in reference cooperatives. An example of this kind of service is the AskNow program, originally called 24/7 Reference, developed by Susan McGlamery at the Metropolitan Cooperative Library System (MCLS),[15] a library consortium in the Los Angeles, California, area.

AskNow

In the late 1990s, Susan McGlamery, head of reference services for MCLS, noticed that Land's End,[16] the catalog and online clothier, offered live sales assistance over its website via chat software. At the same time, she saw that reference statistics were in decline as former patrons turned to web-based services such as Ask Jeeves[17] from their homes instead of coming into the library. What to do? Well, thought McGlamery, why not offer live reference service over the web via chat? And that is exactly what she did. Working with the thirty-two libraries in the MCLS consortium, McGlamery designed a service in which librarians could answer reference questions and share web pages with patrons remotely.[18] The service began as a cooperative volunteer effort, with participating libraries taking electronic reference shifts during business hours. Soon, however, the service evolved into a true 24/7 operation, with paid librarians taking the off-hours. It spread up and down California and into key areas across the United States and Canada including Boston, Maryland, and the University of Alberta. One part of the service specializes in questions asked of public libraries; a second focuses on libraries that serve universities. As of October 2003, according to McGlamery, public and academic libraries in California alone answer about ten thousand questions via this service per month. "We expect this number to rise once we start our publicity campaign," she added.

AskNow!

Australia's first collaborative reference service, AskNow![19] is a pilot initiative of the Council of Australian State Libraries (CASL). Professional librarians from across the nation answer questions in real time using MCLS's 24/7 Reference software. Currently, this service is not offered 24/7 but only during business days and hours. Will the Aussies ever join the Yanks in providing around the clock service from opposite poles of the world, thus creating the first Earth-wide reference cooperative? "The Australians still consider their service a pilot project. We are ready to join them once they feel certain of their success," says McGlamery.

Cell Phone Reference

Suppose we do get that worldwide reference thing going. To get our answers, we still need to have one of those $2,000 computers plugged into the wall and connected, usually by a big blue wire, to the Internet. This is a clunky and expensive way to access the web. So lately, I've had an idea that has grown into a fixation: I want to do reference on my cell phone.

Can It Be Done?

In June 2003, I took advantage of my cell phone provider's deal of a second line for an additional $10 per month. At the same time, I got to choose new phones. My two-year-old basic Nokia was beginning to look antique. Still, I had no idea how far cell phone technology had advanced until I started to play with my new Motorola flip phone. Yes, it has a color screen. Yes, it has good sound quality. But to me, the most thrilling feature of this tiny new device is that it can access the World Wide Web.

Mind you, this is no $600 Handspring. This is a phone that was essentially *free* to me, after sign-up bonuses and a trade-in on my old Nokia. Admittedly, after three months of gratis service, I pay about $7 per month for web access. And the screen is small, and it is very hard to type anything on a numeric telephone keypad. Yes, yes. But the point is, I can now reach into my purse and grab the Internet almost anywhere I go at almost *no* cost, depending on how much I use it. My provider goes so far as to offer an adult chat service, although I find it hard to believe that anyone can have an erotic conversation via a phone dial pad. I have to press 7 four times just to get to the *s* to spell *sex*. On the plus side, the phone does have a vibrating ring option. But I'd have to get a *lot* of calls before I got any fun out of that. No, the real pleasure for me in this phone is that it offers a little bitty version of

Google—what else?—developed especially for mobile phones. If my library's Internet connection was to fail, could I use this miniature search engine to answer patrons' questions?

Wireless Google

Here, Google describes the search services it offers for wireless web users,[20] including those using i-mode and J-Sky. From this page, you can try out the stripped down portal for personal digital assistant (PDA) users.[21] It may be spare, but it is still written in HTML. The problem is that cell phone browsers can't see HTML. These devices communicate via wireless application protocol, or WAP.[22] WAP-enabled pages sport the suffix ".wml" rather than ".html." According to Google Wireless Services,[23] there are currently about five million pages on the Internet created specifically for this "mobile web." Many of these originate from European countries that were WAP pioneers. Thus, if I use my cell phone browser to search for San Marino, the suburb of Los Angeles where I work, I only get results for the tiny Repubblica di San Marino, embedded in eastern Italy, which is considered to be the oldest independent country in Europe. The restriction to WAP-enabled sites would seem to seriously limit the usefulness of my wireless Google application. But wait! Under the Google search box, I can select Search Options. Here, I can choose to search the measly mobile web or I can open up and query the entire three-billion-plus-page Google-universe of regular web pages!

How can Google do that? Well, leave it to the search engine that has been described by the *New York Times* as "a little bit like God" to offer an on-the-fly conversion service that translates most web pages into the language that mobile phones understand. What if I can't stand pushing the 7 button four times to type the *S* in San Marino into my diminutive search box? Google offers an alternative number search on the same Search Options page that allows users to search for San Marino by typing 7 only once, then 260627466. The 0 stands for the spaces between words; users type the number 1 for quotation marks.

Opera

Google solves the question of how to display wide web pages on small screens by converting HTML into WML on an as-needed basis. The Oslo-based Opera Software ASA[24] has come up with a browser featuring an alternative method for wireless devices to surf the regular web.

Eurasian cell phone users either receive the Opera mobile browser as standard equipment or can download it. Although Opera-compatible phones are currently sold only in Europe, the Middle East, and China, one can imagine their market extending to the United States as Opera expands its partnerships.

Whereas the Google mobile portal translates HTML into WML, the little Opera browser looks at a regular web page and displays just a vertical slice of it. This technique, called small-screen rendering, or SSR,[25] strips the graphic elements out of a web page and then displays it as a single column of text. The text in this rendering is stacked vertically according to document order. According to Opera, "Document order is the order the HTML source code is in. In most cases a page is displayed by this order. . . . One exception is tables. Tables are displayed cell by cell left to right for each row going down."[26]

The new version of Opera for *regular* Windows, version 7, is a great improvement from the older versions. It is still thin compared with its rivals, only 3.4 MB, and it continues to be the browser of choice for assistance technology (i.e., screen readers and such). But now, it allows users to seamlessly view pages written in WML. They can even switch to a tiny narrow view of these pages by hitting SHIFT+F11. There you go. Now you can see what your pages look like on a cell phone screen.

Searching Library Catalogs via Cell Phones

Let's face it—mobile communication devices are everywhere. Judging from the distracting rings and the loud yakking of patrons (sometimes seemingly into open air), it seems that wireless phone signals travel through library walls virtually undistorted. Rather than spend our energy playing cell phone cop, why don't we enlist these patron-owned electronics as adjuncts to our OPAC stations, thus adding searching capacity within our buildings at no expense to us?

Jack Blount, president and CEO of Dynix, notes:

> [Libraries get] public funding based on the services that they provide the community, which means Internet browsing from home at night, authoritative data from hundreds of databases, digital access to rare book collections. If they're not . . . letting me use my PDA when I walk into the library to do my search, then they're going to lose their patrons and their funding.[27]

Ouch! Point taken. So, I try to use my library's web-based catalog through the Google mobile web portal. On the same Search Options page is a "Go to URL" link. When I type our catalog URL into this box, I can see all the words on our search page but no place to type in a search term.

Of course, our ILS is a "legacy system" created by a company that no longer exists. Frankly, it is obsolete and awkward to use on even the largest of desktop machines. No amount of Google magic can make it searchable from a cell phone, or a PDA for that matter. When we decide to migrate to a new system, we would like it to be searchable from cell phones in addition to PDAs and regular web browsers, in both English and Chinese. (The population of San Marino is now about half recent Chinese immigrants.) The only way to do that, as far as I can tell, is to convert our sturdy MARC records, designed for the computer systems of 1962, into XML, or extensible markup language. The United States Library of Congress has been working on this[28] and even offers a free MARC to XML conversion utility!

If this can be done, according to State University of New York at Buffalo libraries system manager Mark Ludwig, we will have "found a revolutionary way to integrate all of our content: our full text, our library catalog pages, our image collections, our sound files, our course reserves. We are integrating them using native XML, with a search engine to bring it all together into one common search interface."[29] Ah. So that means that very soon I shall be able to search the entire universe of electronic information by tapping out queries on my cell phone keypad! Or, maybe I could just use my phone to call a reference librarian.

Disadvantages of Wireless Reference

I am so thrilled that Google and Opera have worked so hard to make it possible to see the web on my phone. And I really appreciate that the companies that make automated systems for libraries are doing research to change the way we can access electronic information. But even I, geek that I am, must admit that at least three big structural problems currently make it difficult to use cell phones as reference appliances.

For one thing, mobile phone web networks are notorious for spotty coverage. There are plenty of places, including remote locations, inside buildings, or behind big hills, where the network simply is not available. No network equals no web, and no web equals no cell phone reference. Waah!

Also, at least right now, wireless connections are slow. Finding the answer to one reference question on the phone while sitting in a restaurant or waiting for your plane at the airport may be amusing, but both the laborious telephone typing and the long download times are enough to drive the average user and the busy reference librarian mad with frustrated impatience.

Finally, although a bit of noodling around on the mobile web won't cost you much, a high volume of downloading or extended connection time will take a chunk out of the old budget. On my plan, I pay for the amount of data I download. Other plans charge by the minute or offer a flat monthly fee. Such rates make me thankful I am no chat hound. I could easily double my monthly mobile charges!

In the end, although I just love the idea, using a cell phone to search the web is analogous to Samuel Johnson's comparison of a female preacher to a dog walking on its hind legs: "It is not done well; but you are surprised to find it done at all."[30] Still, it's the future. So start thumb-typing today—at the reference desk!

THE NATURE OF CHANGE

The constant with the web is change. With change comes benefits, but also loss. When the technology of information retrieval changes, we lose the competency that it took years for us to develop. When our knowledge no longer applies, we feel lost and . . . stupid, really. Even what we know about computers rapidly becomes obsolete.

Also, our beloved print collections will shrink as more reference collections come online. We will pay more for the digital versions, yet we will have nothing to show for these ephemeral collections but empty shelf space. Still, offering these products over the web means more of our patrons will use them because they will be available to them 24/7 from wherever they access the Internet, not just inside the library when it is open.

As the new century progresses, libraries must become as easy to use as microwave ovens, as ubiquitous as Google. We have started on that road, offering service not only by telephone but also by twenty-four-hour chat over the web. We need to demand enriched catalogs from our integrated library systems companies, ones that can be searched on cell phones and PDAs, in as many languages as necessary for our communities.

The move from an entirely print-based to a mixed print and digital information environment does not leave librarians in the dirt. Quite the contrary, it is not a tug of war at all but a synergy. The mix can only improve what we do, making both information and our assistance more available and user-friendly. In the end, the web will not defeat us. We will use it to pull ourselves out of the dirt, to wipe off our sensible shoes, and to triumph!

NOTES

1. UCLA Center for Communication Policy, at ccp.ucla.edu (accessed 31 March 2004).

2. UCLA Center for Communication Policy, at ccp.ucla.edu (accessed 31 March 2004).

3. Librarian Avengers, at www.librarianavengers.org/worship.html (accessed 31 March 2004).

4. Search Engine Watch, at searchenginewatch.com (accessed 31 March 2004).

5. Google, at www.google.com (accessed 31 March 2004).

6. Steven Johnson, "Digging for Googleholes," *Slate*, at slate.msn.com/id/2085668 (accessed 16 July 2003).

7. Johnson, "Digging for Googleholes."

8. Health Canada, at www.hc-sc.gc.ca (accessed 31 March 2004).

9. The Invisible Web, at www.invisible-web.net (accessed 31 March 2004).

10. Chris Sherman and Gary Price, *The Invisible Web: Uncovering Hidden Internet Resources Search Engines Can't See* (Medford, NJ: CyberAge Books, 2001).

11. Librarians' Index to the Internet, at lii.org (accessed 31 March 2004).

12. Infomine: Scholarly Internet Resource Collections, at infomine.ucr.edu (accessed 31 March 2004).

13. Academic Info, at www.academicinfo.net (accessed 31 March 2004).

14. The Virtual Reference Library, Toronto Public Library, at vrl.tpl.toronto.on.ca (accessed 31 March 2004).

15. Metropolitan Cooperative Library System, at www.mcls.org (accessed 31 March 2004).

16. Land's End, at www.landsend.com (accessed 31 March 2004).

17. Ask Jeeves, at www.ask.com (accessed 31 March 2004).

18. AskNow, at www.asknow.org (accessed 31 March 2004).

19. AskNow!, at www.asknow.gov.au (accessed 31 March 2004).

20. Wireless User Guide, at www.google.com/options/wireless.html (accessed 31 March 2004).

21. Google Palm, at www.google.com/palm (accessed 31 March 2004).

22. Open Mobile Alliance, *What Is WAP?*, at www.wapforum.org/what/index.htm (accessed 31 March 2004).

23. Wireless User Guide, at www.google.com/wireless/ (accessed 31 March 2004).

24. Opera Software, at www.opera.com (accessed 31 March 2004).

25. Opera Software, "Opera's Small-Screen Rendering," at www.opera.com/products/smartphone/smallscreen (accessed 31 March 2004).

26. Opera Software, "Opera's Small-Screen Rendering" (accessed 31 March 2004).

27. Brian Kenney, "The Future of Integrated Library Systems," *Library Journal* 128, no. 11 (15 June 2003): 39.

28. Library of Congress, "MARC in XML," at www.loc.gov/marc/marcxml.html (accessed 31 March 2004).

29. Kenney, "Future of Integrated Library Systems," 40.

30. Samuel Johnson, at www.bartleby.com/100/249.60.html (accessed 31 March 2004).

2

Library Prophets and Library Pornographers: Some Problems That Arise When We Talk about Libraries and the Web[1]

Stephen Good[2]

What would you say about the future if being wrong meant death? More specifically, what would you say about libraries and the web in the future if being wrong meant death? Would you go with, "The future will be different from the past," and hope that stating the obvious is not the same as being wrong? Would you run with the undergraduate synthesis and say, "Libraries and the web will remain interlocked in a synergistic yet antagonistic embrace," and hope that being noncommittal is not the same as being wrong? Or would you venture out on a limb and say, "In the days of jet cars and android butlers, the web will reign triumphant and libraries will be left in the dirt," and if you are challenged that this scenario has not come true, would you wax prophetical and say, "Ah, but it will, it will"?

PROPHETS AND PORNOGRAPHERS: WHO'S WHO

I will hazard only the most timid predictions, but to begin I would like to introduce three terms to facilitate how we can even talk about "the tug of war between libraries and the web." The three terms are prophet, false prophet, and pornographer. The definitions exist on a spectrum, they overlap, and they are neither clear cut nor simple. A prophet, for my purposes, is not synonymous with "someone who makes accurate predictions about the future." That can be part of it, but both false prophets and pornographers can achieve this feat. An accurate prediction can be based on wishful thinking, intuition, luck, revelation, or keen insight into the past and present. I want to use a more stringent definition of prophecy, where the present is judged in terms of what was best and noblest about the past, and the future will either be consistent with that high standard or a doomsday scenario where the best of the past is forgotten and the worst of the present is carried into the future. Predictions are passive; prophecies are "if . . . then" statements.[3] The prophet's maxim "Repent!" does not mean "Stop!" but rather "Fix your course to line up with your true destiny."

A false prophet then is not someone who makes wrong predictions. A false prophet can be right, but the predictions being made are taking society in the wrong direction.[4] False prophets can be surrounded by "signs and wonders" and appear to be working miracles, but they have no interest in the big picture or what the future should be about. They are in it for the cash and the glory. I think of false prophets as the men in suits who will sell you system A and then sell you anti-system A shortly afterward with complete equanimity.[5]

Pornographers are the loose cannons of the future prediction business. If it's neat, if it's new, if it hasn't been done before, they are all for it. They could not care less about stability, sustainability, destiny, responsibility; they are the "I'm just here for the beer" members of the future fraternity. Pornographers are neither compelled nor even willing to "sell" you on the benefits of system A. System A is simply what you must have to be a player in the web game. So what if system A is a black box that costs $50,000 in a library accounting environment where every $30 book purchase is gone over with a fine-tooth comb. The pornographer wants to seduce you with technological possibilities. Unlike either kind of prophet, the pornographer has no regard for people. Technology is what matters—people are just the rationalization for acquiring the black boxes.

Here's a concrete example of a library/web scenario proposed by a pornographer:

> I, or rather my customized avatar, met with Dr. Knowitall's avatar on the virtual beach. We discussed the compilation of his multimedia bibliography in support of his multimillion dollar grant application. We enjoyed e-cocktails and virtual massages.

When talking of the pornographic versus the prophetic, there is nothing at all to say that the pornographic version of the future is not in fact the one that will come to pass. So the aforementioned scenario is not pornographic because it is false, as in it is unlikely to happen. It may already have happened in some beta form or another. The scenario is pornographic in three ways: how the interaction is portrayed, who the patron is, and who is left out of the scenario.

This scenario is curious because every librarian knows that 90 percent of interactions with people are nonverbal. So what exactly can an avatar tell us about the other person, unless that person is mapped 1:1 onto the avatar, which means that the patron may look like a superhero, but the superhero's eyebrows move exactly in sync with Dr. Knowitall's. The virtual beach is not just a matter of convenience (since we are in different cities, let's meet in this pretend location); it also shows a disdain for any room in the actual library in which the librarian works. As with the infamous *Playboy* airbrush, there is contempt for what is actual, what is physical.

The second level of the pornographic in this scenario has to do with the patron. Dr. Knowitall is obviously an intellectual high roller, a guy with multiple PhDs in the academic fast lane. Dr. K's alleged bibliography is most likely a bogus gesture made to fulfill a grant requirement, not anything he really needs, and Dr. K is probably capable of compiling the bibliography himself, so the librarian is "saving the time of the reader" by doing it for him. But the librarian is not helping Dr. K; the librarian wants to be associated with Dr. K and his extravagant project. There is nothing wrong with this but for the third part of this scenario. In attributing all the "dream patron" qualities to Dr. Knowitall, the librarian is turning his (and I use that gender intentionally) back on the rest of the world who might be in need of education or information. The librarian is including everything he likes about librarianship and excluding everything that bothers him.

In what seems like the distant past, a popular Canadian bumper sticker said, "My Canada includes Quebec."[6] Amid all the gung ho web worship, perhaps we need a series of slogans more along the lines of "My library includes comfy chairs," "My library includes chess sets you can borrow," and my personal favorite, "My library includes story time." There is nothing "wrong" with the web except when everything becomes judged by its IT (information technology) quotient. The previous scenario is not pornographic because it is high tech but rather because it involves an essentially empty and meaningless exchange—library service as gesture. However, some very library-specific scenarios have no IT quotient whatsoever:

> Even though he smelled of urine and cigarette smoke, I asked Elijah to sit next to me during the reading of *Silly Sally*. I could tell after finishing the story that not only was he in fourth grade and still unable to read, Elijah had probably never had anyone read to him and more than that, he had never actually had an adult sit calmly next to him for a long, long time.[7]

If the Dr. Knowitall scenario constitutes "the future," where are the people who are (excuse my political incorrectness) poor, stupid, old, crazy, illiterate, ugly, uneducated, lonely, desperate, homeless—all the things that Dr. Knowitall is definitely not? In our futuristic view are we ignoring them, helping them, "solving" them, or deliberately constructing our web/library "reality" so that they do not figure into it? The corollary of "On the web no one knows you're a dog" is "On the web those who want to can refuse to acknowledge your humanity." Libraries should not be fighting to avoid being thrown in the dirt; libraries should be volunteering to serve those who are in the dirt on the shoulder of the information highway.

VIRTUAL REFERENCE AND THE FALSE PROPHETS

Holographs and virtual masseuses are obviously pornographic takes on the future. To give an example of false prophecy, let's look at virtual reference, without taking the extreme position where "no technology is neutral" and where information "have-nots" are left out of the equation. Let's assume a world of cheap computers and easy access, where any person, library regular or not, can ask a real librarian questions via the web.[8] Virtual reference works best if we perceive all reference questions as an elaborate version of Trivial Pursuit: What is the population of Zimbabwe? Where do I get change of name forms? Who won the Oscar for best actor in 1939?

The danger of virtual reference is that we can think we are doing a good job when in fact we are not. The statistics look good, we are filling in the blanks, but we are not being librarians. The first problem, one that is straight library school textbook stuff, is that the question being asked is not the real question. On the phone, or especially in person, it would be apparent that the person asking for change of name forms is not actually asking for change of name forms—she is being stalked by her ex-husband, and she thinks in some magical way that changing her name will help solve this problem. I know I'm preaching to the converted, but many reference questions are actually the end result of a very long, perhaps tortured, thought process and series of experiences that bear little or no relation to what started the whole thing in motion. And that is where the pornographic element comes in. Rather than deal with the full extent of the dilemma, we pat ourselves on the back for answering the question. However, the information given has as much value to that person as did the bread crumbs in the story of Hansel and Gretel. Virtual reference can be used to extend service or to hide behind technology, and in this "well, I can check that question off my list" scenario, there is more hiding than serving.

The other problem with virtual reference is that a threshold level exists that doesn't exist in an actual library. This threshold is concerned not with knowing how to type or knowing how to use computers but with knowing how to turn the current information obstacle in your life into a question. I have never subscribed to the notion that library patrons are stupid. All of us appear stupid to other people when our limited knowledge intersects with their high level of competence and expertise. Cashiers and bank tellers could think everyone is stupid because the person in front of them has already moved on to the next item in their errand list. I have been the person perceived in that way, and I like to think that I am not stupid. But the reality of many library patrons is that they don't know what they don't know. The average library user, for example, is not aware that there is far more in the library they could use or borrow. As a recent convert to the treasure trove of government documents, I venture to say there are even some librarians who do not know how much cool stuff there is in their own libraries. What has this got to do with virtual reference? Well, you have to know that Wal-Mart sells IBC Diet Root Beer before you think to go and buy it there. Ditto for libraries—you have to know what they have before you can ask for it. As with Dr. Knowitall, virtual reference works best for the initiated. The danger is that if a library becomes too wedded to virtual reference as "the way to go," then everything becomes a matter of pumping up those numbers. What you risk losing are face-to-face, in-person services. The potential problem with virtual reference is that we will buy into the premise that this is *the* way to offer reference rather than *a* way to extend the reference service we currently offer.

DUKING IT OUT—WHO CARES?

The biggest fallacy in "libraries versus the web" is even thinking the question matters. I'm a librarian and this is hard for me to accept, but the fact is the majority of people in the world really don't care about how the web and libraries fight it out with each other. Why? Because for the majority of people in the world the main thing that matters is . . . people. Cell phones have not eclipsed computers simply because cell phones are smaller, cheaper, and easier to use than computers. Cell phones eclipsed computers because cell phones connect you to other people better and faster than computers and the web. Truth be told, the average person on planet Earth is not a postdoctoral student in search of unadulterated data. Technology is made for people, not people for technology.

Let's back up a little bit. Is a library a building full of books? Or is a library a locus where those with information needs interact with those who have information-handling skills? Or is a library whatever the library's budget priorities say it is? I doubt anyone would go so far as to say that a library is a state of mind—partly for fear of being signed up in the employee assistance program because it's just too corny. Ironically, if there is such a thing as a "library state of mind," that is exactly the state of mind that defines the web.

Defining the web is even more elusive than defining a library. Is the web the hardware, the software, the content, the culture, the websites, the weblogs, or the attitude of those who see themselves as webheads? I went to library school (1989–1991) when the web was gopher and e-mail, and it was assumed that private data providers had a death grip on information and we were just going to have to accept those $250/hour connect charges. The web came along like the cavalry and a deus ex machina all rolled into one and spared us from this seemingly inexorable privatization of all knowledge by online database conglomerates. The web and libraries share a common philosophy: A citizen deserves free access to educational information and to entertainment customized to his or her taste. However, the web did libraries one better by saying that like-minded people deserve a chance to find each other no matter where they are in the world. While the library helped readers discover authors, the web enabled 1967 Harley Davidson enthusiasts to find each other.

There is a level of absurdity even in the phrase "libraries versus the web." To point out the first absurdity, picture me sitting at my kitchen table with a laptop hooked up to the web, accessing articles about the web from the full-text journal database hosted by the university computer. I am in my house, I can read the articles on the screen, and I don't need to go to the library. However, I have access to the articles only because the library has worked out an arrangement to obtain the full-text database. So my statement "I don't need the library because I have the web" can be transformed into the logical statement "I don't need X because I have X." Because my library and the web have become so interwoven, I am now confused about which I need and which I don't need, comparable with "I don't need oxygen because I have the atmosphere."

Thus, in the sense of prophecy the real danger of the web is not that it will destroy libraries outright but that libraries will become so hypnotized by technology that they will lose any sense of their past, mission, or destiny and simply amputate whatever parts of library service are not high tech. Libraries are not killed by the web; they submit to a kind of institutional anomie and commit organizational suicide.[9] In this scenario, the web builds the procrustean bed, but the library world, not the web, amputates whatever aspects of librarianship protrude. In this future, either both the web and libraries end up in the dust, or neither do because they have become the same thing.

The other "web versus libraries" absurdity, a second false dichotomy, is to assume there is any competition, a rivalry, an either/or-ness to these two. Superficially, there are discrepancies. The web is young, anarchic (almost criminal), brash, and disrespectful. The tone of the web, created by those who live there without being paid to do so, is cynical, crude, and sarcastic, although it thinks itself witty. Libraries are rule bound, are stodgy, and stay well back from the cutting edge owing to budget, temperament, and necessity. But ideologically, libraries and the web occupy the very same space. Libraries gave practical meaning to resource sharing by loaning books and materials to each other before the web even existed. The web is built on a model of exchanging computer power and digitized information. Just as librarians help each other to best serve their host institutions or communities, so computer people helped each other over the earliest versions of the web. And both the web and libraries define *free* as "that which cannot have a price assigned to it," such as wildflowers and blood, rather than free as in "worthless." The hidden assumption of course is that the web will eclipse libraries as a form of evolution, the same way that television eclipsed radio.

This leads to another fallacy, that we still need to speculate about what the web *will* be like and what its impact on libraries will be. The web is here and has been for seventy years or whatever in "web time," so we don't need to speculate about what the web "will be like." The two books that have impressed me most about what the web is like, not what it will be, are *Small Pieces Loosely Joined*[10] and *Social Consequences of Internet Use.*[11] As neither can be summarized briefly, I will recommend them. As a librarian, what I took from *SPLJ* is that the main achievement of the web is the undermining of authority, similar to the revolutions in culture, religion, society, and so on that followed from the invention of the printing press and the proliferation of small printed books and manifestos. For those who took the "History of the Book" class in library school, this will ring a bell. In this web world where experience, opinion, and hands-on knowledge count for more than degrees and certification, librarians need to learn an important lesson: Our passion, and not our precision, is the proof of our professionalism.

I felt vindicated when I read the survey reported in *Social Consequences of Internet Use.* The hardest thing for the web enthusiast to understand is the nonenthusiast's complete lack of interest in the object of the enthusiast's obsession. In other words, we can't get why they don't get it. Libraries versus the web is the stuff of life and death—but only to us. Confirmation of this came in a survey where the authors prided themselves on having discovered a new category in the Internet population—the dedicated nonuser (often the ex-user and now dedicated nonuser). In the web view of itself, this is an impossibility, an oxymoron of sorts. The only people who could possibly be nonusers are those who have never used the web. The idea that you could have a perfectly wonderful life and never turn on a computer or access the web simply does not compute. I think part of this mystery of the dedicated nonuser is traceable to what I call the "upgrade fallacy." We think that because OPAC 3.1 has solved many of the most glaring annoyances of OPAC 3.0, then 3.1 must be very good. But that is only what people who are "inside the paradigm" think. To someone who does not know the details of OPAC 3.0 or 3.1, the issue is simply, "Why isn't whatever I want right here in front of me?" People who worry about technical upgrades have a relative standard, while those who simply want something to help them get on with their lives have an absolute standard.

WHO ENDS UP IN THE DIRT?

The golden age of the Internet is over. What started as a technological miracle and a micro-democratic revolution is now just a way for the rich to get richer and for power to reproduce itself. The diamond mine of the web is now cranking out cubic zirconium. The educational super-diet of the web turned out to be a combination of steroids, amphetamines, and computer-induced attention deficit disorder. To learn, you still have to sit down in a chair with a book, and to love, you still have to get over yourself and really interact with another person. The web makes you think things are happening that aren't happening, but there's so much noise you think something must be going on. I would give away the entire Internet for one good book, and for some books I would expect change back.

The mission of librarians has never been clearer. We must speak truth to power; we must stand up to the pornographers and false prophets and say, "Not with our budget you don't." Every dollar spent is still a dollar spent, and we need to spend our money in a way we can justify to the generations to come. "Yeah, we spent the equivalent of two years' book budget on some gizmo that we had to replace before we ever figured it out" will not impress posterity. While not to provide access to the wealth of free information on the web would be foolish, to remake and destroy your library to pretend you are part of an information technology revolution is irresponsible.

Librarians have always loved fighting censorship. But there are very different kinds of censorship. The one that gets discussed most often is when someone wants to take all the copies of *Huckleberry Finn* off the shelves of the local school library, or when someone wants the library to put ten copies of *Dianetics*, provided free, on every shelf of every library in the city. Those are both relatively easy fights. Real censorship involves what does and doesn't get bought overall. Real censorship is having your book budget slashed, period. Real censorship is having all your money for salaries and acquisitions eaten up by the IT department. Real censorship is being persuaded that access to electronic content is everything, and the fact that you will have nothing to show when the subscriptions run out doesn't matter. Speaking truth to power in this situation is saying that as a librarian you want only what you can actually hold onto, not just what you can buy into.

Parts of web worship are funny. My personal favorite is when an online article says, "TABULAR OR GRAPHIC MATERIAL SET FORTH AT THIS POINT IS NOT DISPLAYABLE." Okay, I'll bite—if you haven't put the illustrations, graphs, and tables into the online version and I don't own the print version, how exactly do I track down the tabular or graphic material? However, those kinds of objections to the web are subject to technical ("we'll figure it out") responses so are best left alone. The more serious problem is that the web encourages us to buy into a worldview that is inconsistent with good librarianship. Libraries are not a subset of the computer industry; false techno-prophets should have no more say in the direction a library takes than carpet retailers or mini-blind manufacturers. Furthermore, computers are based on a franchise model of existence that does not apply to libraries. You can have a laptop in Bangkok or Boston and run Microsoft Word on either one. This transfers into the view that there exists a big vat of information that all of us tap into. This is a bland, professional bourgeois view of information as an undifferentiated and homogenous accumulation. Identical computer systems generate identical information needs: "Managing Your Wireless Network," "Dealing with IT Staff Turnover," "Recordable Media: The Year in Review." But, and this is the big but, information is not generic. Or more specifically, not all information users require identical information. Libraries are not just strip mall outlets of "Information Inc." For our patrons, geography, history, and local interests are distinct. In Canada, it would be a poor public library that had no copies of Robert Munsch. In Texas, the children's corner will have a copy of *The Armadillo from Amarillo*, which may not be in any libraries north of the U.S. border. In Canada, I would be ashamed to work in an academic library that didn't have a good collection of writings by Harold Innis. In the United States, it would be "Harold who? Oh, now Marshall McLuhan, we have something by him."

The answer is not to digitize every book in the universe and then create local profiles—nice job if it could be done but really a whole lot of unnecessary effort. The answer is to realize that computers deal in hardware/software and not content. Libraries are educational institutions in the broadest sense. Libraries are also linked to museums, schools, and archives. Teachers use computers; computers don't replace teachers. Ditto librarians.

Nicholson Baker, the library Antichrist, warned that paper card catalogs were being trashed out of a misguided macho vision of librarian as digital revolutionary, especially male librarians wanting to bury the notion of librarian as trivia-obsessed, dusting and shushing school-marm.[12] Add to that a desire to be fashionable,[13] the self-loathing of the middle-class elite,[14] and the desire to act as if technology itself is liberating when in fact it perpetuates privilege under the guise of pulling the dispossessed into a bold Star Trek future[15] and you have librarians who are willing to destroy the reality and destiny of libraries so that no one will think they aren't "with it." We need to fight for our right to be traditional, to acquire books and copyright-free electronic information, and to have a building with comfy furniture, chess sets, peace and quiet, and of course, story time.

NOTES

1. This chapter is dedicated to Peter Rukavina for teaching me everything I know about computers and the web; to Barbara McDonald, ditto librarianship; and to my wife, Sheila, who knows more about being a real human being than anyone I've ever met.

2. Reference/instruction librarian at Texas Tech University School of Law in Lubbock, Texas. The letters after his name spell SLIM B-BALL.

3. I got a glimpse of the complexity of the role of prophet from Paul Johnson's *A History of the Jews*. Prophets were predictors of the future but also religious judges; they valued content over ceremony. "His greatest single function was to act as intermediary between God and people, and to do that he must mingle with the masses." Paul Johnson, *A History of the Jews* (San Francisco: Harper & Row, 1987), 51–52.

4. Taking a break from working on this chapter, I picked up Thomas Merton's *No Man Is an Island*. He says, "The false prophet will accept any answer, provided that it is his own, provided it is *not* the answer of the herd." Thomas Merton, *No Man Is an Island* (San Diego: Harcourt Brace, 1983), xiii.

5. False prophets are referred to throughout the Bible. One reference to signs and wonders taking place but where the prophet "must be put to death because he preached rebellion against the Lord" is Deut. 13:1–5.

6. In my hometown the variation was "My Kingston includes Wolfe Island" for those who wanted to replace the ferry with a bridge.

7. I am sure some fancy French theorist would maintain that this scenario is as equally pornographic as the previous scenario, except here we are substituting bleeding-heart liberal social worker pornography for high-tech pornography. Point taken.

8. Of course it seems silly to imagine a person having to go to the library to use a computer to ask a reference question via the web when a librarian is sitting right

there—let's assume that even a poor person has a cheap computer at home or that cell phones with web access are within most people's budgets.

9. Nicholson Baker, who will be forgotten as the author of the wonderful book *Room Temperature* and remembered and vilified as the library Antichrist, sees signs of this institutional death wish in the destruction of card catalogs and old newspapers and will certainly be proven prophetic when we see libraries hauling all their book collections to the dump.

10. David Weinberger, *Small Pieces Loosely Joined* (Cambridge, Mass.: Perseus, 2002).

11. James Everett Katz, *Social Consequences of Internet Use: Access, Involvement and Interaction* (Cambridge, Mass.: MIT Press, 2002). As the web ages, discussion of "the future" is subject to the same kinds of social science statistical analysis and projection as any other human activity. Those who see the web as an all-conquering force have to contend with "net evaders, net dropouts and the truly disconnected" as described in *The Ever-Shifting Internet Population: A New Look at Internet Access and the Digital Divide*, at www .pewinternet.org/reports/toc.asp?Report=88 (accessed 26 March 2004).

12. "[Male librarians] believe that if they are disburdened of all that soiled cardboard, they will be able to define themselves as Brokers of Information and Off-Site Digital Retrievalists." In the next paragraph Baker reminds us, "The function of a great library is to sort and store obscure books." The original article, "Discards: Annals of Scholarship," appeared in the April 4, 1994, issue of *The New Yorker*, but I read it in *The Size of Thoughts: Essays and Other Lumber* (New York: Random House, 1996), 158.

13. "If nothing stands still, then everything—opinions, styles, information, fortunes, success, groups, society—falls victim to continuous change. Snobbery comes to stand as the fickle and arbitrary surrogate of good taste, which is based no longer on the canon of the beautiful but on that of fashion, of whatever is in vogue." Alberto Movaria, "Shelter from the Storm," in *Architecture of Fear*, edited by Nan Ellin (New York: Princeton Architectural Press, 1997), 14.

14. The web can also be dissected as part and parcel of what Saul calls "corporatism." John Ralston Saul, *The Unconscious Civilization* (Toronto: House of Anansi Press, 1996), 21–23.

15. Gay or straight, Marxist or capitalist, north or south, every person and organization *has* to have a computer, e-mail, and a website. All the "isms" are bracketed (perpetuated? reinvented?) in the presence of information technology. See Vicki K. Carter, "Virtual Shades of Pale: Education Technologies and the Electronic," in *Dismantling White Privilege: Pedagogy, Politics and Whiteness*, edited by Nelson M. Rodriguez and Leila E. Villaverde (New York: Peter Lang, 2000), 25–40.

3

The Library Blog: Serving Users and Staying Relevant

Amanda Etches-Johnson

With the recent buzz surrounding weblogs (or "blogs") and the blogging phenomenon, it would be almost impossible not to have come across the term, whether from a vexed journalist bemoaning the loss of traditional journalistic values for which weblogs are often blamed or from a champion of the format praising the democratization of the web that blogs have collectively stimulated. Either way, the blogging phenomenon has turned the world of journalism on its ear, and the impact of this phenomenon, whose popularity arose out of the technology's simplicity and ease of use, is being felt by anyone who deals with the Internet with any regularity.

It is not surprising then that blogs are causing a stir in the library world and that librarians were some of the first to embrace the format as means of personal expression, information dissemination, current awareness, community building, and professional public relations. But what is it about blogs that makes them so popular? Why are librarians and, increasingly, libraries drawn to them, and what are they using them for? Should more libraries be investigating the potential of weblogs in an institutional setting? And what could a library weblog possibly contribute to an institution? This chapter attempts to answer these questions and explores a few of the ways in which libraries can harness the power of blogs to better serve their users and how institutional blogging can ensure a library's relevance within its community and in the broader information landscape.[1]

WHY ALL THE FUSS? DEFINING WEBLOGS

Much like the rest of the Internet, a weblog is in fact different things to different people, and that is what makes defining it so problematic. Most blog commentators agree that the single characteristic that defines most, if not all, weblogs is format: "A weblog or *blog* is a website that's designed to be updated with items in a linear, time-based fashion, similar to a personal journal or diary, except that the contents are meant specifically for public consumption."[2] Comparing a weblog to a personal journal or diary is apropos not only because many blogs are typically personal in their content but also because blogs have become synonymous with a chatty, informal style, with entries (or "posts") arranged in reverse chronological order on the page. While format and additional features are set by the individual blog author (or "blogger"), each post generally includes a date, the time the entry was posted, the name of the author, and a permanent link (or "permalink") for the post. Additional features include the ability to categorize posts by subject, a comment feature that allows readers to provide feedback for each entry, and the ability to generate an RSS feed (a formatted XML file) that can be used to deliver the blog's content to users via an RSS aggregator or to syndicate that content on other websites.

Even those who have never visited a weblog will likely find this definition somewhat familiar because the Internet community in general, and the blogging community in particular, agree in principle that the typical "What's New" page seen on various corporate, governmental, educational, and personal websites was the prototype for the modern day blog. As Paul Bausch, Matthew Haughey, and Meg Hourihan explain, "A What's New page is like a weblog of all the changes and new features added to a Web site, a place to post news about the company. . . . these pages serve as a primary place for news specifically designed for dissemination of information to repeat visitors of a Web site."[3] In fact, one particular blog management tool still markets its service in this manner: "Tired of updating your 'news' page for your Web site and want a page you can update easily, quickly and from any web browser?"[4]

While it is generally accepted that technology does not define weblogs, it is probably safe to assume that technology has made them popular. Bausch et al. note that the earliest bloggers were Internet- and tech-savvy individuals who wrote "their own software to automate the posting and sorting of their sites."[5] It was only when blog management software was released to the Internet public that those without these skills could jump on the blog bandwagon with relative ease. The popularity of weblogs positively exploded when, in 1999, two blog management services were launched in close succession (first Pitas, followed a month later by Blogger[6]), and since that time, the buzz surrounding weblogs has yet to diminish.[7]

This popularity can, in large part, be attributed to the ease with which a blog can be set up and maintained. Presently, the nascent blogger can choose from dozens of free applications that are either centrally hosted or that can be downloaded to a hard drive or server. In either case, the blogger merely needs to go to a website or open an application, log in with an established username and password, and compose the blog entry in the form provided. Little to no knowledge of HTML is required to set up and maintain a blog, and helpful buttons on most of the publishing interfaces provide shortcuts to format text, insert a link to a website, and even spell check the entry before publishing it to the site.

THEY *DO* HAVE BLOGS: WHY THE FORMAT FITS LIBRARIANS

A glance at any directory of library-related weblogs[8] is enough to convince anyone of the exploding popularity of the format with librarians. Some of the earliest weblogs served as filters for the mass of information found on the web. As Rebecca Blood notes, the "classic weblog" was "organized squarely around the link, maintained by an inveterate Web surfer"[9] who was in fact filtering the information found on the web or "pre-surfing" for the benefit of his or her audience.[10] Given this definition, it is not difficult to see why librarians were naturally drawn to the format: From a basic service standpoint, selecting the best resources to serve a library's users is an inherent part of a librarian's daily work. This selection is more than a simple acquisitions activity. Resource selection is undertaken every time a subject bibliography is developed, highlighting a library collection's strengths in a particular area of research; every time a library research guide is compiled as an accompaniment to a bibliographic instruction session; and every time an exchange takes place at a reference desk, where any sort of reader's advisory or recommendation is offered by a librarian.

Examples of the ways in which librarians make filtering decisions are quite literally countless; the point is that filtering information and providing access to authoritative sources is *what we do*. It is what we have been trained to do, and with the emergence of the Internet as a significant information resource, it is perhaps the most time-consuming, if not the most significant, part of our jobs. Librarians were surfing even before surfing became a metaphor for trolling the Internet, and blogs provide the perfect format to present that material. As Blake Carver notes, blogs are "tools to do what we've always done: collect, categorize, and make information accessible."[11]

It is not surprising then that creating, maintaining, and reading weblogs feels like a natural extension of what librarians have been doing for most of their professional lives. For most librarians who maintain weblogs on a regular basis, publishing content to their blogs is part of an established personal ritual of keeping current by reading through library literature, listserv subscriptions, newsletters, zines, and other blogs. Sharing that content rises out of the collegiality that is such a defining principle of the library profession. As Elizabeth Thomsen succinctly points out, "Librarians are natural collectors and sharers."[12]

Furthermore, new librarian-authored blogs continue to spring up on the Internet landscape with surprising regularity. Steven Cohen and Greg Schwartz maintain LIS Blogsource,[13] a blog devoted to tracking new library-related weblogs. Both agree that as a result of their daily web trawling, they find an average of thirty new or previously unknown library-related blogs per month.[14] That librarians continue to start their own weblogs with consistent regularity is a testament to the devoted audience these blogs have, since most blog authors start out as blog readers and, as Walt Crawford notes, "Logs beget logs."[15]

SO, WHAT ARE LIBRARIANS DOING WITH BLOGS?

Weblogs have come a long way from being simple lists of links with accompanying annotations. Librarians have been experimenting with weblogs for a while, and currently a large number of library blogs are targeted to general and subject-specific audiences. General-interest library blogs are those devoted to library news and culture issues, and one of the most popular of these is the long-running librarian.net,[16] maintained by Jessamyn West. With a target audience consisting of librarians, West uses librarian.net to link to and discuss news stories that feature libraries and librarians, as well as to monitor and comment on issues and legislation that impact the mission of the library. Similarly, Steven Cohen's Library Stuff[17] is written for the professional community and highlights current awareness tools and resources for librarians who have an interest in professional development. Gary Price's popular ResourceShelf[18] is a regularly updated list of online resources that would benefit practically anyone who does web searching.

In addition to the general library news and culture weblogs, a plethora of subject-specific library blogs are targeted to specific groups of librarians. For example, David Bigwood's Catalogablog[19] is devoted to cataloging and classification issues, Dan Chudnov's oss4lib[20] provides information on and access to open source systems for libraries, and Randy Reichardt and Geoff Harder's blog, the SciTech Library Question,[21] discusses issues that are of import to engineering, science, and technology librarians.

Other librarians have made a point of using the blog format to build community, as Blake Carver has done with LISNews.com.[22] LISNews .com is a library community site that encourages readers to register on the site and post entries themselves. The added benefit of user comments means that each post does not begin and end with the author but becomes a dynamic discussion. As Carver himself explains, "The comments become part of the stories, adding to it in ways that you can't find anywhere in print."[23]

WITHER THE INSTITUTIONAL BLOG?

While individual librarians have been taking advantage of the power of weblogs since the format first became popular in the late 1990s, library institutions are just beginning to harness the many advantages of weblogs to reach out to their user communities. These institutions are in the forefront, experimenting with new technologies to better serve their users. While many share a common purpose when publishing their weblogs, others are finding ways to use blogs to serve their constituents in varied and creative ways.

What's New Pages

Perhaps the single largest use of the weblog format by libraries is the What's New page. These pages cater to the library's various user groups by posting new resources acquired by the library, changes to the library's programming or physical arrangement, and events in the library and the community. Examples of these include the Adams County Library System weblog,[24] which is devoted to announcing library programs, and Escondido Public Library's What's New page,[25] which provides community news and information on library events, as does the Waterboro Public Library via their h20boro lib blog[26] and the Urbana Free Library weblog,[27] which is used exclusively for construction updates on the library's expansion project. Thanks in large part to the ease with which updates can be posted and content managed, it is abundantly clear why the blog format is suited to this sort of information. Since much of the material on a typical What's New page is only current for a short period of time, using a blog to manage this content and allow older "news" to be archived off the main page makes perfect sense. For this reason, traditional print marketing (in library newsletters or community papers) could likely fall into extinction in favor of a library blog.

Current Awareness

As was the case with individual librarians' blogs, institutions have discovered the benefit of using blogs as a current awareness tool to serve specific communities. Chi Lib Rocks![28] is the blog of the Chicago Library System, a member organization that serves the library community in Chicago. This blog provides its member community with information on the organization and its programming and also includes current awareness information, such as timely news stories and legislation of value to its constituents. The Alberta Gaming Research Institute Library uses its weblog[29] to provide information and news links that pertain to gambling and gaming. Rhys Stevens, the institute librarian and information specialist, notes that the blog attracts others who have an interest in the topic (some of whom maintain their own blogs on gaming), as well as gambling researchers.[30] The Veterinary Medicine Library at the University of Saskatchewan publishes a link-rich weblog[31] for news in the field of veterinary medicine. Jilly Crawley-Low, the department head, maintains the blog and points out that since many of the faculty, members, staff, and students use the Veterinary Medicine Library's home page as their browsers' default home page, the weblog format works well for delivering topical posts that are pertinent to the research in which they are engaged.[32]

READERS' ADVISORY AND LITERARY NEWS

Readers' advisory weblogs provide an effective avenue to bring new book suggestions and literary news to a library's community of users. The Glenview Public Library maintains a blog called the Reader's Connection whose mandate is to provide readers' advisory information and resources to its user group. Another example is Waterboro Public Library's weblog, h20boro lib blog, mentioned previously, which also provides readers' advisory through announcements of fiction contests and literary award nominees and winners. A readers' advisory blog can complement existing reading and outreach programs and would be of particular benefit for patrons who are located a considerable distance from their nearest branch library.

WHAT'S NEXT?

Many unexplored possibilities for institutional weblogs have the potential to revolutionize the way users interact with and receive information from libraries. Mita Sen-Roy, who maintains the blog for the Leddy Library at the University of Windsor, defines an ideal library blog as "one that would tie local and global events to the material and services in the library . . . as a means to demonstrate that libraries can serve a useful purpose, enriching one's day-to-day information life."[33]

Blake Carver notes that "adding a blog to your library's Web site can add currency and freshness."[34] Transforming a library website from a series of static pages into a dynamic portal has advantages in that users may be encouraged to return to the site on a more regular basis if they know the content is updated frequently. As we have already seen, weblogs provide the ideal format and technology that make delivering content simple and fast. Apart from offering fresh library content on a regular basis, weblogs provide all the necessary tools to turn a library website into a collaborative network that encourages, and indeed thrives on, community participation and interaction, two of the cornerstones of the library as a community institution. Rachel Singer Gordon points out:

> With all our talk about knowledge communities, we need to go back to our roots and provide an egalitarian space where both patrons and librarians can contribute. When others are truly able to participate in the

discussions and communities we facilitate, then they begin to feel as if they have a stake in our institutions' success. When we only put up resources and don't allow users the opportunity to join in or comment, it is not true communication.[35]

With weblogs, much of this communication and interaction can be accomplished by making use of some of the advanced features built into most blog management tools.

Invite Feedback through User Comments

Before we can start thinking about a library's website as a place for community participation, we need to stop thinking about the blog format merely in terms of a What's New page and start thinking of it as a dynamic, user-centered, interactive space. The first logical step to accomplish this transition would be to implement the blog's commenting feature. As discussed previously, many blog management tools include a commenting feature that allows readers to append their comments to the end of each post. Those who use applications that do not include this feature (e.g., Blogger) can access many of the free services available online[36] that allow institutions to add a commenting feature to their blogs by adding a line of JavaScript code to their blog templates. At its simplest, this function provides a platform from which readers can comment on library issues. Giving the library user the ability to connect instantly with the library, as well as the rest of the library community, provides for open dialogue and knowledge sharing, two of the basic goals most libraries already aspire to.

Encourage Community Collaboration

Using a library weblog to create community could be achieved by implementing collaborative blogging. Blake Carver's LISNews.com, the collaborative weblog devoted to library and information science news and current awareness discussed previously, provides ample evidence that blogs might be the perfect forum to encourage community interaction. At LISNews.com, readers request an account or login in order to begin posting entries themselves, and as Carver explains, the blogs "follow a semi-open model, where a team of editors screen open submissions and make the final decision on what gets posted. . . . Diversity among both contributors and editors fosters broad content and instigates free exchange."[37]

While LISNews is an example of a collaborative blog for the professional library community, there is no reason why a similar model cannot be successfully implemented for a broader user community. Geoffrey Harder and Randy Reichardt suggest a virtual book club as one way in which collaborative blogging could be used in a public library setting where patrons could post discussion topics and reviews of the book under discussion.[38] Libraries serving communities that are physically dispersed would benefit greatly from this sort of virtual collaborative endeavor, while libraries with a thriving local population could implement a collaborative blog to enhance existing programs. This sort of model opens up the library blog to true collaboration, where library users are actually generating discussion topics and playing an important role in public discourse. How appropriate for a library blog to be a collection of the voices of the community it serves!

If You've Got It, Syndicate It

As one technology commentator rightly notes, "I've been looking at the future of information and part of it is spelled R-S-S."[39] No discussion of weblogs and their potential in the library world is complete without a discussion of RSS. RSS, mentioned briefly earlier, "is an XML format used to distribute content via a self-syndication method. . . . it helps you offer and receive the information you want in a convenient way."[40] Most blog management tools have the ability to publish an RSS feed by simply pressing a button to turn on the option. Once selected, an XML document containing tags that describe the post's content is published to the site's server. On its own, an XML document opened in a standard web browser will produce a page with a lot of text and bizarre code, which is why an RSS reader or news aggregator is required to receive the feeds and translate them into the standard hypertext documents we are used to seeing on the web.

One of the key advantages of RSS feeds is the amount of time saved by having the content you want delivered to you when you want it. As Steven Cohen explains, "Instead of bookmarking various sites and returning to them every day, the user can set up a feed so that the data from those sites are sent to a news aggregator that resides on the user's desktop."[41] Additionally, RSS answers those critics who claim the success of a weblog is predicated on site traffic. Publishing a feed for a blog pushes fresh content out to the user as opposed to forcing the user to go in search of that content.

Currently, RSS is gaining considerable publicity and momentum thanks to the simplicity and ease with which RSS feeds can be created and publicized on the web. Every day, more websites add the syndication feature, and more news sources are publishing RSS feeds and allowing their headlines to be syndicated all over the web (including CNN, the *New York Times*, MSNBC, BBC, the *Washington Post, USA Today*, and the Associated Press[42]). The library world is already embracing XML as "an important tool, with wide-ranging implications for how information will be handled in the future."[43] Because XML powers RSS, it has the potential to become the standard for online content delivery, which is why libraries need to start thinking about getting into the RSS game.

Starting a library weblog is the first step. Publishing an RSS feed for the content of that blog will make sure that along with daily news and other specialized content, library patrons will receive information from their library. Mita Sen-Roy has an idea about the role of a library weblog in the information landscape, and that idea centers around the currency and topicality of the information provided in the blog: "If a particular wacky psychology study was being talked about on the radio and written about in the newspaper, the [library] blog could try to track down its scholarly source."[44] This is not only the perfect example of the optimum synergy that exists between blogs and RSS but also an example of the manner in which the library can fulfill the information needs of its users with the aid of this exciting technology and remain an important player in the world of content delivery.

Furthermore, the more libraries publish their own weblogs and RSS feeds, the more likely that the library as an institution will solidify its place on the information landscape. Gordon justifiably notes:

> The electronic environment provides unique opportunities to get our profession and ourselves onto the public's radar. We librarians need to become more proactive in promoting both our own and the profession's expertise in a variety of online communities, by establishing ongoing connections and becoming as integral a part of community life online as we have traditionally been in the "real world."[45]

RSS provides an ideal platform from which the library can become an "integral part of community life online" through its ability to deliver information to those who want it and to allow interested parties to syndicate that information on their own websites. For example, a library that owns a special collection of interest to a particular area of research could use a weblog to publicize that collection, which would in turn allow other related sites to capture those key headlines and publish them to their audiences. As RSS continues to gain momentum and popularity, more government, business, and nonprofit organizations will be using syndicated feeds to publish content to their own pages. With libraries publishing topical content on their weblogs and providing RSS feeds for that information, these groups will be able to syndicate content from library weblogs alongside news and headline feeds from traditional media sources such as newspapers and media companies, cementing the library's relevance in online information provision.

WHY BLOG AND WHY NOW?

Over the past two years, a number of articles published in the library literature have extolled the virtues of blogs in the library world and answered the question "why blog?" with a simple "why not blog?" This chapter has attempted to show that blog management tools have made the task of establishing and maintaining a weblog so simple that even those libraries that do not have access to vast technological resources can still use a blog to reach out to their patrons in new ways. However, it would be naive to assume that a weblog is the answer to every library's marketing and outreach endeavors. Darlene Fichter points out that one of the first questions a library needs to consider before establishing a blog is "whether your target audience is online in sufficient numbers to make a blog worthwhile."[46] As mentioned previously, adding fresh content to a library's web page can go a long way toward increasing and maintaining traffic to the site, but a library that serves a community without widespread online access would be better advised to maintain its more established marketing and outreach methods while staying attuned to the growing number of online tools that can be implemented once its user community has the access to take advantage of them.

Libraries that serve communities with widespread online access, and whose patrons are accustomed to receiving information from web-based sources, should always be on the lookout for ways to facilitate access to online information. Many libraries have come to the realization that developing their collections and waiting for patrons to come to the library is short sighted and irresponsible. As a result, these libraries are seeking out new ways to service the information needs of their patrons, and blogs provide a fresh, new opportunity to do so. Rachel Singer Gordon equates the need to embrace new technologies with the need for libraries to stay relevant:

> As online interaction becomes integrated into people's daily lives, we need to become involved in these conversations. . . . Libraries have spent years putting information online, but have often relied solely on traditional PR methods such as newsletter and newspaper announcements to get the word out. We need to work instead to make our resources a natural part of users' daily online experiences.[47]

As simple and affordable new technologies such as blogs and RSS become regular components in our users' information toolkits, libraries need to implement these technologies or risk being left out of the information and content delivery loop.

THE FUTURE IS NOW

As we have seen, a handful of libraries have begun taking those all-important first steps in realizing the potential of weblogs. At a rudimentary level, weblogs provide a simple, cost-effective way for a library to update the content of its web pages. At their most ambitious, blogs have the potential to change how libraries serve their users by creating dynamic, interactive, virtual spaces that encourage participation, stimulate knowledge exchange, and create communities of learning. Libraries can no longer be content with supplying authoritative content. Occupying the pole position in an information society and cementing the library's relevance in today's online world also necessitate using bleeding-edge technology to deliver that content wherever possible. Since bleeding-edge technology has rarely before been packaged in such easily implemented tools, institutions have little excuse not to avail themselves of the benefits blogs have to offer.

NOTES

1. More resources on libraries and their use of weblogs can be found at the author's website (www.blogwithoutalibrary.net).
2. Todd Stauffer, *Blog On: The Essential Guide to Building Dynamic Weblogs* (New York: McGraw-Hill, 2002), 4.

3. Paul Bausch, Matthew Haughey, and Meg Hourihan, *We Blog: Publishing Online with Weblogs* (Indianapolis, Ind.: Wiley, 2002), 9.

4. Pitas.com, at www.pitas.com (accessed 15 August 2003).

5. Bausch et al., *We Blog*, 10.

6. Blogger, at www.blogger.com (accessed 2 August 2003).

7. Rebecca Blood, *The Weblog Handbook: Practical Advice on Creating and Maintaining Your Blog* (Cambridge, Mass.: Perseus, 2002), 5.

8. Peter Scott, from the University of Saskatchewan, maintains the most comprehensive of these directories at www.libdex.com/weblogs.html (accessed 23 July 2003).

9. Blood, *The Weblog Handbook*, 7.

10. Bausch et al., *We Blog*, 30.

11. Blake Carver, "Is It Time to Get Blogging?" *NetConnect* (Winter 2003), at www.libraryjournal.com/article/CA266428 (accessed 31 March 2004).

12. Elizabeth B. Thomsen, "Blogging, Anyone?" *Collection Building* 21, no.2 (2002): 77.

13. Steven M. Cohen and Greg Schwartz, LIS Blogsource, at lisblogsource.net (accessed 12 October 2003).

14. Steven M. Cohen and Greg Schwartz, personal communication, 20 September 2003.

15. Walt Crawford, "The E-files: 'You Must Read This': Library Weblogs," *American Libraries* 32, no. 9 (October 2001): 75.

16. Jessamyn West, librarian.net, at www.librarian.net (accessed 3 June 2003).

17. Steven M. Cohen, Library Stuff, at www.librarystuff.net (accessed 1 June 2003).

18. Gary Price, ResourceShelf, at www.resourceshelf.com (accessed 1 June 2003).

19. David Bigwood, Catalogablog, at catalogablog.blogspot.com (accessed 5 June 2003).

20. Dan Chudnov, oss4lib, at www.oss4lib.org (accessed 5 June 2003).

21. Geoff Harder and Randy Reichardt, the SciTech Library Question, at stlq.info (accessed 5 June 2003).

22. LISNews.com: Librarian and Information Science News, at www.lisnews.com (accessed 5 June 2003).

23. Gillian Davis, "An Interview with Blake Carver. Pt. 2" (2002), at www.suite101.com/article.cfm/9460/90957 (accessed 23 August 2003).

24. Adams County Library System, at adamslibrary1.blogspot.com (accessed 28 June 2003).

25. Escondido Public Library's Latest News, at escondidolibrary.blogspot.com (accessed 28 June 2003).

26. h2oboro lib blog, at www.waterborolibrary.org/blog.htm (accessed 28 June 2003).

27. The Urbana Free Library Construction Updates, at urbanafreelibrary.org/bldgblog.html (accessed 28 June 2003).

28. Chi Lib Rocks!, at radio.weblogs.com/0111803 (accessed 28 June 2003).

29. Rhys Stevens, Alberta Gaming Research Institute Library Weblog, at www.abgaminginstitute.ualberta.ca/agrilibrary/blogger.html (accessed 16 September 2003).

30. Rhys Stevens, personal communication, 19 September 2003.

31. Veterinary Medicine Library, at library.usask.ca/vetmed/blog.html (accessed 12 September 2003).

32. Jilly Crawley-Low, personal communication, 19 September 2003.

33. Mita Sen-Roy, personal communication, 23 September 2003.

34. Carver, "Time to Get Blogging?" 28.

35. Rachel Singer Gordon, "Relevant Yesterday, Relevant Tomorrow—But How to Stay Relevant Today?" *Computers in Libraries* 23, no. 9 (October 2003): 47.

36. BlogKomm (www.blogkomm.com) and Haloscan (www.haloscan.com) are two examples of free blog commenting services that can be added to an existing blog regardless of the blog management software being used.

37. Carver, "Time to Get Blogging?" 17.

38. Geoffrey Harder and Randy Reichardt, "Throw Another Blog on the Wire: Libraries and the Weblogging Phenomena," *Feliciter* 49, no. 2 (2003): 87.

39. Dan Gillmor, "RSS Starting to Catch On," *Computerworld* 3, no. 30 (2003): 19.

40. Gillmor, "RSS Starting to Catch On," 19.

41. Steven M. Cohen, "Using RSS: An Explanation and Guide," *Information Outlook* 6, no. 12 (December 2002): 7.

42. J. D. Lasica, "News That Comes to You," *Online Journalism Review* (2003): 14, at www.ojr.org/ojr/lasica/1043362624.php (accessed 31 March 2004).

43. Davida Scharf, "XML Under the Hood," *Information Outlook* 6, no. 12 (December 2002): 21.

44. Mita Sen-Roy, personal communication, 23 September 2003.

45. Gordon, "How to Stay Relevant," 11.

46. Darlene Fichter, "Why and How to Use Blogs to Promote Your Library's Services," *Marketing Library Services* 17, no. 6 (November 2003): 13, at www.infotoday.com/mls/nov03/fichter.shtml (accessed 31 March 2004).

47. Gordon, "How to Stay Relevant," 11–12.

Part 2

WAKE UP AND SMELL THE COFFEE: HOW DO WE REINVENT THE LIBRARY AS PLACE?

For cutting-edge change to take place in libraries, we must recruit librarians to the profession who are not enthralled with today's libraries, even ones that have experimented with new physical spaces, but rather are capable of envisioning the library of tomorrow and a profession more in step with our already changed society.

—Ruth E. Kifer

In recognition of the importance of continuity of library buildings as civic space, we should design and build our libraries to both last and inspire.

—Paul Whitney

The reality, though, is that public libraries are being increasingly called on to fill the void left by inadequately funded school libraries and insufficient teacher-librarian positions.

—Patricia Jobb

4

"Real" University Libraries Don't Have Neon Lights

Ruth E. Kifer

The George W. Johnson Center (initially named University Center), the first university building of its genre in the United States, opened during the fall 1995 semester on the Fairfax, Virginia, campus of George Mason University. The unconventional Johnson Center Library occupies approximately one third of the 320,000-square-foot hybrid academic/student activities building. Now, after almost eight years of experience providing library services in space unlike any other academic library, George Mason University Libraries can begin to evaluate the effectiveness of this innovation on the "library as place" and plan for future enhancements. Because the success of any library is based on far more than its collections and the physical space in which it operates, an examination of George Mason University's Johnson Center Library as "place" cannot be undertaken without also looking at the Johnson Center Library as "people."

A WORD ON "LIBRARY AS PLACE"

The phrase "library as place" is cropping up in the literature with increasing frequency as the profession begins to acknowledge that what libraries offer is not something that today's library users and potential users see as exclusively the library's domain. Although librarians are quick to point out that using an Internet search engine to find authoritative information on a topic is not always sufficient and that people need information professionals more than ever, this does not compute with the average library user, and more important, it may be meaningless for nonlibrary users. With more information and misinformation available free for the taking, the word on the street is that academic libraries are now more irrelevant than many librarians dare to believe. Our proselytizing has not won over the masses, not even those teaching faculty who may dutifully send their students to the library but think it unnecessary for their own research needs.

Some academic librarians are beginning to wonder if perhaps their passion for providing services that they perceive their users need, instead of what the library users want, may be having negative and unintended consequences. Statistics show that as the online world has expanded exponentially, foot traffic and circulation of print materials in academic libraries have declined. And so, one after another, those fashionable coffee shops have cropped up in many academic libraries, and prohibitions against food and beverages are relaxed. Academic library administrators are hoping this acquiescence to popular trends will foster as much of an increase in library use as it has profit for the retail booksellers. This is certainly a move in the right direction, but academic librarians must realize that such conveniences, although well intentioned, are merely baby steps toward making the library relevant within our institutions. Examination of the Johnson Center Library concept (the coffee shop is not in the library, but the library did try moving materials to the coffee shop) at this juncture in its evolution may identify issues for the library profession to ponder in the current discussion of library as place.

A WORD ON "LIBRARY AS PEOPLE"

How students, faculty, and librarians lead their lives today is dramatically different from the lives of many library decision makers when they entered the profession, certainly different from the undergraduate days of most library directors, and even different from the undergraduate world as recent as a decade ago. Students in the eighteen- to twenty-two-year-old age bracket (and even older) have never known a time without computers; are accustomed to being always connected (IM, chat, cell phones); expect 24/7 service (such as retail copy service outlets); and are more inundated with mass media and pop culture imagery than ever before. With more discretionary funds to expend than were available to previous college-age students, this generation grew up in the shopping mall, eagerly sought after by mass marketers and retailers who have catered to their likes and dislikes, seeking to create lifelong brand name loyalists.

Picture the features of many academic libraries. Upon entering a library building, students see admonitions against entering with food and are informed of the facility's closing time; after they have walked through book detection gates, they may be greeted by a security guard; they often encounter an imposing circulation desk; and in spite of their technological expertise and feigned sophistication, they can be intimidated. Students may be in search of a book, a journal article, the location of a required library instruction class, or something unfamiliar to them—a bibliographic or full-text database. If they are self-assured and assertive, they will ask for help. Or perhaps, as is often the case when people of all ages enter an unfamiliar situation, they will pretend to know what they are doing. Many will dart for the first known thing they see, a computer, and attempt to "Google" for the needed resource or seek help from a peer via e-mail or chat. In any library facility, regardless of its physical design, the crucial factor in whether students have a successful experience and will be motivated to return is the intervention provided by the people who work in the library.

Librarians and library staff are often drawn to the library profession because of their love of scholarship, their fascination with technology, their perception that it is an easy first job after graduation, their missionary zeal for being part of a "helping" profession, their aspiration to teach, their dissatisfaction with their first career choice, or any number of other reasons. Whatever the motivation, some in the profession unwittingly live up to the media stereotype of librarians as introverted, rigid, or schoolmarmish. Meeting up with a less than enthusiastic librarian when seeking research help, or a procedure-strapped circulation assistant when attempting to charge materials without the forgotten ID card, results in an unsatisfactory experience for a student, who may choose not to return for the next assignment. Logging on to a "research paper for sale" website may be more attractive and ultimately more productive from the student's perspective.

HISTORY AND BACKGROUND OF THE JOHNSON CENTER LIBRARY

George Mason University is a state-funded institution of higher education in the busy metropolitan Washington, D.C., area and is one of the fastest growing universities in the Commonwealth of Virginia. Established as an independent university in 1972, it has grown dramatically in a relatively short time period. Student enrollment (head count) in the 2003 fall semester was over 27,000, up by 3,000 since 1995 when the Johnson Center Library opened its doors. The student population is diverse ethnically, attracting students with roots in virtually every area of the world. The average student age is twenty-nine, well above the traditional college-age student, although approximately 3,600 eighteen-to twenty-two-year-old residential students live on the Fairfax campus.

In the late 1980s and early 1990s, the university recognized the need for a facility that would meet the academic, cocurricular, and social needs of its ethnically, racially, economically, and generationally diverse student population. At the same time the university's only library was outgrowing its stacks and badly needed additional seating space. These two demonstrated needs, along with a growing desire to foster a sense of community for a growing residential population and a well-established commuter constituency, established the backdrop for the creation of the Johnson Center and the Johnson Center Library. It is significant that the Johnson Center Library is one of four libraries in the university library system and one of two libraries on the Fairfax campus. (It is the view of this writer and others closely involved with the library that the Johnson Center Library as designed would not be effective if it was the only library on campus.)

The purpose of this chapter is not to retell the story of the history and planning of the Johnson Center at George Mason University. However, knowledge of the history of the university and the process employed to plan and build the facility is essential to understand the environment within which the concept of the building and the library's place therein developed. The history, background, and planning of the Johnson Center Library is described in detail by Charlene Hurt, director of libraries (1984–1997), in a chapter of the book *Building Libraries for the 21st Century*.[1]

Special recognition must be given to Ms. Hurt and George W. Johnson, George Mason University president (1978–1996). President Johnson catapulted the endeavor with his out-of-the-box thinking, and library director Hurt provided leadership and extraordinary vision for the integration of the library program throughout the building. President Johnson is quoted as saying:

> Forget anything you think you know and return to ignorance. Retain traditional values and outcomes. We still want a graduate to be schooled in

traditional subjects, imaginatively capable of judgments that are honorable to alternative realities, capable of judgments that are honorable and critical, poised in the face of complexities. . . . But abandon all conventional means for achieving those outcomes.[2]

The Johnson Center is a prime example of this premise in action. Its concept is unique, unconventional, and bold; yet, the planned outcomes are traditional—the support of learning, student development, and community.

Description of the Building

Covering approximately eight acres, the Johnson Center contains twenty-two wired group study rooms, ten large sunny student lounge areas, a 310-seat cinema, a student technology assistance and resource center (STAR), student computer labs, the university bookstore, an art gallery, the university computer store, a large food court, the Johnson Center Library, and seating for over 2,000 throughout the building. The Johnson Center website at jcweb.gmu.edu provides a plethora of factual information about the building, the planning process, and the philosophy underpinning the concept, along with contact information for other units housed in the center.[3] Even more than anticipated, this mall-like building has become the vibrant and always crowded center of campus. (Approximately three million individuals stepped through the building's doors during the 2002–2003 academic year.) Location in this environment gives the library a great deal of visibility, and the unique physical design and configuration of the collections have defined library services.

What is most strikingly different about the library itself? As students approach the front door of the controlled library, they first see the bright, colorful neon lights shining in the six large storefront-type windows. Those neon lights market what is to be found inside: books, web access, videos, DVDs, magazines, newspapers, and more. Once inside the door, more neon directs visitors to the stairway leading to the second floor of the library. Numerous computer pods hold four computers each in a circular fashion, with bright blue hoods drawing one's attention to them. With over fifty computers on two floors in the public area of the controlled library, students often ask, "Where are the books?" Large hanging banners (white letters on bold blue background) direct library users to the media collections and viewing/listening stations, the circulation and course reserves desk, and the reference desk. A small collection of reference books (approximately 3,000 volumes) and musical scores is housed on the first floor, but the design and placement of the computer furniture and the visibility of the media collections (the combined total of media formats and musical scores is approximately 34,000 volumes) overshadow the book collection. This is intentional. "Where *are* the books?" The library emphasizes electronic access over print collections, seeking to present itself as a gateway to information resources and not merely a storehouse of books. However, there is a circulating collection that as of September 2003 numbers approximately 112,000 volumes. The circulating book collection is shelved in open stacks located outside the controlled part of the library, on the second and third floors, and is accessible to anybody walking through the building. Lack of walls around the book collection gives the library a unique feel and makes the collection more accessible to students who visit the building for reasons other than "going to the library."

Another striking difference that most newcomers comment on is the smell of food and the number of students eating a snack or lunch in full view of library staff. Again, this is intentional. Students are not placed in an awkward or guilt-producing situation where they must hide food in large pockets and backpacks in order to elude library staff. With food permitted and smuggling unnecessary, some think there is actually less in the way of spills and damage from food and beverages than in libraries where users must revert to deception. The library is situated very close to the university's largest food court and student gathering place, attracting many students to the library who may have initially come to the building just for lunch. The lack of a prohibition against eating in the library, along with other features such as full wiring of study carrels and extended hours, represents an effort to create a truly open and barrier-free learning environment. Numerous group meeting places encourage collaborative learning, and the building's food court and marketplace atmosphere provide a community gathering place and opportunity for structured and impromptu multicultural activities.

Circulation, Course Reserves, Collections, Reference, Instruction

The library circulation and course reserves desk provides traditional services and is the primary service point for the media collection. Prior to the opening of the Johnson Center, media materials were housed in closed stacks in the Fenwick building, and the media staff took a great deal of pride in their control over the carefully organized media collection. After the merging of media and print formats in the Johnson Center Library and the housing of media materials in open stacks, some library staff members were troubled because of the apparent lack of control. It is true that the media collection is not as protected as previously, and as a result there is a larger loss rate than when materials were retrieved by staff from closed stacks. However, the overall benefit of the new arrangement has been a significant increase in the use of the media collection by students for assignments or for leisure purposes and by faculty for use in teaching. Weighed against a rather low loss rate, the benefit of increased use far outweighs any loss.

Print Collection: Development and Maintenance

The Johnson Center Library also houses circulating books, reference materials, media and multimedia formats, and a small newspaper collection. George Mason University Libraries experimented with a number of approaches to build the collection. At present, Johnson Center librarians lead teams of subject liaison librarians from other George Mason libraries and collaboratively develop the overall Johnson Center Library circulating collection. It should be noted that this has had mixed success and may change at some time in the future. Initially, the Johnson Center Library circulating collection contained core foundation texts, supporting undergraduate study, technology, and diversity in its broadest meaning.

In an article written by Hurt et al., librarian collectors describe the collection development strategies and activities employed in building the collection for this unique open stack space.[4] Since the opening of the library, the focus has changed somewhat, and the university's entire subject collections (both graduate and undergraduate level) in music and education have been shifted from the main research library. A serious space shortage in the Fenwick Library was the impetus for this shift; however, the determination of which subject areas to move was made in consultation with faculty and with consideration given to complementary collections already housed in the Johnson Center. Housing the music collection in the Johnson Center Library provides ease of access for students and faculty in music programs because monographs, scores, and media formats are all in one location. Locating the education collection in the Johnson Center Library, including state-approved K–12 teaching materials for Virginia's public schools, fits well with the learning component of the center's mission.

The circulating collection is housed in the open portion of the library, so security of materials is an ongoing issue. Because of the unique openness of the stacks area, an inventory of the open stacks was conducted annually for the first five years the library was open. Although the loss rate for the collection has remained low, selectors consider cost and potential for loss or theft when deciding where to locate a specific title. As with many traditional libraries with walls, the computer science and technology area is the section with the highest loss rate. Subsequently, selectors now designate a higher percentage of those titles to be shelved in the research library and not the Johnson Center.

The practical matter of managing the collection in this open configuration has been complex and challenging. Initially, self-check machines were located at the outer doors of the building so that students could charge out materials themselves without a trip to the circulation desk located in the controlled library. However, use of this self-check technology was not intuitive for library users, and the units were located far from those who could provide assistance. After several years of attempts to improve the level of customer satisfaction with this technology, the decision was made to eliminate the self-check units. The technology has been much more successful in the public library setting because the units are placed adjacent to service desks where staff are available. However, the size and design of the Johnson Center and the number of doors did not make this a reasonable solution. Now students may charge materials at the circulation desk located inside the controlled library or at the information desk located in the center of the building.

Instruction

A prime goal of the Johnson Center since its opening has been to foster and support learning by creating an environment conducive to collaboration among learners and the development of learning communities. Kevin Simons and James Young, Johnson Center instruction librarians, with Craig Gibson discuss the library's role in this environment at length in "The Learning Library in Context."[5] The physical design of the facility and the nature of the academic tenants in the building have contributed to the success of librarians' efforts to integrate library instruction into the curriculum of at least one major academic program, New Century College (NCC), an interdisciplinary undergraduate degree program that emphasizes collaborative learning. The library assumes a significant role in the first-year curriculum of NCC, and the NCC liaison librarian established collegial relationships with NCC faculty, designed multiple library instruction sessions for the freshman class, and functioned in many ways as a teaching faculty member within the college. This was an expansion of the library instruction program at George Mason University. Significantly, the librarians have played an active role in the assessment of student work, a function most often reserved for the teaching faculty. This library success can in part be attributed to the innovative design of the Johnson Center Library "as place" and the creative librarians attracted to working in this environment.

Reference

Johnson Center's progressive environment has presented librarians and other library staff with a myriad of opportunities and challenges. The library now has a public service philosophy unique to the building's physical environment and provides reference and instruction services in a manner quite distinctive from the university's more traditional research library. As an example, the librarians are often seen away from the reference desk assisting students at public computers. Reference staff members also take the library on the road and periodically set up research assistance stations in kiosks located in the food court. Traditional reference service has evolved into one-on-one consultations, and paraprofessional staff and graduate research assistants are deployed to tasks previously considered the sole domain of librarians. This has occurred simultaneously in the main research library and has been a growing trend in the academic library community as well. This approach requires a public service philosophy different from what has been the norm historically in academic libraries. The success of this endeavor in the Johnson Center Library is indirectly attributable to the physical design of the facility and the individuals who were recruited to work in this environment.

IS THE JOHNSON CENTER LIBRARY REALLY EFFECTIVE?

Reception by faculty, students, library staff, and visitors to this library concept has been as mixed as the university population is diverse.

Those individuals who are more steeped in academic tradition have wondered aloud: "Where are the walls?" "Why is that student eating a falafel in the library?" and "Do 'real' academic libraries have neon lights?" Others, in tacit approval, accept the innovative and inviting atmosphere, as evidenced by the heavy student use. A recent request by graduate students from the art and visual technology department to exhibit numerous art pieces there, during a month-long series of exhibits on campus, demonstrated that students recognize this library as a busy place that would give their exhibit optimum exposure to the university community.

Has George Mason's Johnson Center Library been successful in all it set out to become? The resounding answer to that question is yes! The building (and the library) as a gathering place for the university community has succeeded beyond expectation; the integrated open stack areas and scattered group study rooms are used by students for collaborative learning, and the rooms are always occupied; the neon lights really do draw attention and don't detract from the "academic" nature of the facility; the food is not a problem—we have no more damaged books or computers than any other academic library; and the Johnson Center Library staff, by and large, are committed to the philosophy and concept of the open library. One reference and instruction librarian, who came to George Mason University Libraries in 1996 to work in the newly opened Johnson Center Library, wraps it up by saying, "While there certainly are aspects of the building that hindsight shows us did not work as planned, the overall philosophy of an open, community-based facility has been exceeded."[6]

Gate Counts and Student Use

One indicator of success in a library, at least as far as measuring its ability to attract users and retain them over time, is the volume of foot traffic in and out of the facility. Beginning with 584,171 visits to the Johnson Center Library (controlled library) between July 1996 and June 1997, foot traffic has steadily increased, with one slight downward fluctuation during the 1999–2000 year. The Johnson Center controlled library gate count for the 2002–2003 academic year was 683,338, up by 85,906 from the 2001–2002 academic year. It should be noted that the gate counts for the Johnson Center Library reflect library use within the controlled library only—the area housing the media collections, course reserves collections, circulation and reference services, and library instruction room. The statistics for the building at large include the count of students who use the outer part of the library to retrieve a book, meet with fellow students in a group study room, browse the stacks, study alone at a study carrel, or receive quick library referral from the building's information desk. It is difficult to estimate how much of the total building gate count includes library users. Anecdotal observation indicates that students consider themselves to be "in the library" when they are in the open stack area of the outer building. A student was recently overheard on her cell phone saying, "I am in the library," as she stood in the open area of the building outside of the controlled library.

Comparing the gate counts of the Johnson Center Library with those of the main research library on the same campus can provide interesting comparative statistics. One of the reasons for justifying the creation of the Johnson Center Library was the severe overcrowding in the Fenwick facility. Library lore has it that during pre-exam periods students sat on the floor to study (some say even in the bathrooms) because all seats were taken. The annual gate count for the Fenwick Library reached a high of 1,151,896 during the 1994–1995 academic year. When the Johnson Center opened the following year, the number fell to 817,591 and then dropped to 568,989 and 564,187 respectively the following two years. During that time period, the foot traffic in the Johnson Center Library actually exceeded that of the Fenwick Library. Since then the count for the Fenwick Library has once again increased, as has the count for the Johnson Center Library, but foot traffic numbers in the Fenwick Library have not returned to those prior to the opening of the Johnson Center. Increased use of both facilities is due in part to an increased university enrollment and in part to more aggressive marketing of library services.

Librarians find that the relaxed atmosphere in the Johnson Center Library attracts students who are accustomed to the large, busy, and noisy atmosphere of the modern mall and who are comfortable and at ease when multitasking. Students come to the Johnson Center, grab lunch, take it to the library while talking on their cell phones, meet friends for a study group meeting, seek research assistance in the controlled library, check out a book, check their e-mail, and stop at the information desk to verify the time and place of a student activity. The visit to the library is just one of many reasons they come into the building, certainly not the only one, and for many—we must acknowledge—not the most important one. The multipurpose building allows students to blend their social and leisure time with the library activity necessary for academic success.

Conversely, students and faculty who choose to go to the main research library do so in a very intentional way. They are seeking out a quiet study place or a research consultation with a subject liaison librarian, or they are in need of specific resources held in the collections housed in the building. Many of them are just more comfortable in a traditional academic library atmosphere. Those students who start an assignment using the Johnson Center Library may eventually end up going to the Fenwick Library to access the periodical backfile, government documents, special collections, or the largest circulating collection within the university library system. However, students have self-selected which library environment is best for them, which library best suits their style, and which library provides the most comfort and ease as they conduct their library business. The Johnson Center coordinator of reference and instruction states:

> I have received many comments from students in the Johnson Center Library expressing that they do not feel intimidated in using the library or asking for assistance as they often do in a more traditional academic library. The library space is such an integral part of the building that students do not differentiate between the various physical parts of the building. They are as relaxed in their use of the library as with the bistro or lounge area.[7]

Noise

Even in the Johnson Center Library there are occasional complaints regarding noise. The building utilizes a system to mute noise and for most that is sufficient. Some students, however, want the convenience of the food court, the social setting, and the attractive environment but not the noise that comes along with the activity level in such a building. One interesting anecdote illustrates the ambivalence felt by some students to the environment. One student registered his concern and displeasure over what he perceived as a lack of quiet space in the Johnson Center. When it was suggested that he could find a quieter study environment in the main research library only two campus buildings away, he responded that he did not want to use that library because he preferred the atmosphere of the Johnson Center Library. This non sequitur brings to mind that old adage: "Be careful what you wish for; you may get it." Since opening, the library has made concerted efforts to designate some areas of the library as quiet space. Signs have been scattered in select areas asking library users to be considerate of others, to study quietly, and to refrain from using cell phones. As an aside, the steady increase in cell phone popularity prompted many library patrons to complain about their use in the library, and so in addition to hanging banners, laminated signs affixed in study carrels ask that people refrain from using their cell phones. Although this has helped somewhat, it is impossible to enforce, and staff do not want to become the cell phone police any more than they wanted to be the food police in years past. Some seating areas of the open building have become quieter than others, providing some students a more tranquil space and others the space for noise and robust activity. This has occurred not so much as a result of anything initiated by the building or library management but rather in an informal, almost symbiotic recognition by the individuals using the building that it is for multiple uses—academic and social, quiet and noisy.

Staff: Recruitment, Training, and Development of a New Service Philosophy

It can be said that the "renegade" Johnson Center Library has succeeded in much that the visionaries who planned the building hoped it would accomplish. The library is used heavily, most physical barriers between library users and resources have been removed, instruction is a top priority, the media collection has higher circulation than ever before, and students generally feel comfortable in the space. The role of the committed, enthusiastic staff who work in this unconventional environment cannot be emphasized enough when examining the library's successes. Although there is no empirical evidence to support it, the open physical space and the atmosphere it creates have had an effect on how library users interact with the information resources they use and the information professionals they consult. In a like manner, and probably more important, for that to occur the staff who work within the space must be flexible and open to allowing the space and the users to define the services provided. In this regard, through no fault of the library staff, the library probably has not met the full potential that the innovative building promised. For library staff to develop and flourish within such a different library space, library administration must support ongoing development and training after careful and selective recruitment.

Library administration did recognize that this attention-getting space was not enough to provide the outcomes sought. Staff would have to provide the services in the space in a way that they themselves had never experienced as students in a library setting. Staff could not be afraid to try new things or to make mistakes. And, they needed the support from above to do this. George Mason University Libraries recruited librarians who were energetic and imaginative, who demonstrated a real commitment to the Johnson Center Library concept, who embraced the unusual and at times challenging environment, and especially who understood the importance of instruction within the library program. Upon arrival some librarians were enamored with the library and the myriad possibilities and wanted to move forward quickly. Others, more invested in how the services were provided in more traditional libraries, had difficulty imagining things in a different light, even within a drastically different space.

To support library staff as they explored new ideas and service philosophies, a development program was needed so that all librarians and support staff could buy into the Johnson Center Library concept and learn to live comfortably with the inevitable growing pains the library would create. Although this happened in spurts and starts, it did not take place as part of a comprehensive, continuous, and well-planned program. Unfortunately, we focused more of our energies on the library as physical place and not enough on the development of the people who could either make or break it. It should be noted that the university library system was developing library programs at the university's two distributed campuses (twenty-two miles west of Fairfax and fifteen miles east of Fairfax) and soon had even more growing pains as a result of rapid expansion. Within a five-year time span, thirty-five librarian and staff positions were added to the libraries' staff roster. Soon after the Johnson Center Library opened, several librarians who had been instrumental in the development of the Johnson Center left the university, including the director of libraries who had been a part of its very conception. All of these developments had a significant influence on the development and forward movement for the Johnson Center Library, and over a period of time a certain degree of momentum was lost. This was due in part to budgetary considerations and new priorities taking shape within the library system.

It must be noted that the debate regarding how to provide library services in creative and innovative ways to complement the unconventional physical design of the Johnson Center is still in process. Many librarians love the Johnson Center Library environment: the neon lights, the food in the study carrels, the books outside of the library walls, and even the casual attitudes of the students as they drop in. Some librarians prefer to sit at the reference desk and wait for requests for help to come to them. Others suggest that the librarians should be offering help to library users as they rove among the computer workstations in the library. Yet others suggest the roving could be done outside of the library walls: in the open stacks, in the computer labs, or in the food court. All agree that instruction is a top priority; however, not all librarians feel at ease attempting to make each reference transaction a teaching opportunity, especially if the student resists. This approach can take a great deal of time with one student, and it may increase the need for double staffing and require the development of improved negotiation skills.

A number of implemented service changes have not been well received by all library staff. For example, because the Johnson Center Library is located in a multipurpose building, the library has been asked to provide service during periods of inclement weather or holidays when the rest of the university closes. With a growing residential student body, the university recognizes that even with many resources available via remote access, on-site services must be provided to those students remaining on campus during otherwise down times. Since the Johnson Center Library stacks are located outside the library walls and the library program is promoted as part of the entire mall-like facility, library staff must be available when the doors of the building are open. These staff development issues are not endemic to the Johnson Center Library and are undoubtedly being addressed in academic libraries with both traditional physical designs and those with which the mold has been broken.

How does the profession recruit the librarians and library staff who will be able to move the academic library as an institution forward and keep pace with the vast societal changes we are all experiencing? If any of us knew the answer to that question, academic libraries would look very different than they now do. Perhaps we should begin to look to the retail environment for our recruits and not be afraid to create marketing positions within our organizations—positions that may or may not require a graduate library degree. Perhaps library schools should identify candidates to groom as potential librarians long before they complete their undergraduate degrees—individuals who do not necessarily come from the student library employee ranks but who come from other identified groups of undergraduates. This question is an essential one for all of us who are committed to preparing future academic library leaders.

John N. Berry III reports in a May 2003 *Library Journal* article that informal studies indicate most recruits to the library profession are influenced by practicing librarians to enter a graduate program in library and information sciences. Although this is gratifying to the library staff who have served as mentors and provides for a certain degree of diversity, the fact remains that the library as it exists today is what inspires most new librarians, perhaps making the library of the future difficult to develop and evolve in our current libraries.[8] For cutting-edge change to take place in libraries, we must recruit librarians to the profession who are not enthralled with today's libraries, even ones that have experimented with new physical spaces, but rather are capable of envisioning the library of tomorrow and a profession more in step with our already changed society.

WHERE DO WE GO FROM HERE?

To make the most of our wonderful "library place," continued work is needed to develop staff, build teams, collaborate with other academic colleagues, reach out to faculty, place customer service as a top priority, and meet the always changing needs of today's university faculty and students. One caution to libraries planning to make a move away from traditional library design of facilities, as did George Mason, is that an innovative and unconventional physical space is not enough. Academic librarians must borrow liberally from the public library's customer service philosophy; recognize the need to market collections and services; and create inviting, comfortable spaces. Creation of "library places" such as the Johnson Center Library at George Mason University is only the first step in reengineering the academic library. In addition to an effective physical space, libraries must foster a state of mind not just for the library users but also for the librarians and staff seeking to preserve the academic library as a viable institution.

NOTES

1. Charlene Hurt, "The Johnson Center Library at George Mason University," in *Building Libraries for the 21st Century: The Shape of Information*, edited by T. D. Webb (Jefferson, N.C.: McFarland, 2000), 83–104.

2. Helen Ackerman, Daniel Walsch, and Colleen Kearney Thornberg, "The Johnson Years," at www.gmu.edu/news/gazette/johnson.html (accessed 30 March 2004).

3. George Mason University, Johnson Center, at jcweb.gmu.edu (accessed 30 March 2004).

4. Charlene S. Hurt, Laura O. Rein, Maureen S. Connors, John C. Walsh, and Anna C. Wu, "Collection Development Strategies for a University Center Library," *College & Research Libraries* 56 (November 1995): 487–95.

5. Kevin Simons, James Young, and Craig Gibson, "The Learning Library in Context: Community, Integration, and Influence," *Research Strategies* 17 (2000): 123–32.

6. Kevin Simons, personal communication, 1 October 2003.

7. Sharon Kerr, personal communication, 9 October 2003.

8. John N. Berry III, "LIS Recruiting: Does It Make the Grade? Open Houses, Dual Degrees, and Distance Programs Help but May Not Foster a Vital Future for Librarianship," *Library Journal* 128 (2003): 38–41.

5

A Refuge and a Sanctuary: Vancouver's Carnegie Library as Civic Space

Paul Whitney

The construction of a public library building is often a complex process that entails balancing differing and sometimes directly competing agendas. Some of the influences on the process are practical, including financial considerations and location, and these can influence, if not dictate, the nature of service delivery from the new facility. More enlightened politicians and planners understand the role a library can play as a catalyst for civic pride and a community focal point that generates high foot traffic, along with the attendant commercial and property development benefits this often entails. The long-term service implications of a library building itself are often underplayed. Library space planning is commonly predicated on the assumption that larger and more aesthetically pleasing space is better. This is generally proven correct as new buildings result in higher use levels and user satisfaction.

As North America enters its second century of widespread public library building development, interesting case studies demonstrate that library buildings can have long-term significance as civic space and that a community can change in unanticipated ways that can dramatically affect the uses made of this public space. This chapter examines the central branch of Vancouver, British Columbia, as one example of the transformation of a community and the changing roles of the library building in response. The symbolic and practical role played by Vancouver Public Library's Carnegie branch (hereafter referred to as

Carnegie, as it is known in the community), while unanticipated by its builders, demonstrates the importance of such civic space.

While old buildings can adapt and provide new services to a transformed community, history teaches us that new buildings can create psychological and/or physical barriers that can discourage use by the most disadvantaged library users. Vancouver opened two new central branches in the second half of the twentieth century, and in both instances staff noted the loss of a clientele that did not "make the move" to the new facilities. Carnegie was transformed as a library building when, decades after the relocation of its main library branch functions, it reopened as a community center with a library reading room, bringing library service back to its original local community. How this classically styled public building both came to be and was transformed over its first one hundred years tells us much about the public library as public space, reflecting community aspirations, the political agenda of the day, and the changing needs of the community and the citizens who entered through its grand entrance.

On a sunny Vancouver afternoon in March 1902, 500 Masons paraded to the site of what was to be Canada's first Carnegie library. There, joined by 3,000 of the city's 27,000 residents, the Freemasons' grand master laid the cornerstone for the new building and delivered a "formal and fulsome speech"[1] on the role of the new library. The ceremony concluded with an oration by the Reverend Mr. Tucker on the importance of books: "It is to be sincerely hoped that in due time the choices and works of the greatest minds of all lands and of all ages will find an honored place on the shelves of this new library."[2] The library, which opened to the public in November 1903, would become one of the key symbols of the profound changes that were to transform Canada's major west coast port city in the new century.

James Edwin Machin became Vancouver's librarian in 1880, four years after the city's incorporation, when his predecessor headed north in search of gold. While operating the library out of space above a hardware store, and later the YMCA, Machin introduced free library service and advocated for a library building. Andrew Carnegie's expansive program for the construction of public libraries was having a significant impact by 1901, when 131 buildings were funded and thousands of requests seeking support were being submitted. Vancouver's politicians and library supporters would have been well aware of the opportunity offered by Carnegie, as grants had already been approved for nearby Seattle and Tacoma. Following what were described as "rapid and succinct"[3] negotiations involving library board members and a Vancouver member of Parliament, Carnegie's private secretary confirmed an offer of $50,000 for the construction and furnishing of a public library on the condition that the city agree to provide $5,000 a year in operating funds. The offer was quickly accepted and the process began, resulting in the construction of "the Old Sandstone Lady," a building that figured prominently in the lives of generations of Vancouverites and that continues to play a high-profile and symbolic role in its immediate community, Canada's poorest neighborhood, the downtown east side.

From the perspective of the twenty-first century, it is interesting to note that many of the pressures and issues involved in building a library today were evident in Carnegie's construction. With what strikes the present-day reader as surprising cynicism, the newspaper coverage of the awarding of the construction contract in October 1902 referred to "the usual squabble over the site."[4] Already the young city was dealing with a shifting of both population and commercial activity, and it was recognized that the new library would influence development. A central location with easy streetcar access from all parts of the city was acknowledged as crucial by politicians. But where was the center going to be? Library staff noted that the majority of library users now lived uptown, to the west of the then perceived city center. Council was unable to achieve consensus and decided to call a public referendum with two weeks' notice to choose between two sites, one in the emerging uptown and one in the heart of the old city center. Describing the process that chose the now Main and Hastings site, long-serving Vancouver city librarian Edgar Robinson was disdainful when writing in 1937:

> It is obvious today suitability was a secondary consideration. West End versus East End interests fought it out on a personal and selfish basis with little regard for the welfare of the city as a whole, or for the library either. . . . The Eastenders turned out in force and swamped their enemies by a 746 to 407 vote. This was an important matter settled by a group of voters who know nothing about the factors entering into the location of a central building, and cared less.[5]

In the medium term, the recognized center of town shifted to the west, and the Carnegie Library was increasingly perceived as being on the edge of downtown. City staff and politicians, consciously or subconsciously, learned from this process, and Vancouver's two subsequent main libraries were strategically located both in recognition of and as a catalyst for future growth.

From the outset, the Carnegie Library was conceived of and described as a "monument." Writing in 1992, architectural critic Robin Ward describes the building's "enduring presence": "Its lantern dome, French Second Empire roof, rusticated neo-Romanesque stone work and columned entrance strike just the right note of civic pomp and cultural self-importance."[6]

It is worth noting that the classical "temple dome" design associated with Carnegie libraries reflected the preference of local decision makers and was implemented over the objections of the donor and his staff, who wished to see funds spent on the interior. The impetus to provide an architectural embodiment of civic aspirations and a concrete affirmation of the importance of culture and learning is as prevalent today as it was in 1901, as evidenced by the selection of Moshe Safdie's design, seemingly inspired by the Roman Coliseum, for Vancouver's 1995 central library.

Many of the community aspirations articulated around a library building remain consistent, while others change in recognition of shifting social values. In her study of Carnegie libraries, Abigail Van Slyck notes that the letters received by Carnegie seeking library funding clearly expressed the need for public libraries as part of the struggle between good and evil: "Their tendency to enumerate the church buildings and saloons in town suggests that the score in this struggle was recorded in the physical landscape of the town."[7] Van Slyck views this need for tangible expression of the forces of good as the motivation for the grand exteriors of many Carnegie libraries. As already noted, the laying of the cornerstone of Vancouver's Carnegie Library was accompanied by a paean to the greatness of books. A banquet for the business and political elite followed the ceremony, and the Freemasons' grand master congratulated the citizens of Vancouver for pursuing, in the form of a library building, the highest form of civilization that "most wisely seeks the welfare and happiness of mankind."[8] Reflecting the spirit of the British Empire that shaped much of Canada's history, Sir Charles Tupper delivered what news coverage delicately described as an "exhaustive speech," highlighting the strong sympathies for the Anglo-Saxon race shared by Andrew Carnegie and Cecil Rhodes. That the building being celebrated was being constructed in close proximity to Vancouver's growing Chinatown and that the Chinese community was to be the one constant in use of the library for one hundred years are just two of the incongruities that this perspective represents.

The dichotomy of the grand dinner celebrating the new library and the middle-class and "aspiring poor" residents who were to form its user base is reflected in the library design, services offered, and rules of conduct that it held in common with other early-twentieth-century public libraries. Andrew Carnegie originally envisaged the public library as benefiting the working man by giving him the tools for self improvement. He soon came to realize that it was the children and youth who would most gain from his philanthropy: "The letters received from parents thanking me for libraries established and telling of the change these have made upon their children are numerous. . . . If the young do not acquire a taste for reading, what will they otherwise acquire?"[9]

In common with other Carnegie libraries, the provision of a children's room was an important component of Vancouver's new building. While welcoming children into the library, expectations of middle-class behavior were enforced, "preparing working-class readers to fit in at school, at work, or at church."[10] Genteel behavior was encouraged through interior design and layout:

> Whether aimed at young or old, reading rooms offered readers an orderly space with tables regimented in neat rows. Period photographs depict readers in approved postures, seated with both feet on the floor, chair pulled close to the table, and with their attention focused on the books immediately in front of them.[11]

Regimented as this may seem to the present-day reader, these libraries often became, in the memories of one user, "a refuge and a sanctuary," a place to go "when things got tough or when somebody was after me—which was often."[12] While Vancouver's Carnegie Library's imposing columns, domed roof, and spiral staircase (with its stained glass window depicting Shakespeare, Milton, and Spenser) all depicted the elite view of culture espoused by its civic-minded champions, the building's true legacy now more than ever is a sanctuary for the defenseless and the vulnerable.

For approximately half its fifty-four years as Vancouver Public Library's main branch, the Carnegie Library was viewed as inadequate at best. A newspaper columnist writing in 1982 notes that "by 1945, the Carnegie was a disaster. There was plaster flaking off the walls, the main staircase sagged and had to be propped up with makeshift steel columns, and the roof leaked."[13]

In hindsight, it seems that much of the building's more than half century of service as a main library was marked by adversity, albeit with much fine service delivered and underlying commitment and hard work provided by library staff. Various infestations of rodents and insects, an extended closure due to budget cuts in the Depression, and an occupation by out-of-work protesters figure prominently in the building's recorded history. When it was finally closed as a main library in 1957, over eighty employees worked in the building, which originally had four staff members. The immediate community was now skid row, and the commercial center of town was ten blocks to the east. Undoubtedly, the only tears that were shed over leaving the old building were for Edgar Robinson, who died one week before his long-dreamed-of new central library was to open.

It was clear to library staff that the relocation and enlargement of the central library collections and services would leave behind a cohort of library users who would not visit the new location. They were the old men who lived in long-term occupancy hotel rooms in the nearby area. A newspaper column written when the old Carnegie closed described the move as a disaster; "the old faithfuls of the Public Library will have no place to read, no place to get out of the rain, no place to doze."[14] Most, if not all, of these "shy men" would be dead when, in 1980, Carnegie reopened as the Carnegie Centre, a community center with a public library reading room.

Immediately after the library moved out, the full Carnegie space was occupied by the Vancouver Museum, which operated out of the building until 1968. For a new generation of Vancouver children, a visit to Carnegie evoked memories of a child mummy and aboriginal artifacts, not story times and reading. Following 1968, the building was vacant as the neighborhood around it declined, fueled by the increase in the drug trade and the attendant property theft and street prostitution. One mayor attempted to have the building demolished; another tried to sell it for a dollar, feeling that the costs of reopening it as a civic facility would be prohibitive. With the leadership of an activist community association and the support of left-leaning city politicians, momentum to reinvent Carnegie as public space for its profoundly disadvantaged community grew. As well as providing public washrooms, showers, a cafeteria, lounge areas, and classrooms, the new Carnegie would provide a large public library reading room with collections targeted to the interest of its local users. Despite vocal political opposition, library service was to return to Carnegie.

The Carnegie Centre opened in January 1980 and was immediately embraced by the disenfranchised residents of the downtown east side. Robin Ward described its "volatile, socialist ambience" and continued: "It's as if a dissolute civilization has collapsed and the natives and the poor have infiltrated its relics, like Petrograd after the Russian Revolution."[15] The courses promoted on the opening-day flyer give a clear indication of the users of the new Carnegie:

English for "boat-people"
Cooking on a hot plate (men only)
Nutrition for Indian women
Criminology 101

From the outset, the Carnegie reading room was different from other library facilities. Staffing was funded by the city's social planning department and, over time, its hours of operation extended well beyond those at any other branch, including opening 365 days a year. The facility clearly served in a very real sense as the community's living room, and the hours of operation reflect more than lip service paid to this concept. Library rules and regulations for things such as registration requirements were waived. Described as less than a branch but more than a reading room, the library service met the unique needs of users for whom the main library, sixteen blocks away, was "outside their world,"[16] in the words of a leading politician of the day.

Now having celebrated its one hundredth anniversary and over twenty years after reopening, while light years from Andrew Carnegie's vision of a public library, the current incarnation of Vancouver's Carnegie building is more of a refuge and sanctuary than it has ever been. Many of the over 2,000 people a day who use it are seeking respite from the dangers of the streets and the loneliness of the approximately 5,000 one-room residences in the area. Staff routinely deal with users who are dual diagnoses (mental illness combined with drug or alcohol dependency). North America's first safe injection site recently opened one block from Carnegie, providing another indication of the community's willingness to address its problems in a humane and groundbreaking way. Although social workers are sometimes more prevalent than library workers, the provision of books and information along with the promotion of literacy and Internet skills remain central to the service provided by present-day Carnegie staff.

The Carnegie building stands now as an enduring symbol of the city's early days. Architect Dave Galpin wrote of the reincarnation of the Carnegie building:

> The architecture may not be "correct" within an analytical context, but is expressive of Vancouver at the turn of the century, and recycling such a structure for new use is the most appropriate method of achieving a sense of continuity in our urban fabric.[17]

At the time of writing this chapter, the Vancouver Public Library board was beginning a community consultation process to explore options for upgrading library service in the downtown east side. "Do no harm to Carnegie" has become a recurrent theme to the preliminary discussions. The challenge is to provide meaningful assistance to a unique low-income and pluralistic community without unintentionally changing the community in such a way that the marginalized residents are displaced. More than a century after the pomp of the Freemasons' parade of 1902, boisterous meetings once again mark all consultations in the area, with diverse organizations representing all residents, from parents concerned about their children's learning opportunities and personal safety to those representing the marginalized, including drug users, sex trade workers, and the homeless. At the same time, with the gentrification of the immediately adjoining area and the continuing engagement by the residents of historic Chinatown, there is pressure to provide bigger and better conventional library service from a new building. As this consultation continues, Carnegie stands as a reminder of the tangible and symbolic importance a library building can provide to a community.

It is ironic but nonetheless important to note that while Carnegie's builders could never have envisaged the nature of the building's present-day service and users, the permanence and dignity of the original conception were what insured the building's survival so that it could continue to fulfill its essential role as civic space. It behooves funding agencies and library staff to be conscious of this potential when conceiving new libraries. It must be assumed that how future generations will make use of such buildings is inconceivable to us. In recognition of the importance of continuity of library buildings as civic space, we should design and build our libraries to both last and inspire. Such buildings have the potential to contribute to the well-being of our cities for centuries.

In late November 2003, under the auspices of the Carnegie Community Centre Association, a play was presented to mark the end of the celebrations of Carnegie's one hundredth anniversary. Called "In the Heart of a City," the play was inspired by the stories of the people of the downtown east side. At the play's conclusion, the musicians "accidentally" resurrect Andrew Carnegie and his mother. In true downtown east side style, Carnegie is accused, in the words of the play, "of ripping off his workers to pile up millions for his libraries." The verdict imposed is a tour of the Carnegie Centre and library in order that he "see the liberating work done in the building that's got his name."

NOTES

1. Stanley Read, "The Great Breakthrough: The Library and Carnegie (1900–1904)," *The History of Vancouver Public Library*, an unpublished collection of essays edited by Read (1975), 9.

2. Read, "Great Breakthrough," 10.

3. Stanley Read, "The Vancouver Public Library: A Capsule History," *The History of Vancouver Public Library*, an unpublished collection of essays edited by Read (1975), 2.

4. "What HO! The Library," *Vancouver Province*, 12 November 1901, p. 1.

5. E. S. Robinson, "Half a Century of Book Lending," *Vancouver Province*, 13 November 1937, p. 3.

6. Robin Ward, "Robin Ward," *Vancouver Sun*, 28 November 1992, p. C14.

7. Abigail Van Slyck, *Free to All: Carnegie Libraries and American Culture 1890–1920* (Chicago: University of Chicago Press, 1995), 159.

8. "In Honor of New Library," *Vancouver Province*, 31 March 1902, p. 2.

9. Peter Kraus, *Carnegie* (New York: Wiley, 2002), 502.

10. Van Slyck, *Free to All*, 109.

11. Van Slyck, *Free to All*, 109.

12. Van Slyck, *Free to All*, 214.

13. Chuck Davis, "Carnegie Centre Hums with New Life," *Vancouver Province*, 9 May 1982, p. 3.

14. "Disaster for Old Men—400,000 Books Move," *Vancouver Province*, 19 October 1957, p. 25.

15. Robin Ward, "Robin Ward's Vancouver: Carnegie Library," *Vancouver Sun*, 8 April 1989, p. 2.

16. "Second Renovation Step Approved for Carnegie," *Vancouver Sun*, 6 May 1977, p. 13.

17. David Galpin, "The Carnegie Building," *AIBC Forum* (October/November 1979): 27.

6

Public Libraries and Services to Students: Taking Up the Slack in the Face of Budget Cuts

Patricia Jobb

> Our schools have limited resources, often allowing children only one book per week to read. If we do not make it easy for our children to access literature, they will lose interest in it and this would be truly sad.[1]

There is no doubt about it—since the funding changes of the early 1990s, school libraries and teacher-librarian positions in Canada have been largely decimated. In Alberta alone, the number of teacher-librarians (half-time or more) declined from a high of 550 in 1978 to just 106 in 2000.[2] The fallout has been an increasing expectation that public libraries will fill a role once filled by adequately staffed and resourced school libraries.

Students, teachers, and parents all come to the public library to borrow large quantities of books and videos for classroom and homework use—resources that school libraries no longer have. Increasingly, students are asking public library staff reference questions related to completing their homework assignments. As well, whether looking for a book or magazine article or searching a database or the Internet, students frequently demonstrate poor research skills—an indicator that they are just not getting enough instruction in school.

The role of public libraries all across the country includes helping children and adults explore topics of interest and improve their skills outside of formal educational structures. At the same time, it is recognized that people of all ages enroll in formal courses of study and use public library services, collections, and facilities to support those endeavors. Generally, however, the viewpoint of public libraries has been that, while they have a responsibility to provide a limited number of supplementary resources for individual students, primary responsibility for curriculum support rests with educational institutions. The reality, though, is that public libraries are being increasingly called on to fill the void left by inadequately funded school libraries and insufficient teacher-librarian positions.

COLLECTIONS

The run on collections is often more than a public library can sustain. It is not unusual for parent volunteers to take out large numbers of public library materials to fill classroom needs. Teachers, too, come into the library to borrow materials in bulk to support classroom activities. In Edmonton, Alberta, public library staff recalled a few typical examples of school use of public library collections:

- The teacher who wanted to go over the forty-item borrowing limit so that every student could have three books on birds
- The teacher who wanted to renew (for another three weeks) the seventy-six books he already had out on large cats (lions, tigers, and so on)
- The teacher who established a "library club" in which her students borrowed books from the public library to create a classroom collection
- Teachers who reside in the city but teach in outlying communities and make use of the city's public library collections for their classrooms
- Teachers who haunt the public library's giant book sales to add to school library collections or create classroom collections consisting of damaged or outdated public library discards

As well, students increasingly turn to the public library for materials and information to support their school assignments. Often, after visits by just a few students from a particular class, a branch library's circulating collection on a topic is exhausted, and staff must rely solely on reference and/or electronic resources to meet student needs. To deal with these situations, library staff implement a variety of strategies to "spread the wealth":

- Limiting children to just a few books on a topic—not a very satisfying solution for either the child or the public library
- Developing "homework shelves" (which can be depleted, too) containing materials related to areas of the curriculum currently being studied, with the intent that something will be available for every child—whether in electronic or print format
- Implementing mechanisms to make it easy for teachers to alert public library staff of upcoming assignments so they can prepare booklists and have appropriate resources on hand when children come to the library (Unfortunately, time-pressed teachers rarely take advantage of such programs.)

SELECTING LIBRARY MATERIALS

While the public library's mandate is that of serving the individual child, the demands of students and teachers are generating the purchase of more copies of more materials on certain subjects. For the public library, this has resulted in increasing portions of its materials budget being allocated to the purchase of materials supporting the school curriculum.

There are continual requests for textbooks—math, literature, and social studies, in particular. In some cases, parents have told public library staff that while their child was not allowed to take a textbook home, it was needed for a homework assignment. In principle, public library collections are not designed to provide multiple copies of items supporting homework assignments. In practice, however, the public library finds itself in a position of purchasing multiple copies of some titles.

In a nutshell, public libraries find themselves (a) purchasing certain types of materials, sometimes at the expense of other areas of the collection, and (b) unable to purchase all that is demanded, thereby satisfying neither student nor teacher needs. Public library materials budgets cannot sustain this level of purchasing over the long run without significant shifts in service vision and/or funding.

INFORMATION-SAVVY STUDENTS?

Three grade four students went into a branch of the Edmonton Public Library to research a science fair project. In the process of "distilling" their request, the librarian learned that the school library was used only for recreational reading, and as is increasingly common, there was only a computer lab to support research. Considering those facts, coupled with the lack of teacher-librarians, it is hardly surprising that children have poor library and research skills.

While student usage of public library electronic resources has increased significantly over the years, often this is not done effectively and the information gathered is not evaluated for either its reliability or appropriateness to the assignment. Students often assume they just need to "Google-ize" their search to get what they need.

As well, students often have little or no basic knowledge of how either a library or information is organized (e.g., how fiction is arranged or how the Dewey decimal system works). Consequently, at the request of teachers, public library staff find themselves spending significant amounts of time giving tours that include instruction in library usage and research. Instruction of this nature provides students with the tools required to independently search for information, whether for school purposes or to support lifelong learning. Toward this end, the Edmonton Public Library has received requests to provide half-day research methods courses for high school students.

INFORMATION SERVICES

Aside from the school library, the public library is often the only public service institution in a community that offers one-on-one help to a child trying to do a homework assignment. This involves staff time to understand what is needed, coach the child on how to find information, actually find resources at the right level, and keep the child focused on what he or she really needs. This is a complex communication process that involves time, listening skills, and expertise. Many of these interactions are complicated by the fact that staff must deal with and instruct not only the child but also the parent.

While public libraries have a strong commitment to providing information services and facilitating children's learning, satisfying their needs is often difficult. As already noted, circulating collections are often depleted by the first inquiries, reference collections are not always detailed enough, and information available through databases or the Internet is not always appropriate to this level of audience (e.g., it may be too general or too technical). Insufficient interaction between teachers and library staff means that teachers make assumptions about the materials and information the public library possesses. Library staff, on the other hand, are often caught off guard by unexpected waves of students clamoring for limited resources.

LIBRARY PROGRAMS AIMED AT STUDENTS

Recognizing that students are an important part of their client population, public libraries make concerted efforts to reach out to schools and students. They do this through presentations at schools to introduce children to the public library, to give kids library cards, and to get them excited about reading. In the public library, staff provide reference and homework help, and through the course of the year they offer literature- and learning-based programs. During the summer, public libraries all across the continent offer summer reading programs designed to keep kids reading during a time when, if they did not, their reading skills in all likelihood would slip. As well, public library websites contain extensive areas devoted entirely to young children, kids, teens, and teachers.

WHAT TO DO?

In an ideal world, public libraries envision partnering with schools on an equal basis when it comes to meeting the reading and information needs of students. While public libraries play a role in providing services to students, they do not want to, nor can they, take the place of school libraries, which are integral to the process by which students acquire a love of reading and develop research skills supporting lifelong learning. Strong school libraries

- are staffed by trained teacher-librarians who work with students and in partnership with teachers to provide library services, collections, and instruction supporting the school curriculum;
- are adequately resourced with balanced collections consisting of reading materials and information resources in all formats (print,

electronic, audiovisual) so that students can read and develop a knowledge and understanding of a broad range of subjects, as well as a love of reading; and

- work in a partnership in which public libraries supplement the work and collections of the school library.

In examining the impacts of school libraries, studies have concluded that

- "a properly staffed, appropriately stocked, and well organized school library is a critical tool that allows librarians and teachers to work together to help students achieve higher levels of literacy, problem-solving and information and communication technology skills"[3];
- "a strong computer network connecting the library's resources to the classroom and laboratories has an impact on student achievement"[4];
- "the quality of the collection has an impact on student learning"[5];
- "a print-rich environment leads to more reading and free voluntary reading is the best predictor of comprehension, vocabulary growth, spelling and grammatical ability and writing style"[6];
- "the extent to which books are borrowed from school libraries shows a strong relationship with reading achievement while borrowing from classroom libraries does not"[7]; and
- "a positive difference can be made to student achievement when school libraries co-operate with public libraries."[8]

And the list of benefits and results goes on.

THE REALITY

In reality, as Dr. Ken Haycock points out, there are "no comparable Canadian province-wide studies of school libraries and achievement in Canada."[9] So, while the value of school libraries appears to be self-evident, it is tough to make the case without hard, cold Canadian facts. Compounding that difficulty is the widely held perception among principals and other school administrators that the Internet is a source of reliable and comprehensive information. That outlook, of course, is expedient in that it conveniently suits a school agenda hampered by a lack of adequate funding.

In Alberta, a commission on learning was struck to study and make recommendations regarding the province's educational system (kindergarten through high school). The 226-page report, released in 2003, is encouraging in that it speaks to the concept of schools as "learning communities dedicated to continuous improvement in student achievement."[10] However, what is not encouraging is that it barely mentions school libraries and lumps teacher-librarians in with what it variously describes as either "support" or "specialized" services.

> Today's teacher librarians provide a gateway to a wealth of information available from a vast array of Internet resources. They collaborate with teachers to assist them in selecting and using a wide variety of sources of information and learning resources. Given the vast amount and diversity of information available on the Internet, teacher librarians teach children how to search for information, find what they need, use information appropriately, and make good judgments about the information they access. These skills will be vitally important to students in their future careers.[11]

While one would not disagree with any of the foregoing, the emphasis on the Internet (both here and elsewhere in the report) is glaring. Additionally, the report does not clearly identify any new funding for school libraries or for teacher-librarian positions. In the absence of targeted funds and if teacher-librarians are to be lumped in with specialized or support services, one can only surmise that they will continue to be marginalized in the school setting. (Please note that none of this even begins to speak to the issue of the future of certified library technicians, which is being undermined by school jurisdictions that hire untrained personnel to work in school libraries, provide those personnel with a few days of training, and then classify them as "library technicians.")

OTHER MODELS?

So, if the future of school libraries remains doubtful, what about the other models that have been tried? These include the following:

- The cooperative services approach (such as shared automated library systems, shared licensing of electronic resources, and so on)
- Shared/joint use arrangements (ranging from independent public and school libraries housed in the same facility to shared public and school library space, collections, and staff)

Frequently described as cooperative relationships, more often than not *partnership* is the preferred descriptor for many of these kinds of models. A partnership can be defined as a relationship built on mutual cooperation and responsibility, with the expectation that mutual benefit will result. However, in considering how these models generally work, one wonders whether the term *partnership* is truly applicable.

In early 2003, a report titled "Cooperation between Public Libraries and Schools in Canada" was released. Commissioned by Chief Executives of Large Public Libraries of Ontario (CELPLO), the report includes an examination of the advantages and disadvantages of the various partnership models. In summary, it appears that, among other things, the advantages to both school and public libraries are often in the areas of capital cost savings and favorable leasing costs (for the public library), along with a political perception that partnerships are cost effective. More often than not, it seems the school library benefits from enhanced service provision, convenience, and the longer hours of public library operation.[12]

The report provides a far more extensive list of issues and problems. While many issues might be resolved through careful negotiations and tight contract writing, there is still plenty to be concerned about. A sampling of things to watch for includes, but is not limited to, the following:

- Public library needs being given a low priority when the school board is the bigger partner (which is usually the case)
- Potential funding cuts on the school side (in terms of staffing), resulting in increased pressure on the public library to meet school needs
- Unclear demarcation of authority
- Citizens feeling discouraged or uncomfortable when using the library during school hours
- Lack of communication surrounding staffing changes as a result of holidays or exams
- Collection issues (e.g., whether to purchase textbooks), Internet filtering, and intellectual freedom issues
- Building/facilities design and planning
- Cleaning, maintenance, and environmental control[13]

In summary, there are many difficulties and potential downsides to traditional cooperative services and shared/joint use models. Furthermore, there is little potential for true partnerships with public libraries when the number of "real" school libraries is diminishing, as are teacher-librarian positions, although more schools are being built. All that being said, a partnership might hold some attraction to communities with one school and one public library. However, in a city with several hundred school libraries, often distributed over a couple of school jurisdictions (public and separate, or denominational), the city's public library cannot afford to set up shop in almost every school. There must be a better way!

A NEW MODEL

Conventional thinking has always seen the public library going to, and joining forces with, the local school. As already discussed, this approach largely benefits the school and responds to the political perception of this as the most cost-effective approach. In the long run, if school jurisdictions refuse to appropriately fund and staff school libraries, such arrangements are to the detriment of public libraries that

- have a broader mandate than schools when it comes to the provision of library services; and
- within current funding models, have even less ability than schools to provide individualized on-site school library services.

So, let's turn all of this on its head, fast forward into the future, and imagine another scenario. Christopher, a grade five student, is in his school library working on a homework assignment. Located in the center of the school, the school library contains a mix of resources (print and electronic) supporting the curriculum, along with literacy, reading, and literature. Acquired and cataloged by the local public library, some library materials are part of the school library's permanent stock, while other mini-collections in a range of specific subjects are available in Christopher's library on an extended loan basis; in time, these mini-collections will be rotated to other school libraries. If something isn't immediately available in Christopher's school library, he can place a hold on it, and it will be delivered to his library from any other school library or public library branch in the city. All library materials, whether located in a school or public library branch, are part of one collection supported by one citywide automated library system and a daily delivery system.

The school secretary (or parent volunteer) is the learning resources person in Christopher's school library, and today she has helped him as much as she is able. However, the school's teacher-librarian, Mrs. Macdonald, is not there at the moment. She is either at another school library in the area or at the neighborhood branch of the public library. While Christopher has found some of the information he needs to complete his science project, he is unable to locate a few pieces of information. Because Mrs. Macdonald is not there right now, he goes to her web page, which he can reach either through the school website or the public library website. Once there, he will find lists of resources (including links) relating to a variety of homework assignments from teachers at his own and other neighborhood schools. If he is still unable to find what he is looking for, he will probably ask Mrs. Macdonald for help via e-mail, or he might be able to visit the public library after school or this evening with a family member and ask one of the library staff for help.

In Christopher's city, neither the public nor denominational, or separate, school jurisdictions had sufficient funds for a good school library or a full-time teacher-librarian in each school. Consequently, the public library, with its eighteen branches distributed across most areas of the city, was faced with mounting demands for homework help from students. While the public library was doing a pretty good job of meeting student needs, it required more staff and more funding for curriculum-related resources to help meet those needs.

In a radical move that followed extensive discussions and negotiations, the two school jurisdictions and the public library entered into a groundbreaking contractual agreement:

- The two school jurisdictions pooled the funds they were spending on school library resources, personnel, and support services and paid those funds to the public library in the form of a long-term fee-for-service contract.
- The public library hired teams of teacher-librarians and support staff, including some library technicians, and established its school services division.
- The school services teams were distributed across the city, with each public library branch serving as headquarters to a team (which included anywhere from a couple to several teacher-librarians and support staff). Each team was responsible for providing services to students and teachers, both within the branch

and at local schools, as well as for building relationships with teachers and students in the schools served by its branch.

- While none of the team members worked full time in any one school library, they were able to provide instruction to students (at both the school library and the local public library branch), provide reference service and homework help to students through a variety of mechanisms, and establish working relationships with teachers.
- Through the agreement, school library collection and resources funds were pooled and made to go further owing to the shared school/public library database, shared collections, and shared electronic resources; the ability to share individual copies of library materials; and the ability to rotate specific subject-based collection blocks among schools. This approach resulted in equitable school collection development right across the city, and while a certain amount of duplication was still necessary, this was considerably reduced from the days when school libraries operated as independent entities. Centralized school library selection teams also were established and run by teacher-librarians, thereby reducing duplication of effort. As well, because there was somewhat less duplication between school library collections, the system-wide school library collection achieved greater breadth and depth than in the past.
- As had been the case in schools prior to the agreement, the public library was unable to hire a teacher-librarian for every school. However, as a result of the pooling of funds, the public library was able to create more teacher-librarian positions than the schools previously had and, owing to the term of the contract, was able to provide them with a greater expectation of job security. Because this model was being carefully examined and considered by other jurisdictions in the country, it was anticipated that more teacher-librarian positions might result in the future should additional agreements of this nature be entered into.
- The parties (the school jurisdictions and the public library) recognized that some schools were located farther than others from their neighborhood public library branch. Consequently, they were able to jointly reach an agreement with the city's transportation department that meant that no student would be disadvantaged owing to distance or lack of transportation to the public library.

Perhaps the foregoing presents an idealistic picture of how things could work in the future. In reality, there would be many hurdles to leap, not the least of which would be huge shifts in thinking. The fact is that this scenario would provide students with less than the ideally resourced and staffed school library described earlier in this chapter. However, very few students currently receive ideal service and support in their school libraries, and more often than not what they do receive is abysmal. The foregoing scenario responds to the reality that on a daily basis, public libraries are expected to fill the gap resulting from insufficient funding for school libraries, and despite tight resources, they do a pretty good job of it. It recognizes that public libraries are distributed networks whose branches serve most areas of their cities. Most important, the scenario attempts to level the playing field by providing all students in a city with a more consistent and higher level of service than many of them experience now.

DOING WHAT'S BEST FOR STUDENTS

The desired and best outcome for students would be that of properly resourced and staffed school libraries. The facts clearly indicate that student achievement is directly tied to well-resourced school libraries operated by full-time teacher-librarians working hand in hand, on an equal basis, with classroom teachers. In the unfortunate event that decision makers fail to understand this and fail to demonstrate the political will to achieve this outcome, the need for a new model will become imperative.

The public library is a democratic institution to which both students and teachers already gravitate in large numbers for help. Given their limited resources and a mandate that does not traditionally provide for direct curriculum support, public libraries will need to rethink their role as well as their relationships with school jurisdictions. So, too, will governments and school jurisdictions need to reconsider how to most effectively allocate school library funding, as well as how to build and capitalize on the services already provided by public libraries, so as to achieve equitable student access to expertise and resources supporting the curriculum.

NOTES

1. Mother of two school-age children in a letter to the Edmonton Public Library, 2002.

2. Ken Haycock, *The Crisis in Canada's School Libraries: The Case for Reform and Reinvestment* (Toronto: Association of Canadian Publishers, 2003), 14.

3. Michel Durand et al., *Elementary and Secondary Schools: The Role, Challenges and Financial Conditions of School and School Library Resources in Canada* (Ottawa: National Library of Canada, 2001), 3.

4. Michele Lonsdale, *Impact of School Libraries on Student Achievement: A Review of the Research*, Report for the Australian School Library Association (Melbourne: Australian Council for Educational Research, 2003), 30.

5. Lonsdale, *Impact of School Libraries*, 30.

6. Lonsdale, *Impact of School Libraries*, 30.

7. Lonsdale, *Impact of School Libraries*, 30.

8. Lonsdale, *Impact of School Libraries*, 30.

9. Haycock, *Crisis in Canada's School Libraries*, 11.

10. Alberta's Commission on Learning, *Every Child Learns, Every Child Succeeds: Report and Recommendations* (Edmonton: Alberta Learning, 2003), 65.

11. Alberta, *Every Child Learns*, 74.

12. Sandra Morden, "Cooperation between Public Libraries and Schools in Canada: Research Report" (Westport, Ontario: Chief Executives of Large Public Libraries of Ontario, 2003), 11.

13. Morden, *Cooperation*, 12–15.

Part 3

THE END OF THE WORLD AS WE KNOW IT: WHAT ARE THE CONSEQUENCES OF PUSHING TO THE DESKTOP?

We must stop thinking we can force our users to learn how we wish them to seek information and instead mold our services to accommodate their natural tendencies.

—Roy Tennant

The fact is, delivery to the desktop is absolutely seductive.

—John Teskey

The intellectual and theoretical role for librarians is lost only if librarians abandon it.

—Melody Burton

7

Being All We Can Be:
The Web as Both a Threat
and the Means of Our Salvation

Roy Tennant

Before the web, anyone who wanted information after exhausting any resources at hand (e.g., one's own book collection) would resort to the local library. No other publicly accessible store of information existed. Libraries were, to a large degree, the information resource of first and last resort. That was then, this is now.

In the age of the web, a great deal of accurate and usable information is but a few clicks away from any Internet-connected computer. A quick search using one's favorite search engine can quickly turn up a rich set of information pathways, one of which is likely to solve the particular information need. Even librarians must acknowledge that, when used intelligently, the web is a powerful and often accurate information resource.

So given this, it is little wonder that those who previously sought out libraries for assistance with their information needs now fire up a web browser instead. Even I do it. We would be fools not to. If we can get the answer we need in a minute or two with a web browser, why should we go through more time and hassle to get the same or perhaps even a slightly better answer by going through a great deal more trouble? "Good enough," for many information needs, is exactly that. The possibly incremental increase in accuracy or depth one might get from a library is in many cases simply not worth the trouble. This is human nature, and we can ignore it only at our peril.

Our basic, most fundamental problem is that as a profession we have
not yet owned up to our responsibility. No other profession has as
much responsibility for making information more easily accessible and
usable than librarians. But where were we when the web came along?
Who developed Yahoo!? It was a couple of graduate students who
were avoiding their studies. Who developed Google? It was computer
scientists. In both cases, librarians were nowhere to be found. Had we
done our jobs the way they should have been done, we would have
been the ones to tame the web. We would have created Yahoo! and
Google. Instead, we were bystanders.

THE SOURCE OF OUR SALVATION

But rather than cry over spilled milk, we can still do something about
it. We can use the very source of our troubles to win our clientele back.
We can be for them what we should have been all along—and what we
can be again. We can be the information resource of first and last resort. In fact, only libraries can be, since only we have access to the full
range of information resources to which our clientele is entitled. And
therein lies our salvation.

If we set our minds and resources to the task, we can do Yahoo!
and we can do Google. But Yahoo! and Google cannot recreate the
full-featured collections of resources and services that our libraries
have purchased and licensed on behalf of every person living in this
country—citizen or not. In fact, many of us are valid users of more
than one library—whether it is a school, college, university, or corporate library in addition to our local public libraries.

So what can we do? What should we do? What, in fact, can we not
fail to do should we wish to win back our rightful place in the center
of our users' information universe?

We must build compelling web-based services. We must cover services such as Google and Yahoo! like a blanket, while also offering the
licensed resources that are our bread and butter. We must meet our
users where they are—on the web—with both collections and services
tailored to their specific needs and desires. We must stop thinking we
can force our users to learn how we wish them to seek information and
instead mold our services to accommodate their natural tendencies.
This does not mean pandering to their lack of searching sophistication
so much as it means working diligently and imaginatively to craft ser-

vices that put the intelligence of a reference librarian into a system that is complex on the back end so that it can be simple on the front end.

Let's take a simple example. With the advent of the online library catalog, and particularly with web-based access to such systems, searching by subject has been problematic. Without the Library of Congress subject headings easily at hand, how does one determine what subject heading is appropriate to search? Well, by searching title keywords, finding an appropriate record, and then looking at which subject headings were assigned to that book and using those. Almost every reference librarian has known this trick for years, but no automated system has yet implemented it, despite the fact that it could easily be automated. If a user performs a title keyword search, the subject headings assigned to the resulting records could be gathered, chopped back to their roots, and presented to the user as clickable choices ranked by the number of returned records for each base subject heading. Should one of those headings look good, the user could simply click on it to perform a search on that subject heading. This is but one simple example of the strategies we need to start imagining and implementing.

We can and should strive to implement systems that use what we've discovered about successful search strategies without forcing our users to go through complicated, nonintuitive procedures. We must complicate the back ends of our systems in order to simplify the front ends.

Another simple but effective search system enhancement for union catalogs is sorting items by the number of holding libraries. Think of it—this utilizes the collective intelligence of collection development librarians across all the participating libraries. If an item has been selected in many collections, then surely it is more central to a topic than an item that appears in only a few collections. And yet most of our union catalogs (a notable exception being OCLC's WorldCat) do nothing at all with this information.

But we must go much, much further than simply tweaking our existing catalog systems, which mainly have been optimized for librarians at the expense of our clientele. We need to think imaginatively about how to help people find what they need in any type of information system.

KEY BARRIERS

One of the most difficult barriers to finding information is the sheer number of places to look. Modern library users are faced with a bewildering array of online databases. Simply narrowing in on the one or few that will be the most productive for a given search can be a very daunting task. Librarians have not been ignorant of this problem, and to their credit they have tried to guide users to the best resources through subject pathfinder pages, searchable indexes of abstracting and indexing services, and other such tools for locating useful resources. But these are doomed to fail in two important ways. First, it is not intuitive to users that the first step when looking for information is to find the library website and plow around it until they locate a page that tells them what databases to search. Neither is it made much better by providing a database of databases since the hapless user must still go to each one successively even if he or she is lucky enough to find the best sources.

Let's assume the hapless user has somehow discovered an appropriate set of resources to search. Now the real fun begins. As the user soon discovers, none of these supposedly similar resources look the same. Each resource has a search form that looks nothing like any other, with a different set of options, different names for the same options, and a bewildering array of buttons, links, and explanatory text. The user is, in other words, adrift in a sea of confusion at every step. No wonder the typical reaction is to frantically locate a search box, type in a few keywords, and hit return as quickly as possible, accepting whatever defaults the system has offered.

Now if the person is lucky, he or she will be looking at a screen of search results. This screen is of course laid out like no other screen of search results, and should the user wish to understand much of what appears, time must be taken to study a typical record and determine the identity of each element. Perhaps having done this, the user is typically dismayed to discover that he or she has precious little information to determine if a given entry will be worth the time to hunt it down. This is particularly true of library catalog records.

To compound the problems the user has so far survived, if the item is not directly available online by clicking a link, there is no information whatsoever to help the user determine how long it might take to obtain that item. If he or she is lucky, a link is available that tells if the local library has it—and allows an immediate request if it doesn't. If such a link doesn't exist, the user's troubles have just begun.

This litany of problems may not be completely solvable. But we can certainly do a great deal about them, despite the fact that so far we have done little or nothing to address them.

EARLY ATTEMPTS AT SOLUTIONS

Although we are far from solving the problems I've described, some early trends may point the way to a set of tools and strategies that will enable us to build more robust and effective library services.

One trend is the dawning realization that MARC and AACR2 are well past showing their age. These standards have been tweaked, poked, prodded, and stretched to accommodate certain requirements of Internet users (the use of the 856 field for URLs comes to mind), but this has been neither pretty nor particularly effective. For example, I was recently dismayed to discover it is impossible for the University of California to determine from its MARC21 records which items in its union catalog are available online. It turns out that variations in cataloging practice and the inability of the standards to accommodate a clear and unambiguous statement specifying what a URL points to (e.g., the full text of the item, an online table of contents) make it impossible for us to limit searches only to items available online in full text. Such a situation is both incomprehensible and indefensible.

I am not the only one dismayed with the existing state of our bibliographic metadata infrastructure. The Online Computer Library Center (OCLC) has been recreating the WorldCat database using XML stored in an Oracle 9i XML-aware database. The center has created its own XML format, dubbed XWC for "Extended WorldCat"; the format accommodates both MARC21 and Dublin Core and may soon welcome records using other standards such as ONIX. The Research Libraries Group (RLG) is similarly working to modernize the Research Libraries Information Network (RLIN) infrastructure.

These are good early steps, but such changes will need to sift down to the rest of us before we see how to implement effective solutions. For a more complete description of the type of bibliographic metadata infrastructure I think is required for significant change, see the article "A Bibliographic Metadata Infrastructure for the 21st Century."[1]

Somewhat related is the fact that many of our library catalog interfaces are seriously flawed. Most of the users coming to our systems have experience searching only Amazon and Google—both of which return useful results with one search box and a button—so facing our usually complicated and difficult-to-understand interfaces can be daunting.

A recent project by the Research Libraries Group to address these issues for a college undergraduate audience is encouraging. Dubbed

RedLightGreen,[2] the system is optimized for how undergraduates wish to search and use bibliographic information. For example, besides offering a simple search box and a button, when a book record is viewed, the top ten Google hits on that book are also displayed. Choices for displaying the citation in the most popular citation styles make it easy to copy and paste a citation into a term paper, and it is similarly easy to determine if your local library has a copy.

These projects by OCLC and RLG are encouraging harbingers of a future in which our automated systems make more sense to the users, are easy to use, and perform the functions we expect them to.

Another encouraging trend is the emergence of software tools for creating cross-database search services. Also called metasearching, or federated searching, the basic concept is to minimize the number of separate resources users must search to find what they need. Although these tools are still very much in their infancy, with a number of significant problems to address, they promise to make it easier for many of our users—particularly those who do not care about comprehensive recall or 100 percent precision.

Libraries that deploy these tools may soon discover it isn't sufficient to group all their licensed databases into subject categories that treat all databases in a category the same way. Large libraries especially may find it necessary to provide more tailored portals to serve a given need (e.g., an undergraduate term paper) or topic area (e.g., biosciences).

From there it is but a small step to the idea of creating additional search targets from harvested metadata (e.g., repositories of academic content that comply with the Open Archives Initiative Protocol for Metadata Harvesting) or focused crawling (e.g., crawling a set of highly regarded bioscience websites).

THE WEB AS SAVIOR

The web has placed in our hands the very means of our salvation. Many of our users have left the library for the web, that's true. But why? Because search engines such as Google are both easy to use and fairly effective. But if we can learn from Google and Amazon how to build easy-to-use and effective web services, we are better positioned than anyone to build truly compelling information resources and thus win our users back.

We are, after all, the only ones who can provide access to the widest possible slice of the information universe. We can integrate services such as Google (e.g., Google conveniently provides an API, or application programming interface, for integrating Google search results into other systems, a capability amply demonstrated by redlightgreen.com), commercial database resources, and our significant print collections into one easy-to-use portal.

Doing this well is not easy. It will take a deep understanding of cutting-edge web technologies as well as existing library standards and protocols. It requires imagination and risk taking. It is not for those who think our traditional methods of acquiring and providing access to information are sufficient.

But whether we like it or not, it is both achievable and imperative that we use the very instrument that led our users away from us to win them back—and in so doing serve their needs better than we ever have before.

NOTES

1. Roy Tennant, "A Bibliographic Metadata Infrastructure for the 21st Century," *Library Hi Tech* 22, no. 2 (2004): 175–81.

2. RedLightGreen, at redlightgreen.com (accessed 2 April 2004).

8

The Challenges of Our Success: Consequences of Pushing to the Desktop

John Teskey

The rapid development and deployment of web-accessible databases combined with access to full-text delivery to the desktop has revolutionized life for library users and changed our lives forever. When Scott Carlson's article "The Deserted Library" appeared in the November 16, 2001, issue of the *Chronicle of Higher Education,* our community struggled between denial and claims that it "just ain't so." Carlson describes a conversation with an English major who progressed through several years of her university career without entering the library. All of us can think of similar if not identical examples, but these are not the stories we like to tell. Part of the problem is that we tend to be somewhat evangelical as a profession. We find it difficult to understand why many of our potential clients don't take advantage of our offers to show them the intricacies of the information and publishing cycle or different ways to use databases to achieve the best results. While we are able to save our users valuable time, the fact is many will never become regular clients.

THE RISE OF ONLINE RESOURCES AND A NEW GENERATION OF LIBRARY USERS

Ten years ago we librarians were relatively secure because there were no effective competitors and we didn't need to spend time worrying about our bread-and-butter services. Today threats have taken physical and virtual form.

During the 1970s, commercial databases such as Dialog became part of our service, with mediated access to journal literature readily accessible to our users. By the late 1970s, databases had become available for local use on CD-ROM. In the 1980s, databases on CD-ROM proliferated, and the number of online searches expanded to fill the hours available at the dedicated workstations. These stand-alone workstations were in such high demand that many libraries implemented reservation systems to ensure fair access for all users. At the same time, training programs for the use of various CD-ROM databases were developed. These changes produced a generation of library users who had some contact and experience with database searching. As well, they were the first generation to move from card catalogs to online public access catalogs.

While these technological changes were taking place in the library, the home computer market was established, resulting in the rise of the computer-savvy library user. This was a period of remarkable and disruptive change, but for most of us the changes went unnoticed. One of the results that should stand out for our community was the collapse of the *Encyclopaedia Britannica* as the standby home education investment. The home computer and a CD-ROM encyclopedia named Encarta led to the quick demise of home encyclopedia sales. A new generation of students arrived at universities having grown up during a time when a mouse meant "point and click" and not a furry little animal with big ears. In addition to familiarity with technology, they arrived with their own computers and expectations of instant gratification and remote access.

Several years ago I picked up the library copy of the most recent issue of *Harvard Business Review*. While scanning it, I identified an article I wanted for future use; when I was ready to leave, I started toward the copier before deciding to check whether the article was available online. It was. My choice now was do I point the article to my printer or find a photocopier? It is no surprise that selecting the laser printer was easier, and it will continue to be the vehicle of choice until portable reading devices become the norm. The fact is, delivery to the desktop is absolutely seductive.

The success of libraries in applying technology to expand and enhance our services combined with the arrival of more computer literate users has resulted in a decline in the actual number of people crossing our physical thresholds. In less than a decade, the web has become the main entrance for many of our clients.

> Libraries have reacted quickly to dizzying changes in the information landscape over the past two decades. Indeed, the rapid acceptance of relevant technologies is a library tradition, from the early adoption of typewriters, mimeograph machines and photocopiers to the use of the fax for document delivery and the mainframe computer for online catalogs. In particular, libraries seized on networked delivery as a transformational new conduit to advance a core library mission: the dissemination of information in the pursuit of knowledge.[1]

This new door to library services changes our relationship with a significant portion of our clients. Now those who study in locations remote from campus can be effectively served, with many of these students rising to the honors list. When off-campus students were surveyed, "the greatest percentage of respondents (51.2%) indicated that off-campus access to full-text materials in the library's databases was the most useful service. The second most useful service (51.1%) was off-campus access to the library's online library catalog."[2]

To focus on Canada, here is a description of online services from the 2003 *Globe and Mail*'s university report card:

> This means, for example, that a student can sit at home and read journals on screen at the kitchen table. No schlepping across town to the campus. No searching for the physical journal in the stacks. Warren Ross, 23, who has just finished his fourth year in media, information and techno-culture at Western, said he was flabbergasted when he realized that he could have an on-line chat with a librarian in real time. Once, for example, he couldn't remember which books he still had out. He clicked on the library chat room and a staff member answered back within 10 seconds. She walked him through the on-line instructions to check his books and renew them if necessary. He has also done research by consulting an on-line librarian. He said being able to get information and research electronically simply makes his academic life more efficient. "I just don't want to have to worry about walking all the way across campus to get to the library," he said.[3]

While the world keeps changing, our mission has remained remarkably stable: to deliver the appropriate information to our users in a timely fashion. Librarianship is a pragmatic profession, with service as its main focus. Consistently we adapt the possibilities that surround us in order to improve service delivery to our users. According to Christine Borgman, the "paradox of the networked world is that as libraries become more embedded in the information infrastructure of universities, communities, governments, corporations, and other entities, the less visible they may become to their users, funders, and policy-makers."[4]

We have worked very hard to make access to information as seamless and easy as possible. There is no question that our clients love it, but often they don't know who to thank. Perhaps we've been influenced by science fiction; however, the desire to create the ultimate scholars' workstation has been with us for centuries, as witness the following:

> It is said that Abdul Kassem Ismael, the scholarly Grand Vizier of Persia in the tenth century, had a library of 117,000 volumes. He was an avid reader and truly a lover of books. On his many travels as a warrior and statesman, he could not bear to part with his beloved books. Wherever he went, they were carried about by 400 camels trained to walk in alphabetical order. His camel drivers thus became librarians who could put their hands instantly on any book for which their master asked.[5]

Perhaps Ismael created the earliest implementation of Vannevar Bush's proposed "memex":

> Consider a future device for individual use, which is a sort of mechanized private file and library. . . . A memex is a device in which an individual stores all his books, records, and communications, and which is mechanized so that it may be consulted with exceeding speed and flexibility.[6]

The web has established a discovery and delivery mechanism that allows a scholar to take advantage of electronic publishing and to create a virtual memex to support his or her research. All these forces place the physical library at some risk.

THE RISE OF ONLINE RESOURCES: THE RESEARCH

During the past few years, many anecdotal reports regarding the use of electronic resources have been released. However, the most extensive study I have found was conducted in 2001–2002 at the University of California, where a yearlong investigation into user preference and acceptance of online versus print journals was carried out. The use of 298 titles from the sciences, social sciences, and humanities was compared on two campuses, with the results nothing short of astounding. Campus A made both the print and electronic versions readily available, while campus B provided ready access to the electronic version and printed volumes in storage, with retrieval on request. On campus A, the 298 journals were used a total of 103,537 times, of which 97,493 were electronic and 6,044 were print. In this environment where the user had a choice of format, the electronic version was selected 16 to 1. On campus B, where the print format copy had to be retrieved from storage, the electronic version was used 160,180 times versus 201 requests for the print, a ratio of almost 800 to 1! While there were some differences between the disciplines, it is evident that the online environment was the format of choice for the vast majority of students and faculty in all fields.[7]

At the University of New Brunswick, while we have not conducted a careful study such as the one described at the University of California, our experience is very similar. The following chart demonstrates the rapid growth in use of one full-text database (EBSCO Academic Search Elite) from 1997 to 2002 (see figure 8.1).

One of the titles provided in this database is *The Economist*. During any given year, fewer than one hundred circulation transactions are recorded for this journal, including in-library pickups from the photocopy area and volumes left on carrels. During 2001–2002, approximately 6,500 articles were downloaded from the online version. While there is no intention to ever cancel the paper version, the fact is that when students and faculty search for a particular article, the online version is the format of choice.

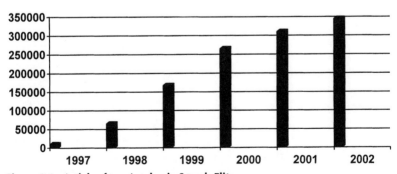

Figure 8.1. Articles from Academic Search Elite

Usage data tells us that our clients love the freedom to access information twenty-four hours a day, seven days a week. Various organizations have conducted surveys to test this statement during the past year, including the Council on Library and Information Resources (CLIR), which commissioned a review of some two hundred user surveys. The conclusions confirm our suspicions and our assumptions. This review, titled *Use and Users of Electronic Library Resources*, prepared by Carol Tenopir and published in August 2003, provides an analysis of the information collected in these surveys published in the past few years, including the Pew Internet and American Life Project's *The Internet Goes to College* and the OCLC's *White Paper on the Information Habits of College Students*. The following are a few of the findings of the council study:

- Users will read articles from a wide variety of journal titles and sources if available to them, although most readings come from relatively few journals.
- Personal subscriptions to journals continue to decrease, with users relying more on library electronic subscriptions and on the Internet.
- While most journal readings are of articles within their first year of publication, a sizable minority of readings come from older materials.
- College and high school students use the Internet more than the library for research, and many believe they are more expert at searching than their teachers.[8]

If we examine these findings in turn they point to various aspects of library operations. The first point, that "users will read articles from a wide variety of journal titles and sources if available to them," was certainly substantiated in an ongoing Canadian project. In Canada, the National Site Licensing Project[9] has provided our users with a substantial suite of full-text journals from a variety of publishers, available at the click of a mouse. A cursory review of the project's usage statistics demonstrates that our faculty and students were interested in articles from all of the journals now available. For most of the sixty-four universities who participated, a considerable number of these journals were new to them. In the print environment, we purchased to the maximum of our financial resources, but our resources always ran out before our users' reading interests were fully met.

Tenopir's finding that personal subscriptions are declining only increases the pressure on the library to provide access to the widest possible range of titles for our researchers. This finding is a reflection of the price sensitivity of the market; however, if the library is expected to be the agency to maintain the "collection in common," our error is to not brand the level of access we provide for our users.

The last point that "college and high school students use the Internet more than the library for research" creates a number of training opportunities for libraries. How many of you have heard the comment, "Why didn't you show me this in my first year? It would have saved me so much time"? Our instruction programs offer considerable value-added lifelong research skills, and I don't see any other group vying for this position.

SUCCESS BRINGS NEW OPPORTUNITIES: INFORMATION LITERACY

The survey information from CLIR makes it clear that our users want to be effective, independent users of information. However, they still have work to do to gain a real understanding of the actual power of the tools available to them. Libraries have stepped up to the significant opportunity in user education. *Information literacy* has become the popular term to describe a set of skills our students need in order to excel in the new economy, and it has been libraries that have taken on this instructional requirement.

The Association of Research Libraries (ARL) maintains statistics of more than 120 of the largest research libraries in North America. They recently published a chart[10] that provides a graphic view of the shifts in library service trends in the past decade (see figure 8.2).

At a glance, the chart appears to support Scott Carlson's arguments in "Deserted Library." The 26 percent reduction in reference and 15 percent drop in circulation indicate a significant reduction in personal library use. However, the library instruction load has increased by some 55 percent, and the number of students attending these sessions has increased by 57 percent. The surprising story is that during the past decade, librarians have taken on a heavier teaching load than many faculty members.

Digitization projects such as Early Canadiana Online[11] have made primary materials available over the web, which has also added to

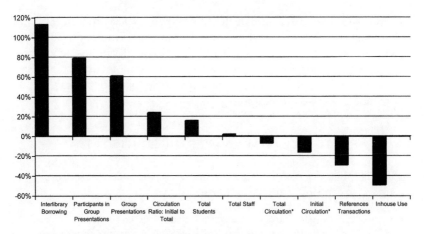

* Includes initial and renewals but excludes reserve circulation.
Adapted from Martha Kyrillidou and Mark Young, *ARL Statistics 2001–02* (Washington DC: Association of Research Libraries, 2003)
http://www.arl.org/stats/arlstat/02pub/intro02.html. Permission to use granted by the Association of Research Libraries, Washington, DC
http://www.arl.org; For more information on the ARL Statistics and Measurement Program, see: http://www.arl.org/stats/

Figure 8.2. Service Trends in ARL Libraries, 1991–2003

our library instruction load. In addition to manuscript material, an increasing number of libraries also provide access to data files from Statistics Canada (Data Liberation Initiative), as well as files from the ICPSR (Inter-University Consortium of Political and Social Research) data archive. For students to access and use these resources successfully, libraries need to devote staff and systems resources to support these materials.

With regard to information literacy, another paradox is evolving that could have a negative effect on the position of the library.

> For the most part, . . . academic libraries have been all too absent in the design, development, and implementation of courseware. As a result, faculty do not think of integrating library resources directly into their courseware-enhanced courses. It is possible that faculty (who increasingly make course-related resources—reading and research assignments—available to students through courseware) and students (who use courseware in conjunction with the Web to search for and obtain their course-related materials) may not see the library as the first or even a relevant place to obtain the scholarly resources needed for their courses.[12]

This is a growth area from which the library seems to be absent when it should be in the position of ownership. We have not spent the appropriate time ensuring that the library plays a lead role in the implementation of WebCT or Blackboard on many of our campuses. Individually and as a group we have not engaged our teaching colleagues in a partnership to make the best possible use of a very changed library that is more than able to provide support to traditional or technology-assisted learning.

IS IT TIME TO TURN OUT THE LIGHTS YET?

There is much discussion about the impact of this shift to electronic resources on the physical library. Carlson notes:

> Clearly, the burgeoning use of electronic databases has sent the buzz of library activity onto the Internet. The shift leaves many librarians and scholars wondering and worrying about the future of what has traditionally been the social and intellectual heart of campus. As well as about whether students are learning differently now—or learning at all. Library journals are publishing articles about the roles of the "old" and "new" libraries, and the tension expressed in those pages is almost palpable.[13]

The ARL chart on service trends reproduced earlier also indicates a 106 percent increase in interlibrary borrowing, effectively demonstrating that our print collections are still in high demand.

OCLC's catalog WorldCat contains some 56 million titles. The vast majority of these titles will never find themselves in a digital repository. With our digitization projects focused on primary material and other out-of-copyright resources, our physical collections will remain the only access to the vast majority of publications. In 2001, members of the Canadian Association of Research Libraries[14] added 1.8 million volumes to their collections. These same libraries had combined holdings of some 76 million volumes at the end of 2002. Our physical collections are still in high demand, and if we add web traffic, electronic access to an ever-widening range of materials, and the number of articles being downloaded from our licensed electronic files, library use is booming!

To ensure that our clients continue to come through our doors in substantial numbers, the real challenge will be to provide the right environment for research and learning. With the expenditure on new library buildings and renovations surpassing $500 million every year in North America, signs are that the physical library is still in very high demand. However, these new spaces often differ from traditional library layouts and frequently incorporate an information commons and other contemporary design features and services.

> Every community seeks to set aside commons, or public spaces, that will be frequented by a broad cross section of the community. . . . Commons create opportunities for people who do not necessarily travel in the same disciplinary, social, political, or economic circles to frequently meet and greet each other. Egalitarian common spaces associated with learning and culture hold a particularly strong appeal for many people, even those who do not use them frequently.[15]

Two Canadian examples of the redevelopment of space to better suit the information needs of students are the Learning Commons at Dalhousie University and the Irving K. Barber Learning Centre at the University of British Columbia. Many have suggested that libraries are now in competition with Chapters' and Indigo's plush seating and Starbucks; I wish it were that easy!

Changing the physical surroundings of the library to keep up with the expectations of our users is a reasonable and necessary response to changing times. The two examples just given demonstrate how the library of the twenty-first century becomes the transformational centerpiece of our universities, providing a new kind of space for individual or group access to the resources needed to advance learning and research. The library now provides not only the materials and the guides to assist users but also the technological components to help them put the pieces together.

IS THERE A FUTURE?

The library provides the tools that allow users to find the right book or article from the mountain of material published annually. Current estimates place the number of journal articles in the range of 2 million annually and the number of new books at over 250,000 every year. This results in information overload and the desperation we all feel in finding the right information with the least effort and the maximum convenience. The library is still the right place!

So is it time to switch off the lights? It is clear from the evaluation of projects such as CNSLP (Canadian National Site Licensing Project) that our users want online access to research literature. Indeed, we learned that they want access to a wider and richer range of journal titles, including deep backfiles. However, our extensive print collections will never be fully accessible in a digital form, and our users will want to use this content for generations to come. As the library continues to provide a growing range of services, both electronic and in person, the library experience is still going to be through welcoming portals, which users will pull or push, as well as point and click, to open.

In addition, many areas provide new or expanded opportunities for growth. For instance, we can respond to current reports of inappropriate use of material available on the web by developing and delivering programs on academic integrity and appropriate use of published materials—how to cite rather than plagiarize. Another area we have not fully explored or exploited is the development of research consulting activities. Such outreach programs could be established as service nodes, increase our participation in interdisciplinary research teams, and create new-style publishing initiatives. These are just a few examples, but the message is clear: The library and librarians are not ready to close the book!

NOTES

1. David Seaman, "Deep Sharing: A Case for the Federated Digital Library," *Educause Review* 38, no. 4 (July/August 2003): 10.

2. Kimberly Kelley and Gloria Orr, "Trends in Distant Student Use of Electronic Resources: A Survey," *College and Research Libraries* 64 (May 2003): 180.

3. *Globe and Mail* in partnership with Uthink and the Strategic Counsel, "University Report Card," at www.universityreportcard.com (accessed 16 October 2003).

4. Christine L. Borgman, "The Invisible Library: Paradox of the Global Information Infrastructure," *Library Trends* 51, no. 4 (Spring 2003): 653.

5. Douglas Greenberg, "Camel Drivers and Gatecrashers: Quality Control in the Digital Research Library," in *The Mirage of Continuity: Reconfiguring Academic Information Resources for the 21st Century*, edited by B. Hawkins and P. Batin (Washington, D.C.: Council on Library and Information Resources, 2001), 105.

6. Vannevar Bush, "As We May Think," *Atlantic Monthly* 176, no. 1 (July 1945): 101–8.

7. Collection Management Strategies in a Digital Environment: A Project of the University of California, at libraries.ucsd.edu/cmi.html (accessed 5 April 2003).

8. Carol Tenopir, *Use and Users of Electronic Library Resources: An Overview and Analysis of Recent Research Studies* (Washington, D.C.: Council on Library and Information Resources, 2003), v.

9. Canadian National Site Licensing Project (www.cnslp.ca) was an innovative project involving sixty-four universities representing some 650,000 students to provide desktop access to a wide range of research publications through multiyear agreements with seven international publishers.

10. Martha Kyrillidou and Mark Young, "ARL Statistics 2001–02: Research Library Trends," (Washington, D.C.: Association of Research Libraries, 2003), at arl.org/stats/arlstat/02pub/intro02.html (accessed 8 April 2004).

11. Early Canadiana Online (ECO) is a digital library providing access to over 1,522,000 pages of Canada's printed heritage. It features works published from the time of the first European settlers up to the early twentieth century. ECO is produced by the Canadian Institute for Historical Microreproductions (www.canadiana.org/eco/english/about.html).

12. John D. Shank and Nancy H. Dewald, "Establishing Our Presence in Courseware," *Information Technology and Libraries* 22, no. 1 (March 2003): 38.

13. Scott Carlson, "The Deserted Library," *Chronicle of Higher Education*, 16 November 2001, p. A35.

14. The Canadian Association of Research Libraries/L'Association des bibliothèques de recherche du Canada (CARL/ABRC), *2001–2002 Statistics/Statistiques* (Ottawa: CARL/ABRC, 2003), 26–27.

15. Sam Demas and Jeffrey A. Scherer, "Esprit de Place," *American Libraries* 33, no. 4 (April 2002): 65.

9

All or Nothing at All: The Consequences of Pushing Electronic Resources to the Desktop

Melody Burton

I lost count a long time ago of the number of revolutions that academic libraries have weathered in the last fifty years. Proclamations of the severity or grandness of change in academic libraries abound. But one innovation resonates with me—the rise of the World Wide Web.

The web signaled profound change for academic libraries. Scholars and academic publishers immediately seized web infrastructure for their own purposes, the publication and dissemination of information. The creativity surrounding the transfer and invention of academic materials in this medium is unprecedented and has only begun to realize its potential. The web's immediate reception in academic libraries has revolutionized how library users access materials. This chapter discusses how the growth of web-based electronic resources is changing academic libraries generally and reference departments specifically.

MEANWHILE, BACK AT THE RANCH

For librarians and university administrators, the introduction, reception, and unparalleled growth of the web and web-based products have raised expectations about how library resources and services can be delivered. Limitless possibilities and high expectations promise to keep librarians and their administrators busy looking for funding to accommodate demand from users and staff.

Arguably, at one time students and faculty were dependent on academic libraries for in-house tools and their representations (books and catalogs). Now electronic versions of library resources distance the user from the library and its representatives (librarians and staff) and put materials directly into the hands of the user. Access from any location at any time is a welcome gesture if still an incomplete service.

The earliest success for academic libraries was the ability to make library catalogs available on the web. Electronic indexes and abstracting databases quickly followed suit, although some library users experience barriers to easy access occasioned by the requirements of licensing agreements and authentication processes. The span of electronic resources grew to include e-journals and, to a much lesser extent, e-books and other products. With all of these materials available remotely, who sets foot in the library?

Studies are unanimous in their assertion that there is no universal user with a common information-seeking pattern of behavior.[1] Discipline affiliation and user status are most frequently cited as predictors of differences. In general, undergraduates are most likely to visit libraries, and researchers in humanities and social sciences still value print collections and the experience of doing research in the library. During a strategic planning exercise at my own institution, a health sciences faculty member's wish to access everything remotely was contrasted with a humanities professor who reads and writes in the library.

Although a no "one size fits all" approach to reference services is warranted, it is possible to consider the overall environment being created in academic libraries and reference departments. As collections librarians acquire increasing numbers of electronic titles and the balance of acquisitions funds swings from print to electronic resources, the real impact of electronic formats has yet to be realized. What factors are likely to influence this impact of electronic resources in academic libraries and their reference departments? How will reference librarians respond, and what service will be created to address the needs of students and faculty?

GREAT EXPECTATIONS: TEN ASSUMPTIONS FOR THE FUTURE

When the editors of this volume asked me to submit a chapter on the consequences of moving electronic resources to the desktop, I asked some questions. Once instructed to be provocative, I tried to develop a portrait of Canadian academic libraries in the future—and failed miserably. The information landscape is a complex environment with multiple variables. Every colleague I consulted singled out a specific trend as an indicator of the future. I captured some of these trends and threw in some of my own speculations. Posing as a devil's advocate and a clairvoyant, here is my arbitrary list of best guesses based on highly suspect methodologies—gossip and speculation. Furthermore, as a librarian in the humanities and social sciences, my point of view is influenced by my experiences serving researchers in these disciplines.[2]

Convergence: Delivering the Goods—Linking Technology

Assumption: Delivering the goods is synonymous with access and retrieval of information.

Take the legwork out of research! Simple, seamless, or intuitive pathways eliminate the drudgery associated with research. Searching and retrieving are the same process. Researchers and librarians welcome with relief the opportunity to skip the multiple steps to actually acquire a text. And although libraries have been expounding the benefits of resource sharing, it remains the "weak link" in the delivery of resources to faculty and students. Imagine that resource sharing among libraries is so automatic and integrated with search tools that it is an easy and *pleasant* aspect of library research. Finally, these improvements, or variations on them, are within reach and not difficult to imagine.

- You have heard this drill before. Vendor-produced periodical databases seamlessly link to e-journals at the article level (if available) or to library catalog records for print holdings (if available) or to an interlibrary loan request screen with one-step access. These links accurately reflect library holdings, and the likelihood of false matches is nonexistent. What's different? It actually works! Some libraries are in the process of realizing this scenario and testing the quality of transactions.
- Variation on the previous scenario: Wherever a library user encounters a citation or reference, it is *easy* to obtain it. If the item is not held by the library, resource-sharing software automatically kicks in, suggesting how the library can receive the item, with accurate estimates of turnaround time, the cost, and the simple option of asking the user to click to submit a request. This is the

long-held promise of resource sharing, but the ability to deliver and deliver fast becomes a reality. The ability to deliver the goods will be an essential component of the future of academic libraries.

Convergence: Federated Searching

Assumption: Advances in search engine technology will continue.

Federated search engines will get smarter and smarter. While reference librarians fret over the loss of database-specific features and criticize federated searching as imprecise and a "dumbing down" or lowest-common-denominator approach to research, students and faculty will celebrate the ability to search multiple databases simultaneously.

Students and faculty will expect research tools to offer the ease and simplicity of Internet search tools, such as Google, and the luxuries of more sophisticated research tools. Specifically, users want a simple search screen and good results from metasearch engines. Experiences with search engines such as Google and Yahoo! are best characterized as overwhelming, time consuming, misleading, miraculous, and easy. Students and faculty will also expect the instant gratification of large result sets without the frustration of weeding through false hits or annoying advertising.

Specifically, librarians and some sophisticated researchers will demand precise searching that is available with a controlled vocabulary, such as Medline, or specialized features such as searching by image. But most students and faculty will be satisfied with sloppy searches. However, in user surveys, these individuals will often cite efficient library research as a desirable state.

Convergence: Virtual Reference

Assumption: Students and faculty who use library resources from their desktops in their homes or offices will enjoy virtual help 24/7.

For library users, remote access to libraries and their collections is wonderful until they need help. Getting started or problem-solving using various resources may require reference service. For some, a visit to campus to chat with a reference librarian may be a simple and easy fix. For others, the distance or ability to reach campus in person may be insurmountable or inconvenient. Other communication methods such as telephone and e-mail reference fail to provide adequate approaches to research. Enter virtual reference.

By shifting reference service away from the static confines of a desk in the library, virtual reference offers help wherever the library user is located. Virtual reference, the call center for libraries, can problem-solve database mechanics, suggest starting points, and help eliminate stumbling blocks.

For library administrators, virtual reference poses a critical staffing challenge. Decisions about who should staff virtual reference desks pivot on identifying needed skill sets and recognizing that not all librarians possess these combinations of abilities. Further complicating the staffing model is the thorny issue of the role paraprofessionals may play in providing reference service. While traditionally seen as the exclusive or semi-exclusive domain of librarians, reference service delivered over the web has the potential to transform the fundamental concept of reference librarianship and erode the role of librarians within it. Unfortunately, instead of a conscious decision to shift a defined set of reference services to paraprofessionals, staffing levels will likely be driven by economic factors.

Convergence: Friends + Library = Information Commons

Assumption: Information commons—the convergence of content, technology, services, and space—will reestablish or solidify the library at the heart of the campus.

Consider the appeal of a consolidated area for electronic resources—one-stop searching and retrieval, service options, and high tech with good furniture. Add students (and coffee) to this scenario and a synergy that celebrates the social aspects of learning emerges.

Imagine a scenario in which students don't *have* to come to the library but *want* to come to the library. Opportunities to meet friends, get motivated, and feed on the atmosphere are tangible outcomes for undergraduates. The introduction of an information commons renews the overall appeal of a library that offers group study, quiet study, comfortable furnishings, and a safe environment.

Although the social aspects of learning may not be compelling for all library users, the concept is a powerful one. As students spend more time on web-based course requirements and less time in the classroom, the environment created by the information commons fills a void. This is a hot spot on the information landscape. It could have happened anywhere on campus, but the action is in the library. This is another success story for the library "as space" and its renewal as cultural center within the university.

Consortia and the Marketplace: Another Kind of Convergence

Assumption: Libraries will continue on a path of consortia collection development in response to international publishing conglomerates and their aggressive pricing structures.

Canadian universities responded collectively to excessive periodical pricing, declining or uncertain funding, and a weak Canadian dollar with the creation of the Canadian National Site Licensing Project (CNSLP). CNSLP delivered the goods—unanimous support from Canadian universities and a single voice to negotiate with some of the world's largest information providers. That CNSLP brokered a favorable deal from these vendors is perhaps less significant than that there is a CNSLP—a single voice for academic libraries, publicly funded institutions who desperately need an edge when up against commercial juggernauts.

If the upside of consortial purchasing is better pricing and a level playing field for key resources, the downside is the potential to create a monoculture among academic libraries and their collections. More may not be better, even if it is cost effective. Specialized libraries may not benefit directly from national, provincial, or regional initiatives but may feel obliged to be good team players and sign on to contracts, trusting that more subject-relevant material will be available in future deals. Adding titles from consortial purchases of subject areas unrelated to the fields of study at a campus simply clutters the catalog with unwanted content.

While the overall consequences of consortial collection development are yet to be assessed, it is unlikely that vendors and academic libraries will abandon the efficiencies and cost savings of consortial purchasing any time soon.

Publishing and the Marketplace: Copyright

Assumption: Intellectual property rights and digital resources legislation will reflect a "fair use" policy for students and faculty conducting research or pursuing independent study.

While little evidence supports this optimistic assumption, librarians will continue to work in an environment where governments and their regulating bodies lag behind the possibilities presented by electronic resources and technology.

The complex issue of intellectual property rights butts up against multiple and contradictory international trade agreements, digital rights management, and David and Goliath–sized creators. Add the wildcards of technological breakthroughs, intransigent organizations, the public, and their politicians, and an unpredictable scenario for the future emerges. Consider the innovation of file-swapping software (such as Napster); the reaction of the recording industry; the wild, enthusiastic, and defiant response of the public; and the "crackdown" legislation from politicians.

A multitude of players populates this landscape—creators, publishers, distributors, users, and politicians. Further complicating the issue is the schizophrenic role of libraries, which have multiple interests in the outcome of this debate. Nevertheless, the future of copyright and its academic twin—licensing of digital content—promises to add a layer of constraint on the access of digital resources in the foreseeable future.

Publishing and the Marketplace: Open Archives/Institutional Repositories

Assumption: Academics and their publishers will choose alternate, publicly subsidized, or cost-recovery venues for distributing their work.

Born out of a strong sense of collegiality and in response to unreasonable pricing for journals and restrictive copyright requirements of periodical publishers, open archives will thrive. Though still a tiny segment of academic publishing, this trend will grow and gather support from universities, academics, and libraries. This "think small, act locally" scholarly response to globalization is empowering for creators who are tired of fighting over the copyright to their own work and want to accomplish something now. These optimistic campus activists have the opportunity to change academic publishing; their success will hinge on their ability to convince their colleagues and administrators of the quality and integrity of an alternative publishing process.

Commercial publishers, faced with this trend, will either drastically revise their pricing schedules or squeeze harder those institutions and their academics who continue to subscribe to pricey periodicals. Or, eager to get a piece of the new publishing economy, perhaps another breed of commercial publisher will be born.

Staffing

Assumption: Although numerous career options are available, enough individuals will choose librarianship as a profession and academic libraries as their workplace.

An aging workforce, lean budgets, and shifting skill sets have changed staffing at academic libraries in Canada in the last twenty years. Fewer staff is the dominant characteristic, but some librarians and administrators advocate different staff altogether. Financial officers, personnel directors, and strategic planners may be better recruited from the MBA program across campus than at a library school. At the same time, support staff members with higher educational attainment than their predecessors are absorbing work that has been the exclusive realm of librarians. Experiencing squeezes on two sides, the composition of an academic librarian's workload is uncertain and will undergo redefinition and negotiation. Still there is lots of work to do, and librarians are not arguing for heavier workloads.

Having won the battle for the center and heart of the campus, libraries may be threatened by a deafening silence—few may choose this occupation. Of those that do, public services such as reference continue to attract more new recruits than technical services or cataloging departments.

Assessment and Accountability

Assumption: Libraries will need to justify resources by submitting valid and comprehensive statistical portraits of resource management and user response to their funding bodies.

Academic libraries, like other academic departments on campus, are required to justify resources. Government-initiated calls for heightened accountability demand that libraries evaluate services and collections and provide better information about how public funds are expended. Furthermore, standard output measures that capture activity (e.g., circulation statistics, numbers of volumes added, and reference transactions) offer an incomplete picture of a library's value to its students and faculty. To measure service quality, libraries have adopted user surveys, focus groups, and sincere attempts to involve students and faculty in strategic planning initiatives and resource planning discussions.

Fortunately for libraries interested in assessment, the Association of Research Libraries (ARL) has introduced LibQUAL+ as a standardized tool to assess faculty and student expectations and perceptions of the library's ability to meet their service and information needs. Many Canadian libraries embraced the survey as a sound methodology on which to base service initiatives and collection priorities. The adoption of a standardized instrument promises to provide an overall view of academic libraries over time.

Size Matters: More, More, More

Assumption: A consumer mentality will drive the direction of academic libraries and their collections and services.

It always has. This is Ranganathan adapted for the twenty-first century and the least controversial assumption here. Mass consumption is rampant. Consider that more quantity is the best selling feature of Google, more selection is the motto for the marketplace, and more quantity and more quality is the collective demand of the consumer.

Students and faculty want more content, more access, more services, and more options. This thirst for knowledge in its multiple formats is unlikely to be satisfied easily or cheaply. Selection—or a *big* menu—is paramount to library users who want services and resources tailored to their specific research needs. Tremendous pressure is placed on library administrators to deliver the quantity and quality of materials users demand.

Libraries have always been champions of users who cry for greater selection, at least in the form of extensive collections. Academic libraries, especially, are committed to building and retaining large collections as long as space can accommodate the growth. However, the faculty and students consistently rank their expectations of library collections at an unattainable level for most, if not all, academic libraries.

Perhaps new in this assumption is a greater demand for services. Help is no longer a luxury but a requirement. Self-service models sometimes provide options for service delivery, but they rarely replace or eliminate services. Within information commons, services from a variety of like-minded partners such as information technology may unite to create a blended, or merged, help desk to address multiple user needs. Add in writing assistance, peer tutoring, data, and GIS (Geographic Information System) consultation, and an irresistible combination emerges.

MAPPING THE FUTURE OF ACADEMIC
LIBRARIES: AN EXERCISE

The aforementioned assumptions help determine the directions that academic libraries may take. Recognizing that I may have proposed overly positive directions for the future, I devised a continuum of possible broad characterizations of a future information-rich society and the academic library's role in it. This map is an opportunity to wear various hats and probe different perspectives. The goal is not to fully capture any perspective but to provide discussion about where academic libraries are headed. What is the consequence of adopting a specific strategy? If the strategy is successful, where does the trajectory lead in ten, twenty, or fifty years?

The middle ground is always the most comfortable and closest to our immediate reality. I challenge readers to contemplate the extremes of the scenarios. The map is an exercise. Create your own continuum of the academic library of the future.

The Future of Academic Libraries: A Continuum of Scenarios

Perspective of Future Growth of Electronic Resources

Utopian view (students and faculty)

- Cultural expressions from around the world are captured and disseminated in real time everywhere. Languages, music, and voices are heard in a diversity never known previously.
- The growth of electronic resources will create an information-rich society where the information needs of all citizens will be directly, immediately, and easily satisfied in multiple languages and multiple formats including exact replicas, facsimiles of the original document in print, and still or moving images complete with sound.
- Remote access equals portability equals freedom for the researcher.
- Anything, anywhere, anytime.
- Technology is available to everyone.
- Free, unrestricted access to everything.

Optimistic view (reference librarian)

- The growth of electronic resources and intuitive search tools shifts work. Less emphasis on mechanics permits more emphasis on information literacy.
- Convergence of technology, content, and service (i.e., information commons) ideally positions the library as a learning community on campus. Students "get it" without advertising.
- All additional resources and their delivery platforms are welcome.

Optimistic view (collections librarian)

- Technology opens doors to endless formats. The availability of resources, especially through consortial purchasing, means the playing field is leveled among universities and geographic regions.
- Small universities blossom in this milieu as having the best of both
  worlds—deep resources and a personal community.
- More resources will spark fierce competition among vendors—
  costs continue to drop as consortia- and government-supported
  initiatives (e.g., JSTOR, open archives) mean core resources are
  available everywhere in Canada.
- Collection development remains an intensive activity as the range
  of products available via the web is beyond imagination, including e-books and e-journals, audiovisual, data libraries, object libraries, and so on.

Moderate view (librarian)

- Growth of electronic resources means fewer face-to-face interactions with students and faculty. Less intermediation is okay, and
  those who seek help genuinely need help.
- Skills and workplaces shift as virtual reference and information
  commons are introduced. Emphasis shifts from mechanics as interfaces improve and technology-savvy students and faculty navigate with ease.
- Less collection development, library classes dwindle, and more
  instruction "on the fly" or on the web.

Moderate view (students and faculty)

- There is more information, a better range and quality of information from which to select, but it's not a perfect world.
- Research must be augmented with print materials, but this is okay
  because it's worth it when doing comprehensive research. But it's
  okay to cut corners if the scope of research permits.

Pessimistic view (collections librarian)

- Information conglomerates worm their way into budgets so com-
  pletely that libraries subscribe to one provider, who turns on one
  information tap for all users.
- Discipline-specific literature is merged into one big database and
  ironically hailed as the triumph of interdisciplinarity.

Pessimistic view (reference librarian)

- The growth of electronic resources either eliminates the role for reference librarians or drastically erodes the professional skills associated with librarianship.
- Librarians fear their skills will be replaced by IT staff or reduced to technological skills only, operating large-scale information laboratories located in libraries.
- Librarians mourn the loss of content as the triumph of technology.

Dystopian view (students and faculty)

- The globalization of information means that electronic resources flood the world, creating a monoculture—a blended point of view that is American, industry based or corporate driven, larger than life, and wholly unmanageable.
- Information is an "all or nothing" proposition. To be information rich means access to this monoculture in its entirety. To be information poor means no access whatsoever. The information "utility" is either on or off.
- All diversity is lost. Creativity is in crisis. It's a "cut and paste" world where information is recycled and is reproduced with diminishing luster.
- The total collapse of the concept of the democratization of information and an informed citizenry.

EXPECTATIONS OF STUDENTS AND FACULTY

There is a substantial mismatch between electronic resources and the expectations of library users. This revelation sometimes occurs in consultation with a reference librarian. "Good" access depends on the availability and speed of delivery of electronic resources, but it does nothing to improve learning. Library users may be numbed or initially delighted with large retrieval sets, but on closer examination another reality sometimes appears. I recently helped a student who found hundreds of matches when searching JSTOR. The student was infuriated to discover that the number of articles retrieved was dramatically fewer than the initial search indicated. Though this is simple misunderstanding, it is symptomatic of how little students understand about the sources they search.

Access cannot be equated with the transfer of information. Printing or e-mailing journal articles is no substitute for reading and learning. Technology has simplified the tasks associated with collecting information, but students still have to read, analyze, and reflect on their findings and the process that yielded them.

Although confident in their keyboarding skills, many students are either unsure of which databases to search or search databases without understanding the content of the search tool. While librarians attempt to provide insight into the content of individual databases or suggest tools in broad disciplinary clusters, students may gravitate to familiar habits such as searching a database that was previously searched successfully or following the recommendations of friends, who may or may not have useful advice to offer. Some stick to full-text sites even if there is little or no disciplinary relationship to their research topic. Others may start at the top and work their way down a list of possible research tools. Faced with hundreds of search tool options, where would you logically begin? Imagine a library website with the option "I'm Feeling Lucky" when faced with a menu of indexes and databases.

It continues to be my experience that students desperately need help to become oriented in this electronic environment. Unlike some of their predecessors of ten or twenty years ago, the vast majority of students have no fear of technology. For students, their high comfort level with computers may be mistakenly translated into a confidence with search engines and research databases. The prevalence of a search box is reassuring, though it is no guarantee that the results received will be understood in the context of the tool itself or within the entire array of research tools appropriate to the discipline. In an introductory sociology class that I teach annually, students routinely assess their ability to conduct library research as extremely low.

THE IMMEDIATE FUTURE OF REFERENCE SERVICES AND LIBRARIANS

Any discussion of the growth of electronic resources immediately poses threats to some reference librarians. The acquisition of new products is outpacing reference librarians' ability to learn them. Stumbling blocks, such as compatibility, frustrate the adoption of multiple products on multiple platforms for library users and library staff. Too often librarians are troubleshooting the printer instead of concentrating on the content of electronic resources. These minor frustrations impede the development of services and roles for reference librarians. However, once past these irritations, planning enhanced reference services is possible.

Most immediate for reference librarians are virtual reference and information commons as methods of inserting or integrating reference librarians into a vital role, as well as relevant space associated with the growth and urgency of electronic resources. Each of these developments represents a medium in which reference librarians may take up residence, but each is insignificant unless services are adapted for the medium or created to reflect the new environment. Exactly how reference librarians respond to information commons and virtual reference will be harbingers of how creative reference services might be shaped in the next five to ten years. Though I am always hopelessly optimistic about reference librarianship, some of my colleagues are much less optimistic. Instead of envisioning an enhanced role for reference librarians, they foresee little opportunity for reference librarians in these scenarios because paraprofessionals or information technology staff may subsume the work.

Information commons and virtual reference are environments that may be short lived and quickly outmoded because of changing technology or demands from faculty and students. Still, other media will appear and the cycle will repeat. Certainly this turnover is not new, though the pace may quicken. Whenever I want to discuss the deeper meaning of the information commons, some of my colleagues groan and insist that reference librarians will do what they have always done, just in a different space. While parts of this argument are compelling, I am convinced that the medium changes the expectations of library users and the work of reference librarians.

Acting as consultants or guides for students who require a framework to conduct research, reference librarians play a vital role in shaping the library experience of students and faculty, even those who never visit the physical library. Information literacy—the ability to map information needs, identify an information-seeking process, perform it, and evaluate the results—is much harder than it sounds. The intellectual and theoretical role for librarians is lost only if librarians abandon it. Though the tangible aspects of academic libraries (e.g., environment and reference tools) may continue to change radically, the role for librarians is unlikely to diminish as long as services are adapted to the changing environment. Relevant services in a dynamic learning environment promise to keep revamped reference areas vibrant and busy.

For librarians, two scenarios loom on the horizon. The optimistic or all-encompassing future demands that librarians be enthusiastic and flexible enough to create a dynamic learning environment. These librarians will be adept at creating an intellectual landscape densely populated with electronic information sources and rich with a variety of services tailored to shifting needs. The pessimistic future is a passive one where our services and spaces are underused and irrelevant to students and faculty. This future is likely to evolve unless librarians respond creatively to the impact of electronic resources in academic libraries. Administrators who fail to make the transition will see their institutions fall far behind their counterparts. Librarians who cannot or will not make the transition will witness the loss of their workplace as they know it and lose their roles in it.

NOTES

1. Carol Tenopir, *Use and Users of Electronic Library Resources: An Overview and Analysis of Recent Research Studies* (Washington, D.C.: Council on Library and Information Resources, 2003), at www.clir.org/pubs/abstract/pub120abst.html (accessed 30 September 2003).

2. Ideas in this section were put together with general references to the following sources: Gregg Sapp and Ron Gilmour, "A Brief History of the Future of Academic Libraries: Predictions and Speculations from the Literature of the Profession, 1975 to 2000—part two, 1990–2002," *portal: Libraries and the Academy* 3 (2003): 13–34; William Birdsall, *The Myth of the Electronic Library: Librarianship and Social Change in America* (Westport, Conn.: Greenwwod, 1994); Lee W. Hisle, "Top Issues Facing Academic Libraries: A Report of the Focus of the Future Task Force," *College and Research Libraries News* 63, no. 10 (2002): 714–15, 730.

Part 4

FROM LIBRARIAN TO CYBRARIAN: CAN CERTIFICATION REDEFINE US?

Do we fight to ensure the longevity of the MLIS or to ensure that, regardless of who libraries hire, employees are cognizant of the library's value systems and perform in a capacity that meets our standards of service?

—Ernie Ingles and Allison Sivak

Let us move our concerns and our literature away from the tired themes of self-justification, certification, image, stereotype, and professionalism and look to the future. Our key strength as librarians is responsiveness, with a touch of the oracle.

—Alison Nussbaumer

When everyone who works in a library of any type has access to additional training and the option of pursuing advanced certification, the level of service to library patrons will be greatly enhanced.

—Barbara K. Stripling

10

Post-Master's Certification: A Case for Responsive Education

Ernie Ingles and Allison Sivak

The education of librarians presents both interest and concern for professionals within the field. A long-standing question debated by practitioners has been the relevancy of MLIS curricula content to professional practice: Do new master of library and information science graduates gain necessary practical knowledge during the two-year program, or is the program primarily a foundation in the philosophy that underlies library service? A more recent question that has surfaced in the past several years is whether libraries are maintaining the MLIS hiring requirement. While a survey conducted in 2000 by the Association of Research Libraries revealed that non-MLIS candidates are generally not hired into librarian positions,[1] there is evidence of American academic libraries increasingly hiring candidates who do not possess the MLIS but have expertise in a particular subject area.

As our society moves into the knowledge economy, a new urgency arises within these debates. It is anticipated that librarians, as facilitators of information and knowledge, will have greatly expanded opportunities within the knowledge economy; however, these opportunities bring their own challenges. Librarians must be able to not only negotiate new technologies on an ongoing basis but also deal with these technologies' effects on our roles in information acquisition, organization, and access. Librarians in traditional libraries must therefore maintain the core values and ethics of librarianship as well as meet a changing work environment with competencies and tools that allow them to forge paths into the wilderness of information.

Without venturing further into potential repercussions of the societal transition we are currently moving through, we can recognize that library workplaces are sites of rapid change in which continuing education and professional development are integral to librarians' roles and responsibilities. Over the past decade, librarians have been negotiating the constant, rapid growth in the amount of information resources, information technologies, and data now available. As well, demand from library users has grown substantially, and users accustomed to the Internet hold higher expectations for immediate access, available twenty-four hours a day.

Concurrent with these changes is the situation of Canadian libraries with respect to fixed or shrinking budgets, experienced at different levels by all types of libraries. In Canada, school libraries have been arguably the hardest hit; however, no library has been exempt from the repercussions of funding restrictions over the past generation. In short, libraries need to meet the challenge of increased user demands with reduced resources. As the financial, information, and human resources available to the library sector continue to shift, it is incumbent upon the sector to examine its own needs for librarian competencies and determine what kind of education and training professionals require—and to take responsibility for providing this training.

Continuing education can be categorized in two streams: formal learning (structured workshops or courses) and informal learning (on-the-job training, work experience, relationships with others, or reading).[2] A recent study by Auster and Chan examined continuing education of reference librarians in Ontario urban centers, and their findings suggest that librarians access informal learning much more frequently than formal learning.[3] While informal learning is an important aspect of ongoing education, we suggest that training should be tied to long-term outcomes in order to realize greater professional goals; formal education is much more conducive to this objective. Even with formal training, questions of assessment and long-term outcomes remain. How do occasional courses or workshops integrate into the competencies and skill sets required in managerial positions, for example? Is professional development in these instances pursued primarily on the basis of immediate need? In this case, how do libraries manage staff educational needs beyond the needs of the immediate present and take a longer-term view?

The rate of change in libraries is so rapid that we suggest continuing education may be too focused on the present tense. Immediate requirements and benefits are thus addressed while overlooking long-term development or future needs (e.g., leadership and management training for existing staff). While we do not suggest that all libraries or educators are ignoring the future needs of either individuals or institutions, providing library service in the face of shrinking or static resources is itself a consuming task, one that demands a greater focus on immediate needs rather than future planning. However, libraries and librarians ignore this future planning to their peril.

We suggest as a solution the need for coordinated continuing education programs that could address this longer-term view. These programs should involve the national and provincial Canadian library associations because they are situated to have a view of the library sector as a whole; this understanding of trends in the industry would allow for greater input on the part of practitioners and result in a greater responsiveness to the sector's needs.

This chapter examines some of the ways the library sector in Canada has changed significantly and the resulting implications for training and education. We write as members of a research team currently conducting a study on various facets of Canadian library human resources, and we make a case for long-term, formalized education through certification. Highlighting this argument will be preliminary findings from the 8Rs Canadian Library Human Resource Study, a comprehensive examination of the current situation of library institutions and their personnel as information and information professionals move into the twenty-first century.

8Rs CANADIAN LIBRARY HUMAN RESOURCE STUDY: PRELIMINARY FINDINGS

A great number of library human resource questions have recently been posed due to changes perceived throughout the sector. Most notably, many professionals have assumed a shortage of librarians due to mass retirements anticipated over the next several years. Researcher Stanley Wilder has published extensively on North American librarian demographics within academic libraries, predicting large numbers of retirements in the next several years and noting that a primary challenge lies in recruitment of new professionals to the field.[4] Wilder further states that Canadian librarians are, on the whole, older than their American counterparts.[5] Based on this research, general assumptions were being made that an impending crisis in Canadian library staffing was looming, with an estimated 48 percent of the workforce set to retire by the year 2010.[6] In response to this concern, short-term studies and discussion of succession management surfaced within the Canadian community.

Taking a step back, we felt it was essential to determine whether a potential shortage does indeed exist within the Canadian context before embarking on a course of action. A research team from the University of Alberta Library began to investigate current trends connected with issues of recruitment, retention, and retirement. Preliminary research and literature reviews demonstrated that in order to answer the broader questions, a study on a large scale was necessary to examine the intersection of a number of human resource issues. This study, drafted under the title 8Rs Canadian Library Human Resource Study/ Étude sur les ressources humaines dans les bibliothèques canadiennes, expanded its scope to include major staffing issues within Canadian libraries: recruitment, retention, repatriation, remuneration, retirement, reaccreditation, rejuvenation, and restructuring. This multifaceted study includes in its methods the surveying of library administrators, librarians, library associates and paraprofessional staff, library educators, MLIS students, and non-MLIS university students. With the support of a number of partners, including at the time of this writing the Canadian Association of Research Libraries, the Council of Administrators of Large Urban Public Libraries, the Canadian Library Association, Patrimoine canadien/Heritage Canada, l'Association pour l'avancement des sciences et des techniques de la documentation, the National Library of Canada, and several provincial associations, the study is creating a comprehensive view of the current issues and trends in library human resources across the country.

The 8Rs study is examining how ongoing trends or factors within the library sector have had an impact on library organizational structures and individual staff. In addition, it will capture how libraries intend to face the future with greater service demands and limited resources. Data collection will include different perspectives from staff within traditional and nontraditional libraries, including analyses of divergent viewpoints. The research will ultimately provide a comprehensive view of human resources within the library sector, creating a better understanding of the needs of both individual library personnel and library institutions across Canada.

The phase of the study dealing with perceptions of library administrators has revealed a body of thought around the future of librarians and staffing library institutions. Notably, some survey respondents defined succession management not only in terms of replacing senior librarians as they retire but also with respect to the overall long-term health and development of libraries and librarians. In other words, administrators are looking beyond the demands of the present tense, attempting to build a vision for future requirements. While certainly not of a size that allows final conclusions to be drawn, this does underscore the need for a longer-term view of the needs of the library profession and professionals—including ongoing professional development and education—and how these needs should be addressed.

EDUCATION: FROM THE GROUND UP

The most standardized and formalized avenue for library education—the MLIS degree—takes place at the beginning of a librarian's career. The two-year degree (found more commonly in Canada than in the United States) provides a foundation in library and information studies while socializing students into the professional values that librarianship possesses. However, few educators would dispute the fact that librarians require industry-specific training and education beyond this point. Further education, it is understood, will build on the foundation of professional values over the course of librarians' careers.

While the MLIS requirement has been a minimum standard for staff in librarian positions, preliminary results from the 8Rs study suggest that library administrations are in fact looking for specific skill sets and competencies rather than strictly the degree. Some respondents stated they consider candidates who do not possess an MLIS but have other necessary competencies. This appears to be a trend across the continent. A number of American academic libraries, for example, have hired non-MLIS candidates who possess PhDs for positions requiring subject specialization.[7] Some Canadian public libraries have made a practice of hiring senior management who possess a master's degree in public management (also known as a master's in public administration) or relevant experience in government or other nonprofit sectors. In other words, the MLIS degree is no longer seen as the fundamental, final requirement to competently perform library work.

Within the profession, practitioners frequently debate the discrepancies between the theory of graduate library and information studies programs and the practice of library workplaces. Some argue that the MLIS provides a broad-based education in the core values and major issues within the library world and that most specific skill sets can only be gained through practicums, work experience, and internships.[8] In the 8Rs study, a sample of library administrators stated that librarians often lack concrete management skills. While most Canadian schools of library and/or information studies provide courses in this area, these interviewees suggested that theory means little if students have not had to deal with real workplace situations. One could further argue that by trying to cater to all needs, MLIS programs would adequately serve none of them and so should focus strictly on philosophical foundations of librarianship. Regardless of these various perspectives, library administrators, like many educators across the country, note that the master's degree is only the first stage of library education; continuing education is cited as fundamental for librarians.

Returning to the questions raised by Auster and Chan's study, librarians and administrators must consider where their investment in ongoing education should be targeted. Are annual conferences adequate, or is a more intensive program necessary to meet their needs? Further, is the function of professional development to address present institutional needs or to provide a strategy for building longer-term competencies that can serve both the library and the librarian into the future?

POST-MASTER'S CERTIFICATION

An educational approach that could serve both purposes is post-master's certification, a formalized education process in which the librarian gains specific training strongly linked to professional practice. This approach would allow professionals to access education with a strong degree of relevancy to the day-to-day workings of their jobs. As a form of further specialization, certification could offer a standardized set of educational competencies and could incorporate the teaching of specific skills, building on both the foundations laid by the values taught in MLIS programs and some of the practicalities informally learned in the workplace.

Post-master's certification is a desirable approach for continuing education in the library sector. We are a profession experiencing a sea of change as we move into the knowledge economy. New technologies, financial constraints, and greatly increased user demands all present major challenges for the library sector and have in part led to the need for specialized knowledge in such areas as information technology and management. We can be assured that the only constant of our workplaces will be that of continued, rapid change. Librarians will require development that is current, responsive to their environment, and specific enough to be applicable to real-world situations.

One of the interesting preliminary findings from the 8Rs study is that administrators identify the need for ongoing training and skill development for all professional librarians in the workplace, including entry-level staff, middle management, and upper management. In fact, while new librarians were identified as needing the most training, 80 percent of respondents noted that senior librarians also need at least some ongoing training. In other words, ongoing training needs are not restricted to a particular position held within library systems. This suggests a need for a holistic examination of the library workplace and an assessment of training needs across the board.

Both informal and formal post-MLIS training as it exists in Canadian librarianship tends to be self-contained units of education; professionals attend conference sessions or courses that provide specific focus on a single skill or aspect of technology. We argue that this view of education targets immediate goals; while this approach is important in its ability to address current needs within libraries, a longer-term cohesive education program would fill needs for longer-term planning, while still retaining a flexibility that is harder to achieve within MLIS programs.

One of the primary benefits of certification would be its emphasis on specific and standardized skill sets that correspond with particular streams of librarianship. Certification in broad areas could provide both core modules (to deal with basic competencies and long-term issues) and electives (to provide structured education on timely topics). A certification program could therefore address both identified general position competencies for the so-called soft skills of communication and management, as well as hard skills in specific applications.

With such a strong connection to the educational needs of librarians, it is not surprising that library associations have taken the lead to investigate this method of education. The American Library Association, as the largest North American association, has initiated the formation of a body to provide some specialized certification of librarians. The Canadian Library Association is, at the time of this writing, conducting

its own research into the potential of certification, seriously considering an active role within continuing education beyond the annual
Canadian conference. Certainly, much work remains before a Canadian certification program could be effectively brought into existence.
However, we believe that a formalized education structure with an eye
to the overall needs of the profession will be the primary key to the
long-term health of libraries and library professionals.

It is important to note that ongoing budget freezing or cutbacks experienced by a great number of libraries in all sectors (special, public,
academic, and school) often mean that small libraries cannot compen-
sate their staff to the degree that is standard for Canadian librarians.
Thus, staff with no previous library experience often perform in these
capacities. Recognizing this reality, associations such as the Ontario Library Association North and the Southern Ontario Library Association
have presented flexible educational opportunities for staff who are
working in the field but do not have a formal background in library education. The EXCEL program in managing a small public library provides a set of courses through which staff without the MLIS can achieve
a provincially recognized certification. The EXCEL program also provides flexible delivery, allowing students to complete the program over
a period of five years. The Southern Alberta Institute of Technology, in
conjunction with the Calgary chapter of the Association of Records
Managers and Administrators (ARMA), now offers a records and information management certificate of achievement, an industry-specific set
of courses appropriate either as continuing education for records managers or for those looking to move into the field.

A similar program built around the professional needs of MLIS graduates could provide a bridge between the foundation in library values
(provided by schools of library and information studies) and the competencies cited by administrators as necessary to the field. While the potential for different streams of certification could certainly be limitless,
we suggest that only major areas, identified through industry needs, be
covered through post-master's certification. An obvious example would
be that of management certification, a currently identified area of need.

A MODEL FOR POST-MASTER'S CERTIFICATION

Who should be responsible for initiating and developing a certification
program? The most obvious choice is the professional associations, na-

tional and provincial, working in tandem. Associations have a tradition of offering occasional professional development, and the larger organizations, such as the Ontario Library Association, often have a regularly scheduled education program in place. Working together, provincial and national associations could consolidate their resources toward a greater, more cohesive service model for Canadian library professionals, avoiding program replication and increasing its overall relevance for library professionals. Further, situating certification with these bodies allows greater input from practitioners, as opposed to the academic MLIS model. Thus the program would be directly accountable to stakeholders within the library profession.

The simplest and most flexible model for a post-master's program would be certification based on a certain number of coursework hours completed (coursework in this instance is defined as formal training of any length) within a set number of years. Credit based on hours of completion or study would allow for diverse content and flexibility. A range of presentations would be suitable, from stand-alone workshops to institute settings to weekly classes over a period of time.

Should all courses originate within professional associations? Not necessarily, particularly in the early stages of building the certification system. Continuing education programs offered through ALA-accredited library school programs (such as the University of Toronto and the University of British Columbia) should be counted toward the completion of an individual's hours. However, nonassociation education should be recognized through the umbrella of the association-led certification program, which would call for an approval system.

We suggest that associations, in consultation with library professionals, designate high-priority areas (e.g., management) that will be required by librarians on an ongoing basis. However, other modules of professional education can be built over time. This model would also allow a choice of electives that would be more attentive to the realities of professionals in small institutions who often perform in multiple capacities.

This structure is similar to that of continuing professional development (CPD) offered through the Australian Library and Information Association (ALIA).[9] Members of ALIA identify their training and development needs, pursue them (both independently and through their workplaces), and accumulate their hours of education to achieve CPD compliance. The association concurrently maintains resources for members, such as a career development kit that outlines the steps involved in pursuing CPD. ALIA, acknowledging the demands of the workplace, has instituted a triennial assessment, allowing an adequate time cycle to achieve CPD goals. Further, areas for CPD are sufficiently varied (including strategic development, information systems and technologies, and management of resources and personnel), with a minimum of four categories required by each participant (two from the generic skills and two from the LIS-specific skills). Hours spent in pursuing a particular CPD subject are weighted to reflect the value placed by the association on that area.

This model provides a useful basis on which a certification program could be built in Canada. A significant difference, however, is that the ALIA CPD program is pursued on a voluntary basis, and we are advocating that certification be required for specific positions within Canadian libraries (such as management). How would this be monitored? Certainly, certification programs could be tied to performance expectations and integrated with defined competencies already in place at individual institutions for specific positions. When recruiting, certification will obviously be weighed against experience: A candidate with ten years' management experience may be selected over a candidate with certification but less experience, for example. However, the inclusion of certification as a hiring qualification will fulfill several purposes. It will encourage participation in formalized training and development. It will also allow newer professionals to gain recognized experience they may not have access to within their workplaces; this would facilitate the fast-tracking of librarians who have strong potential but little opportunity for management. As well, certification can provide institutions with a clear understanding of what the candidates' education means in practical terms.

The ALIA CPD program also allows for informal activities, such as professional reading, as a form of professional development. It is indeed important for librarians to update their knowledge of current trends and research in the field. However, we would not weight hours of informal learning activities on their own. Research and study or supplementary reading could be counted if required reading for coursework or preparatory reading for a project to be completed for the course. However, the goal in certification is to maintain a formal structure of professional development to the greatest extent possible, and so we suggest that informal learning not associated with the certification process be excluded from the final assessment of hours completed.

Education accessibility and assessment are further questions to ponder. Canada's vast geographic span, combined with a significantly smaller librarian population than that of the United States, presumes that distance education would play a major role in delivery. New technologies that provide variations on Internet-based delivery (including weblogs for class "discussion," listservs, and so on) would have the farthest reach to ensure that librarians in rural or remote communities could participate in the program.

LIBRARY SOCIALIZATION

Of course, seeing the rising trend in academic libraries of hiring the functional specialist who may not possess an MLIS, we could envision a slightly different approach to education for librarianship. If the knowledge economy offers more attractive opportunities to MLIS degree holders beyond the traditional library sector, how will we fill positions in our libraries? We may need to make a practice of hiring more functional specialists in librarian positions to staff our institutions.

If library administrators start to hire functional specialists, how will they learn about libraries and how they function? We propose an alternative scenario to that of post-MLIS certification: post-hiring schooling in professional values of librarianship. Functional specialists could be hired where appropriate, then learn about the values of the sector and institution that employs them through short-term professional development. Schooling in professional values could easily be integrated into on-the-job training structures and could ensure that new staff are familiar with both institution-specific and profession-specific information, ethics, and values.

Examples of institution-specific information would include the organizational mission statement, the strategic plan, the budget, codes of conduct and/or service statements, and client demographics. Profession-specific information would include the American Library Association's Library Bill of Rights, the Canadian Library Association's Position Statement on Intellectual Freedom, the publishing industry, and literacy in Canadian libraries. The training's integration of these two bodies of knowledge into daily on-the-job learning would be an exciting exercise, bringing theory directly into practice and increasing its relevancy for the staff.

We argue that the amount of education necessary for socialization into librarianship (or more specifically, socialization into the values and practices of the individual library institution) would not be as intensive or extensive as either a two-year master's program or a certification program. Since libraries as institutions also differ, depending on their context and client group, we suggest that responsibility for schooling in professional values lies with the institution, with supplementary resources and documentation from the professional associations. Potential areas in which the library would benefit from functional specialists could include senior management, information systems, funding development, and marketing. Such a system would prioritize position competencies, ensuring that the person with the most relevant skill set would be the person to do the job.

This scenario assumes that the hiring of functional specialists is a practice that will eventually replace the fundamental MLIS hiring requirement—a controversial proposal, to be sure. How unrealistic is it? To what extent are libraries moving toward increased hiring of functional specialists? This is a question as yet unanswered within the Canadian context; however, Wilder notes that the functional specialist is the second largest job category among new hires for North American research libraries.[10] The question remains: Is this a trend to be circumvented in order to preserve ideas of the profession of librarianship, or is this a trend to be met on our own terms? Do we fight to ensure the longevity of the MLIS or to ensure that, regardless of who libraries hire, employees are cognizant of the library's value system and perform in a capacity that meets our standards of service?

EDUCATION FOR INNOVATION

Certification programs could act as a centralized means for providing relevant and specialized skill sets that are currently not being found through either the general MLIS degree or through occasional training. Certification has the potential to address educational needs in both major areas of library education that require greater attention, as well as hone specialized skill sets and competencies necessary to fulfill the complex needs of today's library workplace. Should this option replace the philosophical foundation in librarianship that the MLIS provides? We might argue that the increased user demands within a highly complex world of information will not solely be met through philosophical foundations. Regardless, forces of great change continue to have an impact on the library world. We believe the attempt to standardize continuing education on a large scale will be fundamental to ensuring that librarians—or those working within information organization and retrieval—are able to navigate ongoing change effectively, allowing libraries to continue to forge paths of innovative practices.

NOTES

1. Julia C. Blixrud, *SPEC Kit 257: The M.L.S. Hiring Requirement* (Washington, D.C.: Association of Research Libraries, 2000), at www.arl.org/spec/257 sum.html (accessed 1 October 2003).

2. Ethel Auster and Donna Chan, "Continuing Professional Development in Ontario Public Libraries," *Feliciter* 48, no. 5 (2002): 230–32.

3. Auster and Chan, "Continuing Professional Development," 230–32.

4. Stanley J. Wilder, *Demographic Change in Academic Librarianship* (Washington, D.C.: Association of Research Libraries, 2003), 7.

5. Wilder, *Demographic Change*, 8.

6. Derek Weiler, "Libraries Face 'Skills Gap': 48% of Librarians Could Retire by 2005," *Quill & Quire* 66, no.1 (January 2000): 10–11.

7. Norman Oder, "New Movement for Ph.D.'s to Work in Academic Libraries," *Library Journal* 128, no. 11 (2003): 16–18.

8. Robert P. Holley, "The Ivory Tower as Preparation for the Trenches: The Relationship between Library Education and Library Practice," *College and Research Libraries News* 64, no. 3 (2003): 172–75.

9. Australian Library and Information Association, "Continuing Professional Development," at www.alia.org.au/education/cpd (accessed 11 February 2004).

10. Wilder, *Demographic Change*, 21.

11

Door #1: Certification. Door #2: Not! Door #3: Real Solutions

Alison Nussbaumer

This is not a new statement or issue, certification has been discussed, reviewed, analyzed, pondered and mulled since the days of
Melvil Dewey . . . as far back as 1923 the Williamson report suggested that graduate education be followed by certification. The
route that was chosen was accreditation of the educating organization instead of certification.[1]

CERTIFICATION—A FALSE VISION

It was a pleasure to be asked to participate in a project that ponders
the future of our profession. As I began to peruse the library literature, I noted with interest that publications of this sort occur on the
average of once a decade, leading me to believe that we anticipate,
expect, and perhaps even long for real change, of the paradigm-
shifting sort, to occur. Have we changed? I regret to say, not that
much. In fact many of the themes espoused in works about the "future of the profession" are at best cyclical and at worst a continuous
review of the same unresolved issues. Certification, professionalism,
image, status, value—these themes dominate our literature. We have
invested a lot of energy in reporting our perceived shortcomings and
little in either changing them, putting them to rest, getting over them,
or moving on.

The themes just identified boil down to one central idea, that librarians as a profession undervalue themselves. Librarians focus on a negative image they believe is held by the world, one that labels them as "bun-heads." They see themselves as a group locked in a woman's profession, suffering from low status and low salaries. This external picture will not change until our internal one does. Therefore, instead of writing endless apologetics for our existence, we need to blow our own horns and tell everyone how great we really are. Within this context, I do not see how the process of certification will contribute to the profession.

This chapter reviews the key outcomes of certification, including better salaries; improved value, status, and image; and better-quality practitioners. I will show that certification is not the means to achieve these goals and will suggest alternative strategies. Finally, the chapter challenges the reader to "get over it" and move on.

CERTIFICATION/ACCREDITATION: WHEREIN LIES THE DIFFERENCE?

Everyone has his or her own definition of certification. I will use the following definition offered in the *American Archivist*:

> Certification is a process by which a nongovernmental agency, such as a professional association, confers a title on an individual to indicate that he or she has met certain minimum predefined criteria . . . [using] one or more of the following screening devices: 1) successful completion of an approved course of study, 2) passing grade on one or more exams and 3) completion of a specified amount of work.[2]

There is nothing inherently wrong with this definition. Where it gets sticky is in the unfolding of the certification process and the claims that hinge on the results. There is no agreement as to what is to be tested, when, and by whom. Where certification programs exist they are voluntary. The process is not standardized, is not overseen by any central authority, and does not follow specific timelines.

For all of our complaints about the accreditation process, it is at least standardized in that is has a defined set of goals and objectives, set timelines, and a central organization overseeing the process, which spans state, provincial, national, and even international boundaries. The certification process can boast none of these characteristics.

What is the difference between certification and accreditation? At its most basic level the difference is one of orientation—the process of certification focuses on the individual, while the process of accreditation focuses on the institutional program. Accreditation addresses the needs of the librarian community by "certifying" the institution, providing a process of accountability, a mechanism for change, and standards by which the institution is measured. Certification, on the other hand, evaluates a set of individual competencies. I would argue, however, that librarianship is far more complex than the sum of individual competencies. Librarianship is the vision, thinking, blending, and innovating that weaves competencies together and enables the whole to surpass the sum of its parts.

WHAT ARE THE DESIRED OUTCOMES?

Proponents of certification claim that the following benefits will flow from the process: better salaries, enhanced value and status, improved image, and better-quality practitioners. While the goal of certification is to improve the situation for the individual professional, it seems to me the problems it attempts to address focus on the community of librarians. Salary scales, stereotypes, and qualifications are superimposed on the whole, on the community. Although individuals may suffer the effects of these problems, they exist because of the group, and they will only change as the group directs and even forces change.

Better Salaries

Let us consider some of the perceived benefits of certification, beginning with increased salary. Those who support certification believe that librarians' salaries will improve if librarians are certified. A 1983 study of certification for personnel administrators (one of very few studies assessing the results of certification) found little correlation between certification and salary scales.[3]

In fact, salaries are influenced by the macro- and microenvironments, which are outside the control of certification. At the macro level, economics, demographics, and the shift from an industrial-based society to a knowledge-based one are key factors that influence the salaries of any profession. Librarians are well positioned for salary increases because demand is currently greater than supply, a large cohort of librarians is retiring, and our society is increasingly relying on information and the skills of those who can manage it. These factors are inextricably intertwined and form the macroenvironment in which librarians work and live.

Salary is also a function of the microenvironment. What kind of organization is the librarian working in? Different salary scales exist for corporate, special, school, public, and academic libraries. Indeed, with the emergence of market differentials for some positions—typically IT and systems specialists—we may be witnessing the establishment of a hierarchy. For example, at this time the University of Northern British Columbia is paying a market differential to its electronic services librarian. At the micro level, salary is also determined by an individual's education, experience, degree of responsibility, and negotiation skills. It may also be bound to predetermined remuneration scales that reflect the relative value of positions within the organization.

It would seem, therefore, that salary is determined by macro- and microenvironmental factors that are not influenced by the process of certification.

Value

One of the perceived benefits of being certified is that it will enhance the value and status of librarians. What does it take to *enhance* one's value or status? Recognition from one's peers. What does it take to *change* one's value or status? Recognition from nonpeers and our clients, hereafter referred to as external communities.

As a profession we recognize our peers, present awards, and celebrate successes; we acknowledge each other and affirm, "We are good." The result is that from time to time our value or status has been enhanced. This is the most that the process of certification can ever expect to achieve—simply another way of recognizing ourselves.

But has our value changed? Are we satisfied with the value and status we have been accorded by the external community? It is all very well that *we* know the value we bring to the lives of our patrons/consumers/students/end users/clients, but do *they* know? Do others know? Do key decision makers in the organization know? Municipal councilors? Provincial and federal bureaucrats? Private investors? They do not.[4]

The proponents of certification believe that if librarians attain the internally awarded designation of "being certified" it will cause the external community to change the current level of value/status they accord to the profession. However, being certified will not achieve this change because the impetus for certification lies solely within enclaves of the profession and has not been demanded by the external community. As John N. Berry III states:

> I'm not sure certification will deliver the improved status or image its proponents claim it will. I was shocked to realize that I know absolutely nothing about the level or currency of the certification of my accountant, lawyer, doctor, cardiac specialist, plumber, auto mechanic or any other professional whose services I use. My perception of them is unaltered by their certification or lack of it and that includes my librarian. If my librarian were certified, I probably would never know.[5]

The key word in the previous quote is *perception*. To change how the external community values librarians, we must change their perceptions. So rather than seek a credential that will have little, if any, influence on their perceptions, we need to concentrate our energy on identifying factors and strategies that will change these perceptions. Our strategies must be creative, consistent, client focused, constant, and clear.

Ultimately what will change the perceptions of the external community is knowing what they expect and consistently exceeding their expectations, be it telling a story, assisting in research for a thesis, or saving a corporation millions of dollars. We need to continuously demonstrate, communicate, and market our value to those we serve. It is through developing and implementing strategies to continuously meet and exceed the expectations of those requiring our services that we will change how we are valued, not through certification.

Status

As evidenced in our literature, status is a thorny issue for many librarians. The literature abounds with declarations that librarians are professional, confusion over what is meant by professional, and lamentations that we are not professional. Does our need to call ourselves professional librarians reflect an uncertainty over whether we have attained professional status? You never hear lawyers, doctors, or accountants add the adjective *professional* before their occupational designation. The issue increases in complexity when you consider that anyone can choose to work in a professional manner, irrespective of their educational background, qualifications, or occupation.

This bears consideration. Are librarians professional because of their educational qualifications or because of the way they perform any given task in the workplace? The meaning of the term is no longer as clear as it was in the early Victorian days when *professional* was identified with and applied to individuals imbued with a defined set of characteristics. Those who support certification see it as means to reestablish this defined set of characteristics and control the application of the word. As a result, only those who demonstrate mastery according to the process of certification are able to use the term *professional*. Ergo if you become certified, you will not have to worry about whether you are professional or not.

Perhaps the evolution of work and the changing values of our society as reflected in the use of language create the ambiguous environment in which we live and work that is the real cause of our confusion, not the word *professional* at all.

I don't think being certified will eliminate the uncertainty reflected in our literature regarding the question of professionalism. But I do think it's time we let go of our anxiety concerning whether or not we *are* . . . and just *be*.

Improved Image/Stereotype

I am the first to admit the harm a stereotype can inflict upon a profession. During my initial foray into a library school open house, I encountered more "buns and sensible shoes" than I could assimilate.

> In books, films, TV, cartoons, comic strips, the unmistakable impression emerges of a very dull, earnest body, usually female, with glasses (probably those little half glasses), her hair in—yes here it comes—a BUN, wearing sensible shoes, support hose, tweed skirt, droopy sweater . . . need I continue? You name something uncomplimentary, and it's probably been said about a librarian somewhere![6]

Unfortunately the reinforcement of the stereotype frightened me away from entering the profession for several more years. Image and stereotypes are important because we attribute value and status to certain images and stereotypes. We have correctly ascertained that the stereotype of the librarian is detrimental to achieving our desired value and status. If we're not happy with the image we have, what image do we want? Do we want it enough to ensure that we get it?

I am happy to report that the image/stereotype of the librarian, while not changing at breakneck speed, is being challenged. A recent, very successful challenge was made by the Library Association of Alberta, Canada, who created a provocative calendar for 2004 featuring librarians in leather, getting tattoos, soaking softly in bubbles, and wall-climbing, to name a few. The calendar achieved national status in the media and international acclaim via various links on the Internet. Of course, we all know that librarians have lives, ride motorbikes, and soak in bubbles, but if we want to change our image/stereotype, we have to let others in on it!

The media are in a state of confusion over our image. They were quite happy with the bun and sensible shoes—but as information has become sexy and the web has overwhelmed the powerful, the librarian has entered as the techno-savvy, web-designing, network-building guru. A classic example of confusion over the librarian's image has been highlighted in the press with the recent release of the "librarian action figure." On the one hand it is quite a coup to enter the realm of toy action figures, including such noteworthies as the Jesus action figure, the Shakespeare action figure, and the Nico barista action figure. It's fantastic to be part of the action figure series, and as Seattle city librarian Deborah Jacobs says, "Anyone who doesn't view a librarian as a potent force doesn't understand the job. Ideas are more powerful than bombs. . . . Information is the way to take over the world."[7]

While the idea was great, an outcry has stemmed from the actual image. The librarian action figure was designed based on the digital image of a living librarian, Nancy Pearl. Pearl is described as modest and unassuming; however, she believes in the superhero qualities of librarians. Too bad she didn't insist that the librarian action figure reflect the "inner superhero." The outrage is based on the details. The action figure, a "frumpy-looking librarian who moves her index finger to her lips with 'amazing push-button shushing action,'" is prompting many librarians around the world to raise their voices in protest. "The shushing thing just put me right over the edge," said Diane DuBois, library director of Caribou Public Library in Caribou, Maine. "We're so not like that anymore. It's so stereotypical I could scream."[8] So while librarians as a group have achieved the illustrious status of being an "action figure," the message remains mixed. My favorite example of the "new" librarian is an advertisement from Bacardi rum showing a glamorous and fun party girl, wearing an outfit that highlights her back, complete with a little tattoo near her tailbone. She commands the attention of those in the room. The slogan proclaims, "Librarian by day. Bacardi by night."

It will be one T-shirt, action figure, advertisement, position description, and nonstereotypical librarian at a time that will ultimately enhance our image and remake our stereotype. The certification process has nothing to offer in improving the image and combating the stereotype of the librarian.

Better-Quality Practitioners

The final claim to be addressed in this chapter is that certification will produce better-quality practitioners. I find this to be one of the weakest claims of certification. Better than what? A new graduate? A practitioner three years away from retirement? While I agree that we must continuously learn and enhance our knowledge, skills, and abilities, I do not believe this will be achieved via certification.

If we have recruited, attracted, and graduated individuals who are committed to the values of our profession, we will have librarians who assume that continuously improving, developing, and enhancing their abilities is a given. And if we accept our responsibility to mentor, encourage, and support each other, we will foster the commitment to lifelong learning, personal leadership, and accountability that ensures a higher-quality librarian than could ever be achieved through certification.

BEYOND CERTIFICATION: ALTERNATIVES FOR SUCCESS

I have reviewed some of the claims made by the proponents of certification and have indicated that while the goals they want to achieve are laudable, the process of certification is not the means by which to achieve them. If this is true, then what strategies will provide the desired outcomes of an enhanced image, a desirable salary, and better-quality practitioners? I suggest that library school recruitment, the curriculum, mentoring, and personal responsibility will be effective strategies.

Recruitment of Library and Information Science Students

Gone are the days when the "if we build it, they will come" approach sufficed as a graduate school recruitment strategy. Geographic boundaries are no longer as limiting; distance education, the web, independent facilitated learning, and globalization all increase the opportunities for prospective students to attain a higher level of customization for their education than ever before. It is within this fluid and dynamic context that library schools are faced with developing strategies for recruitment.

The following key questions need to be addressed: Who do we want? Where will we find them? And how will we attract them?

Who *do* we want? What qualities are employers looking for? We need to look for leaders (innovators, agents of change), lifelong learners, entrepreneurs, good communicators, flexible and forward thinkers, and individuals with a high degree of personal responsibility.

Where will we find them? People with these attributes are found across all fields and all socioeconomic strata. When they are already within our universities, they are fairly easy to identify as the leaders of student groups, social action committees, and outreach programs. The challenge is that many graduate programs will be vying for their attention and offering them incentives, so the market for these individuals is very competitive.

If we look outside the university, we are likely to find a cache of talent just waiting to be tapped into. It will require us to change our traditional thinking from wooing undergraduates into our graduate programs to finding ways to attract individuals from off campus. Once we leave the campus we may find these talented individuals studying in colleges, working in various occupations, serving on associations and boards, and already working in our libraries.

How will we attract them? Consultation and contact with career counselors and researchers is necessary to identify measures that people use when making a career choice and the factors they consider when selecting a specific profession. This information will enable library schools to develop a variety of targeted marketing strategies that will craft and present the benefits of the profession to a broad range of candidates with differing interests, backgrounds, and values.

Michael Rogers and Peter Shepherd have written about successful, innovative programs for recruiting to library schools, including funded internships, tuition reimbursement, and library support staff recruitment.[9]

We will need both short-term and long-term recruitment strategies. Short-term strategies target current undergraduates and market our graduate programs to them as the means of adding to what they have already attained, with the onset of a career path at the end of it. Long-term strategies will include recruiting those without a bachelor's degree and helping them obtain one, then leading them into our graduate programs. This will require library schools, career counselors, employers, government job centers, and so on to work together. And finally, a pool of potential librarians is at our fingertips—those who have already chosen to work in libraries, our support staff.

The Curriculum

In 1995, Herbert White said, "The process of educating students is a delicate balance between preparing them for a productive job in tomorrow's marketplace and a career in whatever the profession turns out to be ten or 20 years down the road."[10] This statement is as valid today as it was then.

The curriculum of the MLIS needs to provide a firm foundation in our values, be forward looking in technology, and be cast broadly regarding thinking, strategies, programming, and services needed to meet people's information needs.

Values form the underpinning of any profession. Those of librarianship need to be woven throughout the curriculum to enable the graduate to apply them to the myriad decisions made during daily operations and long-term strategic planning.

Technology has become a driver in our profession. The library science curriculum now offers courses on web design and development, network systems, digital archives, the Internet, virtual reference, and open source software to name a few. Technology has gone beyond a tool to provide access to our collections. Technology has opened the doors for librarians to provide new services and take on new roles, including those of web specialists, knowledge managers, and CIOs (chief information officers).

What librarians do best is connect people with the information they need—and this can take any form. With the spotlight on technology it would be easy for library schools to drop the perhaps less-esteemed courses on children's literature, storytelling, and young adult programming. However, that would be shortsighted because the children of our generation become the future decision makers that influence the value of librarians, libraries, and information in our communities.

It is important for the curriculum to also offer a stream on developing self, studying leaders and leadership, personal responsibility, and accountability. Because we expect librarians to take on leadership roles in the profession, this will equip those we have recruited with a shared framework for leadership. The profession is only now embracing the importance of developing library leadership; let's take this new awareness and begin to develop it where we begin to develop librarians.

One can't underestimate the value that practitioners can bring, both to the overall development of the curriculum and as teachers, as guest lecturers, and perhaps most importantly as mentors to library school students.

Mentoring

Mentoring has many guises, from formal to informal, organized to serendipitous, within professions and across them. However a mentoring relationship or mentorship moment is established, the core function of mentoring remains constant—nurturing and challenging the individual mentee (and often the mentor as well).

Regardless of the establishment or duration of a mentoring relationship, some common factors are useful in defining the relationship.

For the mentor:	For the mentee:
Giving time	Respecting time
Communicating from experience	Communicating from need
Listening	Asking questions
Encouraging	Sharing discouragement
Challenging	Accepting challenges
Storytelling	Not falling asleep
Introducing to others	Engaging in conversation
Buying beer	Drinking beer
Asking questions	Formulating answers
Assisting in practical matters	Asking about practicalities
Allowing mentee to make mistakes	Not fearing mistakes
Learning from each other	Realizing your mentor is learning too

The benefit of engaging in mentoring/menteeing is that it applies to us at any given point in our development and is not limited to a point in time (as is certification). Mentoring and being mentored are as important to library science students and new graduates as they are to practitioners in midcareer and those approaching retirement; the only difference is in the detail.

By committing our profession to mentoring we commit ourselves to moving forward, addressing new challenges, and managing our individual and collective future.

Personal Responsibility

While having organizational support for continuing education activities is very advantageous, in the end it is an issue of personal commitment. In my own experience, I identified early on (six months after graduation) that I was going to be in a supervisory position, responsible for helping others succeed in a changing environment. The best way to prepare for this role was to take a supervisory development program, during evenings and weekends, paid out of my own pocket. I learned, I applied, I connected, and I made a difference.

A few years later I moved beyond a supervisory role, and this brought its own set of challenges. Once again I elected to take a formal approach to get some additional education by completing a business management certificate. This course gave me insights into concepts of organizational culture and exposed me to subjects that broadened my experience. Once again this was done at personal expense.

Several positions, provinces, and cities later, I have just completed another education program, the ACRL/Harvard Leadership Institute, and was fortunate to have my travel and time supported by my employer. The institute challenged me in new ways and provided me with the tools and models for working effectively in an academic environment.

I have had numerous formal and informal opportunities to learn and develop. I mention these examples to emphasize that no matter what the culture of your organization, it is up to the individual to ensure growth as a professional.

MOVING FORWARD

This discussion demonstrates that certification will not help our profession achieve its stated goals of enabling librarians to enjoy better salaries, improved image, and enhanced value and status, nor will it provide better-quality practitioners. In fact, I think it is clear that only through the implementation of more specific strategies in the areas of recruitment, curriculum, mentoring, lifelong learning, and personal responsibility will these goals ever be achieved.

Let us move our concerns and our literature away from the tired themes of self-justification, certification, image, stereotype, and professionalism and look to the future. Our key strength as librarians is responsiveness, with a touch of the oracle. We continuously redesign ourselves to meet the needs of our user groups and to respond to and help create the ever-changing environment in which we live and work. We can continue to achieve this without imposing a certification model on our profession. Our knowledge, abilities, approachability, flexibility, risk-readiness, and vision have well equipped us for our future. I have no fear for the future of librarianship without certification; after all, we are the future.

NOTES

1. Holly Willett, "Certification and Education for Library and Information Science," *Journal of Education for Library and Information Science* 25 (Summer 1984): 13.

2. William Maher, "Contexts for Understanding Professional Certification," *American Archivist* 51 (Fall 1988): 410.

3. Maher, "Understanding Professional Certification," 421.

4. Alison Nussbaumer, "Alison's Article," *BCLA Reporter: The Newsletter of the British Columbia Library Association* 48 (January/February 2004): 3.

5. John N. Berry III, "Certification: Is It Worth the Price?" *Library Journal* 126, no. 3 (2001): 96.

6. Professional Status and Image, at home.earthlink.net/~cyberresearcher/status.htm (accessed 5 April 2004).

7. Jack Broom, "Toymaker Finds Librarian Who's a Real Doll," *Seattle Times*, 15 July 2003, at seattletimes.nwsource.com/html/localnews/135224851_librarian10.html (accessed 5 April 2004).

8. "Librarians Oppose Shushing Action Figure," *CNN Offbeat News*, 8 September 2003, at edition.cnn.com/2003/US/West/09/08/offbeat.librarian.ap (accessed 5 April 2004).

9. Michael Rogers and Peter Shepherd, "Tackling Recruitment," *Library Journal* 128, no. 2 (2003): 40.

10. Herbert White, "Educating for the Now and Future Profession," *Library Journal* 120, no. 9 (May 1995): 44.

12

The Certification Debate: Will You, Won't You, Will You, Won't You, Will You Join the Dance?[1]

Barbara K. Stripling

Certification in the library field presents interesting dilemmas that reflect dynamic and sometimes conflicting pressures within the profession itself. Debate about the merits and demerits of certification has been brewing for several years within the American Library Association (ALA) and out in the real world of school, academic, public, and special libraries. A careful look at the issues underlying certification should help all librarians decide to "join the dance" for certification yet at the same time realize we are all learning the new dance steps while the music is constantly changing.

Certification in the context of this chapter means that a recognized organization or agency attests that an individual has voluntarily acquired a specified set of knowledge and skills. It is not to be confused with accreditation, which is the validation of a particular educational program according to a set of standards, or with licensure, which is the governmental and mandatory permission to practice in a certain field.

ENTRY INTO THE FIELD

Governmental Certification/Licensure Requirements

Currently, a form of certification or licensure is often state mandated for both school and public librarians, but not for academic or special librarians. Although some of these requirements are called *certification*, all of them fit within the definition of *licensure* because they are government-imposed requirements for entering the field of librarianship. For school librarians, most states require basic certification in elementary or secondary education, with an additional degree or coursework requirement, for endorsement. Some states allow school librarians to receive certification through a library degree in lieu of teacher preparation courses. In 2000, thirty-five states required some form of testing in addition to degree and coursework requirements.[2]

In 1999, twenty-three states required some certification of public librarians, sometimes just for the director or head librarian, sometimes for several levels of librarians. Eighteen additional states specified preferred qualifications or voluntary certification; only nine states had no certification for public librarians.[3] Again, these certification requirements are similar to licensure because they are mandated or recommended by the states for entry into specific job classifications of the public library.

Academic librarians are not licensed by the state, but the educational requirements for academic librarianship have been clearly delineated by the Association of College and Research Libraries (ACRL). In 1989, ACRL issued a statement outlining its position that entry into academic librarianship must be only through an ALA-accredited master's degree, not through certification or licensure.[4]

For librarians in special libraries, an ALA-accredited master's degree is generally the standard for entry into the field. Eighty-five percent of law librarians hold a library science graduate degree. Almost one third of law librarians have a law (JD or LLB) degree in addition to a library degree.[5] Medical librarians must also hold graduate degrees in library science. The Medical Library Association (MLA) recognizes graduate degrees from both ALA-accredited and COPA (Council on Post-Secondary Accreditation)-accredited programs.[6]

Certification of Advanced Specialization

For a number of years, librarians have recognized that the field of librarianship and information science is changing rapidly, placing high demands on professionals to gain additional expertise beyond their initial professional degrees. Librarians began investigating the feasibility of developing certification programs in areas where specialization is needed (e.g., information technology, public library administration).

The Medical Library Association established the Academy of Health Information Professionals (AHIP) in 1978 to provide professional development and career recognition to MLA members. Three areas of achievement (academic preparation, professional experience, and professional accomplishment) are assessed based on submission of an application packet and portfolio. Five levels of credentialing, based on the applicant's professional experience and accomplishments, provide a pathway for medical librarians to continue their development.[7]

As interest in national certification increased and organizations such as AHIP were developed, librarians recognized that a national association such as the American Library Association was the logical forum for offering certification programs for all types of librarians—public, school, academic, and special. ALA's 501(c)(3) tax status as an educational organization, however, forbids a concentrated level of work on personnel, rather than professional, issues. Therefore, in 2002, the American Library Association established the Allied Professional Association (APA), with a 501(c)(6) tax status, to pursue personnel issues related to librarianship (e.g., salaries, status, and certification).

For ALA-APA, certification was designed to build on, not undercut, the initial professional degree. Certification will be granted upon proof that a librarian has developed competencies in an area of specialization. Through ALA-APA, divisions within ALA will be able to design certification programs to meet the specialized needs of their members. All programs will have three goals:

1. To improve professional practice in librarianship through the establishment of continuing professional development goals
2. To identify a body of knowledge and skills necessary to the practice of librarianship and/or to a specific specialization within librarianship
3. To recognize those individuals who have demonstrated both mastery of a body of knowledge and skills and continuing commitment to ongoing professional development[8]

The first proposal for a certification program (and the impetus for creating ALA-APA) was presented by three divisions of ALA (PLA, LAMA, and ASCLA) for a public library administrator certification. That program is being developed as a model that can be followed by other divisions. ACRL has already stated publicly (in its 1989 document) that it is not opposed to certification of librarians beyond the initial professional degree.

THE ISSUES

On the surface, certification seems like a very positive step for advancing the level of competency in the library field, but certification has numerous complex issues and few clear-cut answers.

Issue #1: Will certification help fill critical needs within the profession?
   In the next ten years, a large number of current librarians will retire. At the same time, greater demands for specialized service will emerge as our country's population becomes increasingly diverse and information continues to explode. Recruitment and continuing education of diverse individuals to staff our libraries have, therefore, become high priorities for our profession.
   Because certification programs will define specialized roles and competencies, they essentially will describe pathways for advancement in the field. High school and college students investigating career options will see opportunities for the future through these pathways. Published information about becoming certified as a public library administrator, children's services specialist, or school library/reading specialist could double as recruitment brochures.
   Certification programs also encourage continued professional development. The benchmark of success—certification—will hopefully be recognized and rewarded by employers as a sign of increasing expertise and value to the organization. One example of a certification program that has led to heightened status and increased pay is the National Board Certification program for school library media specialists.
   School librarians have struggled with recognition for years because they straddle two worlds (teaching and librarianship). Their expertise in teaching is often not valued by other types of librarians, and their librarian competencies are not even understood by their fellow teachers. A new national certification program for school library media specialists, launched by the National Board for Professional Teaching Standards, has been enthusiastically received by school library media specialists across the country, with over eight hundred applying for certification in the first year.[9]

Early evidence from the medical librarian credentialing process and the school library media specialist national teacher certification indicates that certification programs can have very positive effects. A voluntary national certification program seems to open up opportunities for advancement and continuing education by building a collective vision of specialized roles and the competency pathways to get to those roles. Certification programs also strengthen professional development at the local level by coalescing the resources for training. Local libraries and library systems do not need to provide all the training in-house if courses are available online or at local universities or regional or national workshops.

Issue #2: Should certification be reserved for librarians, or should certification programs also be designed for paraprofessionals in the field?

An important certification issue that has not been decided by ALA-APA is the possible certification of paraprofessionals, or library technical assistants (LTAs). At the present time, no national certification program for LTAs exists. The ALA-APA Certification Task Force considered the efforts by several entities to define competencies for library support staff but recognized that certification of library paraprofessionals needs further study.[10] This study is currently being conducted by ALA Library Support Staff Interests Round Table (ALA LSSIRT), the Council on Library/Media Technicians (COLT), and representatives from ALA divisions, committees, and staff.[11]

The library field has not even identified the basic educational preparation every library paraprofessional should have before employment. After the basic educational preparation, library support staff must develop another level of skills on the job. Unfortunately, because the job responsibilities of library support staff vary tremendously from library to library, the identification of common competencies is an extremely difficult task. In "Issue Paper #1" from the World Book-ALA Goal Award Project on Library Support Staff, several questions about certification for library paraprofessionals have been identified:

- How will the standards be determined?
- How will individuals demonstrate they have met the standards?
- How will the program be administered—voluntary versus required, funding?
- Will provision be made (e.g., a grandfather clause) for paraprofessionals with experience or library education?

- How will those receiving certification be recognized or rewarded in their own work situations?[12]

Some professional librarians are resistant to the idea of certifying support staff, fearing that it will accelerate an alarming trend of cost saving by replacing librarians with support staff. These alarmist voices must not prevail. When everyone who works in a library of any type has access to additional training and the option of pursuing advanced certification, the level of service to library patrons will be greatly enhanced. Professionals will be able to fill more specialized roles that build on their advanced education because other roles in the library are being well performed by trained and certified support staff.

Issue #3: Who should offer certification, and who should offer the training for certification?

The concept of *certification* differs from the idea of *certificate*. Certificates can be granted by any entity that offers a proposed course of study and verifies that someone completed it (not necessarily with high-quality work). Certification, on the other hand, implies that a reputable national or state body has specified standard competencies and verifies that only those who can demonstrate those competencies will be certified.

Certification will have national impact when a carefully coordinated national program is developed, specific competencies are established, access to training and competency evaluation is distributed equitably throughout the country, measurement of competency level is valid and reliable, and the process of certification is standardized and well administered.

Certification is probably most effectively used for specialized roles in the library world, such as public library administrator or children's services specialist, rather than for specific subsets of skills within those roles. Yet library workers are increasingly being called on to develop very sophisticated and targeted skill sets, often associated with specific products, such as databases, software programs, or hardware. Although ALA-APA will not administer a certification program for management of specific software or hardware products, library workers and vendors recognize that library and information jobs today require specific skills tied to the programs in use by each library.

Vendors are increasingly filling this gap in certification by offering their own programs. They offer a series of workshops on one of their products, and participants who pass a vendor-designed test receive a certification (e.g., certified system administrator for a specific vendor's system). Although the cost for this certification process can be quite high,[13] most vendors offer compensating discounts on annual maintenance charges.

The practice of vendors offering certification programs on specific software seems benign and useful to the field—library staff do need specialized training in order to manage very complex software most effectively. The practice becomes much less benign when vendors offer certification for simply using a product for a specified period of time. This certification is clearly tied to the sale of the product, not the development of skills within the user. For example, a widely used reading motivation software program in the school library field offers students points for reading and passing computer-based tests on specific books. If educators implement the program for twelve weeks, they get one type of certification; for eighteen weeks, they get master certification. School librarians are therefore receiving certification for operating a program for several weeks, with expectations set by a vendor, not the profession, and with no relationship to the development of professional competencies.

Vendors could have a more beneficial effect on the field by aligning with certification programs administered by a national association such as ALA-APA. When certification programs are established and competencies are developed, vendors whose products are related to that certification area could align their training with the specified competencies. With vendor approval and support, training could be coherently organized and consistently distributed throughout the country. As long as each training session is focused on the same overall competencies, it will not matter which specific programs or products are used.[14] Everyone benefits—the vendor is able to train users in meaningful ways, librarians receive training for certification, and the certification programs flourish.

The effect of certification training on library schools must also be considered. Controversy has arisen largely because the process of approving providers has been misunderstood. ALA-APA will register/approve any provider who plans to deliver professional development for certification based on a simple application and a nominal fee.[15] Any entity may apply—libraries, library schools, individuals, other associations, and vendors. Rather than being a threat to library schools, certification programs can broaden the number of people seeking continuing education.

Units (e.g., divisions, committees) within ALA will enhance the significance and depth of professional development offered at regional and national conferences when they design workshops to prepare attendees to meet competencies for certification. Experts in the field may also be approved to conduct relevant face-to-face or online workshops. Training offered by vendors that is specifically targeted toward the competencies required for certification will provide another venue.

Since certification is based on demonstration of competencies, not the completion of specific courses, those seeking certification could even rely on previous on-the-job experience or on independent study. In fact, many certification programs will probably require three to five years of experience in addition to their other requirements. For certification to be widely accessible and attainable, all of the possible venues for professional development should be made available.

Issue #4: How should the competencies for certification be measured and monitored?

Certification implies quality assurance. To assure quality, one must define the attributes of quality performance and then devise a measurement tool to assess achievement of those attributes.

The attributes for national certification can be described as competencies—what an applicant should know and be able to do. For example, the proposal for the certified public library administrator program identifies knowledge and skill competencies for serving diverse populations, including knowledge about the perceived role of libraries and education in various ethnic cultures and the skills to recruit and retain a culturally diverse workforce and library board of trustees.[16]

If it is difficult to identify competencies that are applicable across the country, then it is even more difficult to develop a measurement instrument that is valid, reliable, and equitable. The evaluation of competency could be accomplished through a test, portfolio process, references, validation of experience, or a combination of methods. Table 12.1 outlines the advantages and disadvantages of these evaluation approaches.

ALA-APA certification programs will probably use a combination of test, experience, and portfolio for initial certification and a combination of references, experience, and continuing professional development for certification renewal after three years.

National certification will not measure applicants' ability to interact well with others, their ethical or moral behavior, or their work habits or

Table 12.1. Evaluation Advantages and Disadvantages

	Advantages	Disadvantages
Test	Versions of the test can be calibrated for validity (does it measure what it is supposed to?) and reliability (will the same person taking two different versions of the test get the same score?). Scoring involves minimal or no judgment. Testing can be conducted equitably throughout the country. Few arguments will ensue about results.	Tests can only measure certain types of knowledge and skills—they more easily measure knowledge about a subject than the skills to create something with that knowledge. Tests measure performance at one point in time. Some people may be able to demonstrate competency in real situations but have difficulty showing this on a test.
Portfolio	Portfolios allow demonstration of competency in applying knowledge to real situations. Portfolios can be job-embedded because an applicant can compile a portfolio of actual projects completed on the job. Portfolios are built over time and foster growth and development. Portfolio reflections reveal the voice of the applicant putting the work in local context and identifying his or her own growth.	It is difficult to maintain standards of validity and reliability with portfolios. Assessment of portfolios is extremely time- and labor-intensive. Assessors must be trained. Results can be challenged.
References	References can provide information about work habits and application of competencies in the workplace. References can provide context for the application.	References provide little information about competencies. References are inherently biased. References may tell more about the person writing the reference than the person being reviewed.
Experience	Information about experience may show the development and application of knowledge and skills. Experience provides practical grounding so the competencies are reality based.	Experience may be as much about luck as it is about competence. Experience shows the opportunities for application of skills; it does not show the quality of work.

diligence. Although some in our field believe that ALA-APA should monitor the behavior of those who have been certified as competent and censure those who violate the ethics and values of the profession, that is not a role that ALA-APA has been designed to assume. The certification process will measure competence in specified knowledge and skills and will grant renewed certification for continuing professional development.

Issue #5: What is the added value of certification?
The verdict is still out on the effect of national certification on the library profession and on library service to patrons and communities. All of those involved in the creation of ALA-APA have high hopes, but they also realize it will take continuing effort, especially in the formative stages, to bring those hopes to reality. Whatever system is developed, it must be flexible enough to adapt to the changing world of libraries.

The effects of successful implementation of a national certification program include the following:

- Increased and equitable opportunities for advanced training, leading to certification for all levels of library workers
- A ripple effect in the local workplace, with the certification of one library worker leading to increased interest in professional development and advancement by others
- Higher status and pay for certified library workers and, by extension, for the whole library field
- Increasing numbers of potential librarians entering the profession because of the possibilities for advancement within the field
- Enhancement of library schools because of the addition of continuing education courses for certification and the increasing numbers of library workers seeking additional education

JOIN THE DANCE

Certification will provide new and equitable opportunities for library workers to build their skills and advance in their jobs. This cannot be a rich-get-richer situation. Certification programs must be developed for all levels of library workers. Training opportunities must be distributed throughout the country and in a variety of venues. Pathways for advancement within the library field will provide recruitment incentives and lead to more diverse library staffs. The net result of library certification programs will be heightened professionalism and better levels of service for our patrons in every type of library.

NOTES

1. Lewis Carroll, "Alice's Adventures in Wonderland," *Oxford Dictionary of Quotations* (Oxford: Oxford University Press, 1979), 134.

2. Patsy H. Perritt, "Getting Certified in 50 States," *School Library Journal*, at www.schoollibraryjournal.com/index.asp?layout=articlePrint&articleID=CA153 043 (accessed 28 March 2004).

3. Public Librarian Certification Standards, at www.slis.ua.edu/ala/cert.html (accessed 16 November 2003).

4. Statement on the Certification & Licensing of Academic Librarians, at www.ala.org/ala/acrl/acrlstandards/statementcertification.htm (accessed 12 September 2003).

5. Task Force to Enhance Law Librarianship Education, Education for a Career in Law Librarianship, at www.aallnet.org/committee/tfedu/education.html (accessed 29 November 2003).

6. Academy of Health Information Professionals, General Information FAQ, at www.mlanet.org/academy/acadfaq.html (accessed 29 November 2003).

7. Academy of Health Information Professionals, at www.mlanet.org/academy (accessed 29 November 2003).

8. ALA-APA Certification Task Force Mission and Goals, at www.ala-apa.org/certtfmission.html (accessed 27 March 2004).

9. Rick Margolis, "A Measure of Respect," *School Library Journal* 48, no. 9 (September 2002): 56–58.

10. ALA-APA Certification Task Force, Certification of Library Technical Assistants, at www.ala-apa.org/certtflta.html (accessed 29 November 2003).

11. Sandy Brooks, "Competencies and Certification: Where the Profession Stands," *Library Mosaics* 11, no. 6 (November/December 2002): 8–9; ALA Library Support Staff Interests Round Table (LSSIRT), Stand on Certification, at www.ala.org/Content/NavigationMenu/Our_Association/Round_Tables/LSSIR T (accessed 15 November 2003).

12. American Library Association Office for Library Personnel Resources, Standing Committee on Library Education, "Certification for Support Staff: Issue Paper #1," at www.ala.org/ala/hrdrbucket/3rdcongressonpro/certification .htm (accessed 27 March 2004).

13. Certification as a Dynix system administrator through Ameritech Library Services in 1998 cost $3,290. In "Ameritech Library Services Offers New Dynix System Administration Certification," *Information Today* 15, no. 1 (January 1998): 44.

14. Barbara Quint, "What Vendors Can Do for Us Now," *Information Today* 19, no. 10 (November 2002): 8–9.

15. ALA-APA Certification Task Force, Guidelines, at www.ala-apa.org/certtf guidelines.html (accessed 29 November 2003).

16. LA/LAMA/ASCLA Certified Public Library Administrator (CPLA) Program Core Course, at www.pla.org/projects/certification/certification_diverse.html (accessed 15 April 2002).

Part 5

MIXING THE OLD WITH THE NEW: HOW DO LIBRARY ASSOCIATIONS SURVIVE?

If library associations were not in existence, would anyone now be agitating to form them?

> —Mary Ellen K. Davis and Helen H. Spalding

TLA is an association that can be called on to get things done.

> —Barry M. Bishop

Association agendas will focus not on what matters to the leadership but on what matters to the potential membership.

> —Madeleine Lefebvre and Don Butcher

Many librarians in my peer group have little interest in associations beyond doing what their employers expect of them.

> —Gillian Byrne

13

Changing Roles for Library Associations

Mary Ellen K. Davis and Helen H. Spalding

Service-oriented, people-centered, and intellectually curious, librarians want to share their expertise and resources, sustain their professional development, and network with other professionals. In Canada and the United States, librarians have formed a variety of associations to enhance the ability of their members to deliver quality services to their library users, to further professional development, and to leverage their impact on issues affecting libraries and library users. Increasingly, collaborative bridges among library associations and across international borders are being formed. The key to addressing the challenges of the library's future will be building relationships among librarians to mobilize their creativity and skills to solve the new problems they confront. Associations able to reposition themselves effectively in a rapidly changing environment will provide the ideal structure to facilitate members meeting these goals.

Readers looking for brief overviews of library and information associations are referred to Thomson Gale's *Encyclopedia of Associations*, which describes hundreds of library associations, as well as thousands of other nonprofit membership organizations.[1] Many of these library associations have more detailed current and historical information on their websites.

FORMATION OF ASSOCIATIONS

The eighteenth century was a period when learned societies formed in the United States. Their scope was general, in reflection of the broad knowledge an educated person would have been expected to master. By the mid-nineteenth century, higher education was moving from the general, classical curriculum to specialized fields of study. Learned societies followed suit in the formation of organizations focused on more specialized areas of study. As professions formed in relation to these specialties, universities provided much of the training that distinguished professionals. As a result, academic learned societies increasingly became professional societies that were the means by which a profession and its working conditions were defined. Who was admitted to the profession was determined by specialized knowledge, institutionalized training, and/or licensing. Over time, professional associations became the groups of specialists who sanctioned the field's professional standards and membership.[2]

While other professional groups were being formed in the mid-1800s, a discussion in New York began to develop the plan for a professional meeting of librarians. At the resulting Philadelphia conference in 1876, the 103 attendees elected Justin Winsor, of the Boston Public Library, as president, and Melvil Dewey, Columbia College librarian, as secretary of the American Library Association (ALA). Official incorporation was finalized in 1879 in Massachusetts.[3] Since then, ALA has grown to almost 65,000 members. There are eleven divisions and nearly 1,300 committees within this large, complex association, with fifty-seven affiliated chapters, which are state and regional library associations.[4] Canadian librarians, active in ALA since the late 1800s, formed the provincial Ontario Library Association in 1901. After several attempts at forming a national organization, the Canadian Library Association was incorporated in 1946. It has five divisions (academic libraries, public libraries, school libraries, special libraries, and library trustees), and its membership includes 2,500 individuals and 600 institutions.[5]

Other library associations have formed in the United States around common professional issues and services to particular user groups. For example, the Medical Library Association was incorporated in 1898, the American Association of Law Libraries in 1906, the American Merchant Marine Library Association in 1921, the Music Library Association in 1931, the American Theological Library Association in 1946, and the

Asian/Pacific American Librarians Association in 1981.[6] Early in the twentieth century, state and regional library professional groups formed. A group of librarians in businesses in the New York City metropolitan area pulled together a group of corporate, municipal, and other "special" librarians at the 1909 ALA conference and formed the Special Libraries Association.[7]

CHALLENGES FOR ASSOCIATIONS

Beginning an association with colleagues who have the same enthusiasm for the cause and the possibility of addressing needs that are not being met in other forums is exciting. As an organization grows, its membership, staffing, and programs become more diverse and complex. Each association division and committee is formed because a group of members feels a particular issue or task needs specific attention. Over time, these parts can become large, complex organizations of their own. Smaller library associations may have no paid staff and rely on volunteers, while larger associations require more structure and professional staff. The Music Library Association relies on volunteer leadership, but it outsources management and conference planning functions, without retaining any full-time staff. Having formed as a subunit of a larger association, the Association of College and Research Libraries (ACRL) is now the largest ALA division, with a membership of over 12,000; a full-time executive director and staff; and a broad array of services, conferences, publications, and opportunities for member participation.

Like people, organizations have life cycles. The typical organization life cycle is a gradual beginning, followed by a period of rapid growth, and then a period of slowing down. Unless fresh vision and energy emerge, the organization may face decline.[8] A challenge all associations face is that the history and bureaucracy of the organization may grow to the point where members and staff spend more energy on the life of the association than on its primary purpose. How does the organization remain essential to its purpose in a changing world but responsive to member expectations? Organizational structure may be perpetuated beyond its usefulness because "that's the way we've always done it" or because individuals have become so personally invested in a particular activity that change is difficult. The vision, energy, and leadership that volunteer leaders are able to devote to the effort also play major factors in whether significant change is possible.

Another challenge is the size of the organization. The efforts of a large organization to provide equity in serving a greatly diverse membership may be perceived by some groups of members as not giving appropriate priority to their specialized interests. This stretching of resources and attention may encourage some members to form a separate association more focused on their concerns. Does this splintering into more subunits or completely separate associations present a problem for the larger association? When are the responsiveness of the organization's structure and the size of membership and resources in balance? What effect does it have on an association if a professional joins different associations at different times but holds no long-term allegiance or engagement in any one association? When are there too many or too few library associations? To build membership, should nonlibrarian library workers or library supporters be heavily recruited and encouraged to form their own interest groups and activities? As library associations increasingly collaborate and mobilize resources behind common goals, when should they consider merging to form larger, and perhaps more effective, associations? Keeping the passion for their purpose, relevancy for current and potential members, and responsiveness to change are challenges for all member organizations.

INCORPORATION IN THE UNITED STATES

In the United States, an association files its incorporation papers in the state in which it is formed. For instance, although its headquarters is in Chicago, ALA is incorporated in Massachusetts and thus is bound by the regulations of that state. Nonprofit organizations are exempt from federal tax under several sections of the Internal Revenue Code (IRC). The section of the IRC under which a nonprofit organization is categorized also determines the extent to which it can participate in certain activities. Once incorporated, it is a legal entity that can conduct business in accord with its bylaws and the regulations of state and federal governments.[9] Not only its activities but also its sources of revenue must be directly related to its stated purpose.[10] Educational, religious, literary, or scientific organizations in the United States are given 501(c)(3) tax-exempt status. Trade associations, professional societies, and chambers of commerce are classified as 501(c)(6) organizations. However, each type of organization may find that it must consider establishing separate legally qualified organizations to address its members' needs.

ALA illustrates this concept. Some ALA members, particularly librarians in public libraries, expressed the need for ALA to provide certification of expertise beyond the ALA-accredited master's degree in library science or the NCATE (National Council for the Accreditation of Teacher Education) accreditation in school library media. Other members wanted the association to provide more salary and pay equity advocacy for all library workers. ALA's status as a 501(c)(3) organization does not allow it to provide certification of individuals, but it may accredit programs of education. Neither is ALA allowed to provide direct support of comparable worth and pay equity initiatives nor other activities designed to improve the salaries and status of librarians and other library workers. But it may advocate for library funding, for policies that promote equitable access to information resources, and for First Amendment rights. Because members wanted ALA to provide services such as those not allowed by its 501(c)(3) status, in 2002 ALA formed the Allied Professional Association (APA) under the 501(c)(6) status in the state of Illinois. This trade association will be able to provide specialization certifications and work for better salaries for library workers. Legally separate from ALA, the ALA-APA must sustain itself without financial support from ALA.[11]

MEMBER ENGAGEMENT

Despite efforts of librarians to form and participate in library associations relevant to their professional lives, to what extent are library associations faced with the zeitgeist that Robert D. Putnam describes in *Bowling Alone?*[12] His research has relevance for associations and concerns the decrease in social contact and civic engagement in the United States. He believes that with less community involvement, Americans are losing "social capital," the glue that holds us together in networks of trust and the oil that greases the mechanisms that make our educational, cultural, economic, and political lives run smoothly. Americans do not join bridge clubs, go on picnics, or hold neighborhood potlucks with nearly the frequency they did in the past. If the personal networks that build social capital are not in place, quality of life is affected. Social interaction makes business and political support easier to generate, for it builds trust and reciprocity among its members. What effects will society feel if people do not join organizations as they used to do?

Putnam notes that membership associations face declining memberships, fewer attendees at programs and conferences, and difficulty recruiting volunteer leaders for boards and committees. Membership committees agonize over whether it is the format or message of the recruitment letter that needs refinement. Or are other organizations doing a better job of competing for the same members? (At their June 2003 conference, the Special Libraries Association seriously debated removing *Libraries* from its name in an effort to broaden its appeal to information professionals who are not librarians.[13]) Program committees are convinced that if they could just get a more appealing speaker or choose a better meeting time or day, then surely more people would attend their programs. What the committees may not realize is that they have done no worse than other organizations in membership recruitment or programming. Membership and program committees in most member organizations are having the same self-doubts. A hopeful sign for library associations is that Putnam's research found that those with college degrees are twice as likely to volunteer as those with a high school education or less.[14]

Prospective and current members are making different choices about what they want to do with their time, money, and volunteer effort. People are finding their lives faster paced. Families increasingly rely on two incomes, adding the stresses of balancing home, work, and childrearing within tight schedules. In an economy of budget cuts and staff downsizing, fewer workers must absorb more workload, often lengthening the workday and workweek for professionals. Less funding is available to support professional development and travel, forcing library association members to evaluate carefully how much additional personal investment they can afford from often stretched budgets. Local and regional organizations may find a rebound in membership as librarians seek to put more energy into professional groups closer to home. In *Sharing the Journey: Support Groups and America's New Quest for Community*, Robert Wuthnow notes that people join and switch among smaller, single-purpose groups without building the long-term membership or increasing commitments in a larger association that has been more true in the past.[15]

In evaluating the worth of joining an organization, prospective members want to be sure of what they will gain from the effort. The value of professional networks within library associations for learning, mentoring, advocacy, and getting jobs may provide the basis for continuing relevancy and build the social capital and reciprocity that makes a group effective and provides personal member satisfaction. Library associations should examine where they can build the learning and knowledge communities for their members, similar to those their members are building in their libraries and in their libraries' communities. Putnam advocates strong bonding within an organization, but also "bridge building" with other groups so as to avoid becoming too insular.[16] What bridging potential has not been exploited among the many library associations that may generate mutual benefits, including increased membership for those working together?

Unless library associations are able to respond to the changing behaviors and needs of their members, they may find fewer members and fewer participants at their conferences. Some of the questions associations need to consider include the following: What are the real benefits members derive from their associations? If library associations were not in existence, would anyone now be agitating to form them? If so, how can existing associations capture those motivations and needs in their strategic planning? Is the scope of membership eligibility broad enough? Do nonlibrarian library personnel see career benefits to joining library associations? Would current association members be able to capitalize creatively on the contributions that a more diverse membership would offer them? How can associations take advantage of the ways technology is changing how members use their personal and work time and how they communicate? What consideration needs to be given to how television, computers, and sound systems are affecting how, where, and with whom people spend their time away from work? What changes in the culture and organization of libraries lead associations to rethink their own cultures and organizational structures to be more synchronized with the new relationships their members share with their coworkers, administrations, and library users?

Of all the factors Robert Putnam identifies as having an impact on the decline of civic engagement and social capital, he attributes generational change as the most significant.[17] The generations of citizens most involved in social, religious, civic, and professional groups are not being replaced by the younger generation.

MEMBERS OF THE FUTURE

It may be helpful to look at association members through a generational lens. What current members expect of an association may not match what their parents or children expect. While previous generations may have joined "because it was the right thing to do," subsequent generations may have a more "what's in it for me" approach. As associations struggle to adapt their programs and services to meet their members' needs, they must remember how much more diverse their members are and devise ways to acknowledge and serve this diversity.

A Look at Members by Generation

Here is a quick overview of the characteristics of the generations:

Mature adults (World War II generation, or Silent Generation)

- motivated by duty, tradition, and loyalty
- tend to join and stay members of associations because "it's the right thing to do" and "I've always been a member, so I'll always be a member"

Baby boomers (1946 to 1964)

- have been described as self-absorbed, materialistic, and externally motivated; as they age they are becoming more introspective and subjective
- think of professional advancement as a series of sequential steps ("paying your dues")
- are very pressed for time due to personal and professional obligations
- make up vast majority of association members

Generation X (1965 to 1976)

- most similar to the World War II generation
- tend to be skeptical, realistic, responsible, pragmatic, self-confident, independent thinkers who are not easily intimidated by authority
- believe work should be fun and value quality of life—working to live not living to work
- might ask, "What's in it for me?" or "Does this support my beliefs?" when making decisions about association involvement
- more loyal to individuals to than organizations

Generation Y and millennial generation (1977–)

- tend to be more materialistic than Gen X; generation of consumers
- brand conscious; brands must reflect their lifestyles

- offspring of the digital age
- don't define themselves by their work
- expect a 24/7 society
- group oriented; enjoy working in teams[18]

Many library associations matured under the influence of the World War II generation, who may have joined associations out of a sense of duty and expected to be members for life. This influence continues today, although baby boomers currently make up the largest percentage of members for most associations.

As associations undertake strategic planning efforts, they need to reflect on assumptions made about the members they serve. If associations expect members to join out of a sense of loyalty and if association products and services have been devised to fit the boomer needs, how well will these assumptions work as associations prepare to welcome the Gen Xers, who think work should be fun and who are more loyal to individuals than to organizations?

DIVERSIFYING THE ASSOCIATION AND THE PROFESSION

Associations also should consider racial and ethnic diversities as well as generational differences. A 1998 status report using the five basic racial/ethnic categories defined by the U.S. Equal Employment Opportunity Commission shows that nearly 90 percent of librarians in the United States described themselves as white, about 6 percent as African American, 4 to 5 percent as Asian/Pacific Islander, and 1 percent or less as American Indian or Alaskan Native.[19] 2000 U.S. Census Bureau data and projections indicate that these percentages are not reflective of the general population. The traditional white majority in the U.S. population is decreasing; as just one example, the Latino/a population grew 58 percent over the past decade, according to the 2000 U.S. Census.[20] The U.S. Census Bureau projects that the number of whites in the U.S. population will be a smaller percentage than the number of nonwhites.

Library associations have several challenges in the area of racial and ethnic diversity: first, to recruit a broader mix of racial and ethnic groups to the profession; second, to convince these new recruits they should join and become active in library associations; third, to ensure that there really is an opportunity for all members to have a voice in the association.

Members of an association want to feel that their professional association understands their needs and concerns. It will become increasingly difficult to convince members the association does understand them "if no one in the organization looks like them, sounds like them, or is close to their age. The ability to convert student members to regular members, never an easy task, becomes harder as the student population becomes more diverse."[21]

RECRUITMENT TO THE PROFESSION

Associations must consider the much trumpeted loss to the profession due to the large number of retirements expected to take place in the next ten years. Although predicting when individuals will retire is not a simple task, it is possible to project when individuals in the profession will turn sixty-five. An ALA report indicates that 20 percent of librarians will reach age sixty-five between 2010 and 2014, along with an additional 18 percent in the five years following.[22] Associations are concerned that not enough qualified individuals will be available to fill the vacancies.

ASSOCIATIONS FOR ALL LIBRARY WORKERS

Increasingly, libraries are hiring nonlibrarians to do work that has traditionally been "librarian" work, as well as to perform functions new to libraries. New professionals being hired in libraries include fund-raisers, grant writers, information technologists, instructional designers, and planning experts. Librarians also are delegating more of their traditional work to support staff. Library associations must consider the role they play in providing educational, networking, recognition, and other traditional services to others working in the library. In addition, should the association assume new roles to enhance the careers of library workers who do not have an accredited library or media specialist degree?

ASSOCIATION PRODUCTS AND SERVICES

What do members want an association to do for them? Why do they join, and how do they hope it will benefit them? As noted by Sue

Kamm, "Little research has been done on librarian behavior in professional organizations. Literature searches reveal only a few articles on librarians' or other professionals' relationships with their organizations."[23] While different generations may hold varying expectations, associations have traditionally provided a core of products and services that have included some or all of the following:

- Networking—associations give individuals a way to find others with similar interests
- Setting standards—associations develop benchmarks and guidelines for the services of the profession and the education of its professionals
- Data collection and research—associations collect data about the industry/profession so that members gain benchmarks against which to measure their own institutions and to answer research questions to better the profession
- Professional development—associations offer the means for keeping current in the profession and enhancing career and job skills by offering conferences, workshops, institutes, and seminars and by providing volunteer leadership opportunities
- Publications—associations publish books and articles to share information about the profession
- Advocacy—associations offer a collective voice to speak out on topics affecting the profession or influencing legislation
- Career development—associations offer job services, notices of vacancies, career advice, resume services, mentoring programs, and leadership programs
- Recognition—associations offer achievement awards and provide recognition through election to leadership positions

With hundreds of membership associations related to libraries and information, all offering similar core products and services, how do librarians select which associations to join? Librarians may also choose from a plethora of other professional and subject discipline associations related to their interests (e.g., media associations, technology associations, subject associations, unions). Kamm posits that the decision is based on a return on investment: How much are the dues, and what services am I getting for my money? Kamm reminds us that, unlike attorneys who may be required to join their state associations in order to practice law, librarians join associations voluntarily without any legal compunction to do so.[24] Library associations must be cognizant of the number of associations competing for a finite set of members' dues, registration fees, and fees for products and services.

Relying on a variety of revenue streams for funding, associations have been providing face-to-face settings for the accomplishment of the work of the association, as well as for professional development (e.g., conferences, meetings, and working groups). As budgets are cut, as time is seen as increasingly valuable, and as the importance of balance in work and life takes greater hold, associations must develop means to provide these services in the most time- and cost-efficient manner possible.

FUNDING THE WORK OF ASSOCIATIONS

Associations do not live on membership dues alone. Conference registrations, exhibits revenues, sales of books, subscriptions to publications, donations, and advertising revenues are among the many revenue sources associations have come to depend on. As they change their products and services to meet changing member expectations, associations must become creative about developing new revenue streams.

If members prefer a virtual meeting environment, will they be willing to pay fees that replace the revenues earned from exhibit booth and registration fees generated by the annual face-to-face conference or convention? Most likely, associations will keep some of the traditional face-to-face conferences and workshops because "the Internet, however robust, cannot duplicate the serendipity of a roomful of experts on a given topic spontaneously inventing new policies, tools, or protocols."[25] Associations should be prepared to increase their efforts to promote educational sessions yet expect fewer individuals to attend because institutional budgets have been slashed and because of the ever-widening array of programs competing for members' time and monies.

Declining resources may change how members fund their participation in association events. While many members pay a large share of their own expenses, another percentage of association members receive funding support from their institutions. As the economy shrinks, the value of endowments declines, and library budgets are cut, one can expect to see declines in monies available to spend on association products and services.

The shrinking of libraries' budgets makes an impact on the association in several ways. The library not only provides less individual funding but also has less money to spend on products and services offered by the vendor community. The vendor community then experiences a decline in sales and thus has less money available to support the association through donations, exhibit space rental, and advertising.

This simple illustration demonstrates the interconnected relationship of the librarian, library, association, and vendor communities. Associations have begun to feel the effects of this interdependence as donations have declined along with the downturn in the economy. A recent survey by the Association of Fundraising Professionals reports that 40 percent of the charities raised the same amount of money or less in 2001, compared with 2000. Nonprofit organizations supporting the arts, humanities, or the environment have been particularly hard hit.[26]

The fiscal health of an association is not affected by economic trends alone. The attitude of its members on issues can affect the way an association does business. For example, the recent move to open access publishing received great support in the library and academic community. Traditionally, many professional associations depend heavily on the revenue they enjoy from publications, advertising, and ancillary products. If the revenues from the sale of association publications are forgone by moving them to open access—and are not replaced with other revenue streams—how will it affect the programs the association offers? Some posit that making more materials freely available on the Internet will stimulate sales of related items, thus enhancing revenue streams. How this plays out in the library community remains to be seen, for librarians have not typically published articles under the common open access procedures (e.g., paying author fees).

Associations also enjoy some income from the rental of members' names and addresses to outside parties (typically vendors wanting to reach a particular market). As privacy concerns grow more prevalent, members may be reluctant to give permission to rent their contact information, thus reducing another revenue stream.

If an association's revenues decline, its staffing may need to change. The American Society of Association Executives (ASAE), the association for individuals who manage associations, recently experienced a sharp decline in revenues and cut its budget 15 percent, instituted a salary freeze for employees, and left a dozen positions vacant. "We are a mirror image of what our members are experiencing," said ASAE's current president.[27]

Associations will need to reduce expenses and be conservative in estimating future revenues. New products will have to be evaluated carefully to ensure there is a clearly identifiable value offered and a market for the products, thereby increasing the prospects of success in difficult economic times. More knowledge and skills in strategic marketing will be necessary to better understand and to effectively meet the needs of current and potential members.

PARTNERSHIPS AND COMPETITION

Traditionally, associations have been the primary source for education beyond graduate school. Associations developed and offered the conferences, workshops, seminars, and institutes that members paid to attend. Today brings many more choices for our members. Library schools are partnering with libraries to offer continuing education. For-profit providers, including our member leaders, are offering stand-alone conferences as well as virtual conferences. Associations should look for creative partnerships with library schools, other associations, libraries, state agencies, and commercial enterprises to successfully deliver education to its members. As one illustration of this concept, the Association of College and Research Libraries successfully partnered in 1999 with the Harvard Graduate School of Education to offer the ACRL/Harvard Leadership Institute.

RESEARCH AGENDA

Research is another area that would benefit from partnerships. The academy of library educators, library practitioners, and the associations themselves need to collaborate in examining the role, the impact, and the influence that library associations can have in fostering excellence in library services. Funding agencies may be interested in partnering to examine these issues. The following questions represent the beginnings of a research agenda:

- What essential role do library associations play in the improvement and repositioning of libraries and library services for the future?
- How can library associations convey the importance of libraries and librarians to the public when there is a sentiment that "everything is freely available on the Internet"?

- What partnerships should associations be forming to best offer their products and services?
- Are there too many or too few library associations, given the member market and product customer market?
- When members are focused on the part of the association or specific association products relating to their needs, how can they transform their library association to address members and services outside of their specialized interests?
- How can collaboration among library associations be reciprocal and equitable when they often must compete for members' and customers' limited time and resources?
- How can associations restructure their boards, staff, and organization to become more flexible and responsive?
- How can associations' staff keep their knowledge and skills current with changing tools and member needs?
- How can associations develop a full array of products and services for each generation?
- Should associations focus more on one generation than another?
- What are the leadership, management, and programmatic implications of the differences among member groups?
- What dues structures and pricing models are most effective?
- What relationship will library associations have with the increasing number of nonlibrarian professionals and paraprofessionals who work in or on behalf of libraries?[28]

THE ASSOCIATION OF THE FUTURE

Future generations will want a place where they can experiment with new methods of work, community, and involvement[29]: "The next generation of leaders and members will expect associations to use technology to enable them to participate in the organization's work without having to travel to a certain place at a certain time."[30]

The library association of the future will retain the traditional goals of the association—networking, standards setting, data collection, professional development, publications, career development, advocacy, recognitions—but will look to a wider variety of delivery mechanisms.

The new generations expect an online 24/7 community. Associations will need to develop online communities of practice (i.e., clusters of members with common professional practice interests who "meet" virtually). The communities will be very fluid, coming and going to meet the current needs of the environment. To be successful, these communities must be driven by member volunteers. Members will come to see them as indispensable opportunities for networking, sharing experiences and best practices, creating libraries of resources and references, problem solving, and developing leadership skills.[31]

John Seely Brown refers to these virtual communities as a "new, powerful fabric for learning . . . that combines the small efforts of many with the large efforts of the few. . . . Indeed its message is one that learning can and should be happening everywhere—a learning ecology. All together a new, self-catalytic system starts to emerge, reinforcing and extending the core competencies of a region."[32]

If associations retain their traditional service goals and incorporate the virtual community component into their work, they will be able to respond much more quickly and more flexibly to the changing needs of their members and will receive the opportunity to become more inclusive organizations.

As long as librarians are concerned about issues, want to learn, and are willing to share their expertise and experience to better the profession, library associations are assured a place in the future. The challenge for these associations is to be attentive to member needs, be willing to change their array of products and services, and be willing to stop doing things despite the fact that "that's the way it's always been done."

NOTES

1. *Encyclopedia of Associations*, 41st ed., s.v. "International Organizations" (Detroit: Gale, 2004); *Encyclopedia of Associations*, 41st ed., s.v. "National Organizations of the U.S." (Detroit: Gale, 2004); *Encyclopedia of Associations*, 15th ed., s.v. "Regional, State and Local Organizations" (Detroit: Gale, 1978).

2. Anne Ruggles Gere, "Learned Societies and Professional Associations," in *Encyclopedia of American Cultural and Intellectual History*, 3rd ed., edited by Mary Kupec Cayton and Peter W. Williams (New York: Scribner, 2001), 291–94.

3. Mary Ghikas, "American Library Association: Organization and Structure," in *Encyclopedia of Library and Information Science*, 2nd ed., edited by Miriam A. Drake. (New York: Marcel Dekker, 2003), 117.

4. *ALA Handbook of Organization 2002–2003* (Chicago: American Library Association).

5. Elizabeth Hulse, *The Morton Years: The Canadian Library Association, 1946–1971* (Toronto: Ex Libris Association, 1995), 1–2.

6. *The Bowker Annual: Library and Book Trade Almanac*, 48th ed., edited by Dave Bogart (Medford, N.J.: Information Today, 2003).

7. Special Libraries Association, Virtual SLA: Historical Highlights, 26 September 2002, at www.sla.org/content/SLA/History/highlights.cfm (accessed 26 August 2003).

8. Philip Kotler, *Marketing for Nonprofit Organizations*, 2nd ed. (Englewood Cliffs, N.J.: Prentice Hall, 1982), 81–83.

9. Bruce R. Hopkins, *Starting and Managing a Nonprofit Organization: A Legal Guide*, 3rd ed. (New York: Wiley, 2001), 72.

10. Hopkins, *Nonprofit Organization*, 180–81.

11. ALA Allied Professional Association, ALA-APA Q & A, at www.ala-apa.org/qa.html (accessed 26 August 2003).

12. Robert D. Putnam, *Bowling Alone: The Collapse and Revival of American Community* (New York: Simon & Schuster, 2000).

13. Special Libraries Association, Virtual SLA: SLA Press Release 20, 17 June 2003, at www.sla.org/content/memberservice/communication/pr/pressrelease/2317c.cfm (accessed 26 August 2003).

14. Putnam, *Bowling Alone*, 186.

15. Robert Wuthnow, *Sharing the Journey: Support Groups and America's New Quest for Community* (New York: Free Press, 1996), 6.

16. Putnam, *Bowling Alone*, 22–24.

17. Putnam, *Bowling Alone*, 283.

18. John Gunn, "Generational Marketing," *Forum* 86 (November 2002): 14–15; Lisa Aldisert, "Here Comes Gen Y...," *Convene* (July 2002): 64.

19. Mary Jo Lynch, *Racial and Ethnic Diversity among Librarians: A Status Report*, American Library Association, at www.ala.org (accessed 25 August 2003).

20. Diversity Inc., at www.diversityinc.com (accessed 16 December 2002).

21. Mark Levin, Three Critical Trends, at www.asaenet.org (accessed May 2003).

22. Mary Jo Lynch, "Reaching 65: Lots of Librarians Will Be There Soon," *American Libraries* 33 (March 2002): 55–56.

23. Sue Kamm, "To Join or Not to Join: How Librarians Make Membership Decisions about Their Associations," *Library Trends* 46, no. 2 (Fall 1997): 295–306.

24. Kamm, "To Join or Not to Join," 295–306.

25. Edward J. Valauskas, "The Virtual Association," *Library Trends* 46, no. 2 (Fall 1997): 411–21.

26. James Zaniello, "Fundraising Gets Rough," *Association Management* 54 (September 2002): 57–61.

27. Neil Irwin Washington, "A Closely Associated Struggle: Nonprofits Face the Same Recession-Related Financial Problems as Their Members," *Washington Post*, 4 February 2002, p. E1.

28. *Exploring the Future: Seven Strategic Conversations That Could Transform Your Association: Executive Summary for Association Executives,*

Leaders, and Staff (Washington, D.C.: American Society of Association Executives, 2001), 7.

29. Glenn Tecker, Jean S. Franckel, and Paul D. Meyer, *The Will to Govern Well: Executive Summary* (Washington, D.C.: American Society of Association Executives, 2002), 7.

30. Tecker et al., *The Will to Govern Well*, 10.

31. Lorraine Smalley et al., "Developing and Nurturing Communities of Practice" (paper presented at the Association Forum of Chicagoland virtual seminar, 12 August 2003).

32. John Seely Brown, "Growing Up Digital: How the Web Changes Work, Education, and the Ways People Learn," *Change* 32 (March/April 2000): 11–20.

14

Texas Library Association: A Success Story

Barry M. Bishop

The Texas Library Association (TLA) has over seven thousand members. It is the largest state library association in the United States and oscillates between being the second and third largest library association in the United States. The exhibit hall at TLA's annual conference is the second largest library show in the world, and the association has enjoyed almost a decade of continual growth. What is the key to our success?

Our success lies partially in our size, strength, and history. Most state library associations represent just one type of library, usually public. School and academic librarians often form their own associations. The Texas Library Association, on the other hand, includes librarians from all library types (academic, public, and special) as well as library supporters (trustees, friends of the library, vendors, and users). Although almost 50 percent of the members are school librarians, leadership in the association and membership on committees are equally balanced between school, public, academic, and special librarians. About 1 percent of the members are vendors.

The association provides these different types of library stakeholders with opportunities to network and cooperate. For example, school librarians provide the public librarians with insights about teaching children. In return the public librarians provide advice on advocacy. The academic librarians move the technical agenda forward, and the school and academic librarians work together to improve information literacy skills. Everything that TLA does includes members from all types of libraries, from all across the state.

There are also special interest groups for different types of members. Two different special interest groups cater to the friends, trustees, and lay members of the profession: Library Friends, Trustees, and Advocates (LiFTA) and Friends of School Libraries. The membership in these groups is close to 6 percent of the association. Vendors also have their own special interest group called T-PALS (Texas Professional Association for Library Sales). The TLA executive works closely with this interest group. When TLA was thinking about making some changes to the conference that would affect the vendors, TLA consulted with T-PALS. As well, this interest group works closely with the exhibits manager to make sure vendors are satisfied with all conference arrangements.

TLA is an association that can be called on to get things done. It was there when the Fort Worth Public Library lost a wall to a tornado. A group of librarians convinced the TLA leadership to form a temporary committee to raise money to establish a disaster relief fund. Soon, over $25,000 was raised (the amount needed to create an endowment by association rules). This temporary committee has become a standing committee of TLA, with the sole purpose of providing financial assistance to libraries damaged by physical disasters.

The success of TLA also resides in the association's ability to build effective working committees that have representatives from all parts of the state and all types of libraries. These strong ties often lead to new opportunities for the association. For example, when First Lady Laura Bush invited school leaders to the White House Conference on School Libraries, a few Texas school librarians were invited to attend. With the knowledge gained at the conference, TLA participants were able to broaden the association's focus to include advocacy. The focus of the conference, held in Washington on June 4, 2002, was to demonstrate the importance of school libraries to state and local leaders in education (e.g., principals, superintendents, and state agency educators). TLA members who attended the meeting in Washington were able, through mini-conferences at the state and local levels, to disseminate the information to the entire membership.

As a result of the White House conference, the Texas Library Association proposed a series of advocacy plans for librarians to help them get information about libraries to decision makers. Detailed advocacy planning strategies were distributed to members via the district conferences, as well as via the association's publications and listservs. Plans are also in the works to replicate the White House conference for school librarians in Texas.

In addition to advocacy at the local level, another result of the Washington experience was expansion of the advocacy program to state legislators. Energy was focused on saving the TIF (Telecommunications Infrastructure Fund), a law that provided libraries in the state with funding for online resources. To make legislators aware of the importance of the legislation, a website was set up[1] and information from library staff and users was posted. As a result of this advocacy plan, in a year when 10 percent of the budget was cut rather than increased by the usual 10 percent, the libraries were not worse off than any other group. As well, legislators all admitted there had been enough communication with constituents that they were well aware of the issues and the needs.

TLA is successful because it is open to the ideas of its membership. When librarians in the Houston area suggested courting the legislators, TLA established a legislative breakfast for all legislators and candidates to be held in October, the month before the state elections. The event was so successful that the association held similar breakfasts in other regions of the state and continues with some kind of action prior to all elections to bring issues to the legislators and candidates. The association also expanded the program to include legislative days, days for librarians to merge on the capitol and talk library issues all day long. The results of these activities are real. After years of advocacy, school libraries received direct funding in the amount of $0.25 per student if at least $1 was spent by the local school. Although this was only a quarter of what was asked for, it was the first time the state directly funded school libraries. The funding increased in the next legislative session to $0.30 per student, or about $1 million. In 2002, legislators authorized the Loan Star Libraries initiative at about $2.9 million.

A broader impact of the advocacy program has been that in good budget years libraries receive fair funding, and in bad years library budgets are cut no more than the budgets of other departments. The advocacy program has demonstrated to legislators that the Texas Library Association is a serious player. It should be noted that this program could not have been initiated or have been successful in a less member-focused association. The fact that TLA speaks for all individuals interested in libraries (all types of librarians, friends, and users) makes it a strong lobbying voice indeed.

Success also depends on responding to the needs of the members and providing real benefits for membership. TLA members receive reduced registration rates for the annual TLA conference, subscriptions to the *Texas Library Journal*, membership in a division and interest group, continuing education programs, online job information, access to the TLA advocacy program, and more. TLA also offers some rather unique services such as liability insurance, discounted long-distance telephone service, and a TLA MasterCard.

The liability insurance program[2] was set in place because some librarians were taken to court by users for possessing certain materials in their collections. As a result, the association implemented a program whereby a librarian facing litigation could depend on the association for moral support as well as up to $1 million in legal fees. The telephone and MasterCard programs provide members with discounts and TLA with a little extra revenue. Because TLA has so many members, it is able to negotiate these discounts. It is a real win-win situation for both TLA and its membership. By finding an outside source for revenue, TLA can minimize rate hikes. Members are happy because in addition to discounts, these revenues offset some fee hikes.

> I belong to TLA because . . . it is the only professional organization that represents me and the issues I care most about. TLA provides me with legislative information, professional updates, and now, with professional liability insurance.[3]

> I belong to TLA because . . . it is the only organization which can speak effectively for and to all kinds of Texas librarians. TLA's legislative efforts have met with repeated success.[4]

TALL TEXANS

Continuing education also plays a crucial role in the success of any library association. The Texas Library Association's leadership training retreat is one example of successfully identifying and fulfilling a continuing education need. TALL Texans, as it is known, is in fact so successful it has become the model for many similar programs around the nation. Professionals in Texas became concerned that the state might run short of library leaders. The solution was to create a leadership program that has produced a number of librarians interested in leadership roles in the association.

The TALL Texans Leadership Development Institute started in 1994 and is designed for TLA members with at least five years' professional experience in the library and/or information science field and for library laypersons with at least three years' service to the library community. The five-day institute focuses on leadership development activities. All participants are asked to make a two-year follow-up commitment to the institute through a personal action agenda that includes active participation in the work of the association and the completion of a special project. There are six mentors in the program, including the president-elect of TLA. It is evident that the program has been a success:

> During the 2002–03 term, there were six TALL Texans on the TLA Executive Board. Eleven of the thirty-one standing and ad hoc committees were chaired by TALL Texans, as were two of the four TLA divisions, six of the twenty-five round tables/interest groups, and four of the ten TLA districts. TALL Texans make a difference![5]

Special projects completed by the TALL Texans have made significant contributions to the association. The topic of one project was the staff development programs offered by the various divisions. This project rejuvenated the continuing education and development committee and the staff development and continuing education providers interest group.

CONFERENCES

The focus for TLA is to host a conference that as many members can attend as possible, to keep costs low, and to hold it at a time that is convenient for many. TLA makes a concerted effort to help members from all over the state participate in their conference programming. Stipends have been created and are offered to help members attend.

When deciding when to hold the annual conference, in typical TLA fashion, the decision revolves around the membership. In addition to member preference, TLA also considers the timing of other library conferences to minimize conflict. Another consideration that factors into the decision is the cost of holding the conference. A survey of convention centers determines if there is a less expensive time to meet. It is for this reason that TLA often meets Sunday through Tuesday—this is when you get the best rate.

In addition to the main spring conference, fall conferences provide quality programs on a local level to meet the needs of those librarians who are not able to travel to the large spring conference. TLA has divided Texas into ten geographic districts. In the fall there are ten district conferences. A representative from the TLA executive board attends each district's fall conference. Each district has its own chair and chair-elect who are responsible for planning the fall conference program. Attendance ranges from seventy out in the vast reaches of West Texas to three hundred in the urban areas around Houston or Dallas. The number of sessions ranges from three to fifty. These meetings are held on Fridays or Saturdays in order to minimize the time participants need to take off work. Recently implemented was the "best of the best" program that provides funding so outlying fall conferences have the opportunity to bring in some of the more high-end speakers from the annual conference.

THE ORGANIZATION

While a great deal of success revolves around member-based issues, success is also dependent on the organization and running of the association. TLA has been around for over one hundred years; it celebrated its centennial in 2002 and has a long history of overlapping leadership (a three-year cycle that includes the leader-elect, leader, and past leader), providing continuity of leadership for the association. This concept of overlapping roles is now also applied to committees. Committee chairs are now appointed a half year earlier, and the president-elect is encouraged to appoint chairs from existing committee members familiar with the work of the committee. Chairs therefore serve for at least half a year as "pre-chairs," learning the role and assisting the current chair.

An effective executive director has also made a great impact on the success of TLA. Pat Smith has been a librarian in Texas since 1973 and has been the executive director of the Texas Library Association since 1987. Her respect for all people and her ability to diffuse potentially tense situations, combined with a strong work ethic and a willingness to fly all over the state to meet with groups, make her a very effective leader.

COMMUNICATION

TLA uses the latest technology to facilitate the work of the association. Nowhere is this more apparent than in our communication with vendors, most of which is handled electronically. Each vendor has an electronic profile that includes contact information and product descriptions. The profile is used by TLA to contact vendors and to give them information about upcoming conferences. Vendors can get logins and passwords so they can update their profiles, make and change hotel reservations, pay new and review paid invoices, and register for conference badges. Vendor profiles also feed into a buyer's guide, another tool members can use to find information about products displayed at the conference.

TLA also uses the latest technology to communicate with members. Electronic distribution lists help members stay current in their particular areas of interest. Exhibit hall maps are posted so that librarians can do some advance exhibit hall planning. Newsletters are sent regularly to the vendors to let them know about plans for upcoming conference exhibits, as well as provide information about new and innovative selling techniques. Sponsorship opportunities are posted on the web so that vendors can decide how to use their conference time and money most effectively. As well, TLA maintains a job line and is in the process of setting up online voting.

THE FUTURE OF TLA

How can an association that is so large and strong improve? The answer for TLA is clear—focus on the membership and remain open and flexible. In addition, I can see future direction roles for TLA in areas once managed by the state government. Very recently, TLA took over the maintenance of a school library list once managed by the state agency responsible for school libraries. Given recent changes in funding and management at the state level, there may be more roles for TLA in the area of administration of government-funded programs. In the spring of 2003, the government removed school funding for online databases. One way to rectify this situation may be for TLA to take over the coordination of online databases for all libraries in Texas. In addition to lobbying the local decision makers and state legislators for additional funding, TLA committees could negotiate statewide pricing for online databases. This degree of integration would enable the association to bargain from a much stronger position and get access to resources faster, as well as ensure better pricing. Why will TLA continue to grow? Because the association is willing to take initiatives in many areas. TLA is always willing to step in and do something innovative to ensure that the membership, the profession, and libraries in Texas continue to grow and thrive.

NOTES

1. Texas Library Association, Government Affairs, at www.txla.org/html/govt_aff.html (accessed 24 February 2004).

2. Texas Library Association, Professional Liability Insurance, at www.txla.org/html/insurance.html (accessed 24 July 2003).

3. Ruth Dahlstrom, Member Testimonials, at www.txla.org/html/testimon.html (accessed 25 March 2004).

4. Al Cage, Member Testimonials, at www.txla.org/html/testimon.html (accessed 25 March 2004).

5. Texas Library Association, TALL Texans Round Table: Past Classes, at www.txla.org/groups/ttrt/classes.htm (accessed 26 January 2004).

15

Lighting the Way: Can Library Associations Shape Our Future?

Madeleine Lefebvre and Don Butcher

Canada is a vast country with a relatively small population of 32 million. In 1999, 19,000 libraries and 38,000 full-time equivalent staff delivered services to Canadian library users through 22,000 service points. Librarians accounted for 22 percent and library technicians 19 percent of library workers.[1] The Canadian Library Association (CLA) is Canada's national English-language library association, while l'Association pour l'avancement des sciences et des techniques de la documentation (ASTED) is the national French-language association.

As in many countries, the influences on the Canadian library and information science (LIS) community are many and complex. Governments at three levels provide funding and employment. The public and special interest groups (students, university faculty) are consumers. Private-sector firms, who provide employment, are the greatest source of services and supplies to the community and are also consumers. Internally, the sector faces its challenges: demographic challenges generic to North American society and some specific to the LIS community.

An association can be defined as a collective of people sharing the same values who have come together voluntarily for mutual benefit and to advance a greater good. It is our thesis that a strong national library association can identify the challenges and, with the power of a collective, work to lead the community. This chapter focuses on the role of the Canadian Library Association while making reference to other associations. It sets out the major challenges facing the Canadian LIS community and offers views on how and why the association can lead.

CHALLENGES FACING THE LIBRARY SECTOR IN CANADA

The "baby boom" population bulge is working its way through the LIS community: Statistics Canada estimates 48 percent of library workers will retire by 2010. These retirements are likely to reinforce the current blurring of lines in professional positions and responsibilities. An example of this blurring is the offering of combined MLIS/LLB, MLIS/MBA, and MLIS/MPA degrees at Dalhousie University, designed to not only capture students with interests in other professional areas but also promote expanded career options. Public-sector funding cutbacks have already meant traditional functions and positions are being combined, being realigned, or disappearing altogether. Different sets of competencies are and will continue to be sought.

Professionals with other training and qualifications are entering the library workforce: specialists in human resources, accounting, or computer technology. Just as these functional specialists choose to work in libraries, library school graduates are now using their diverse training in other careers. Lynne Howarth, former dean of the Faculty of Information Studies at University of Toronto's library school, notes that "45% of our students go on to careers other than libraries or archives, as Web designers, researchers in competitive intelligence, information brokers, content managers or knowledge managers."[2] Common wisdom indicates that this generation will change careers many times over the course of their working lives. Research evidence suggests that disenchantment with the corporate world may bring LIS professionals back to the library in later life, when higher-level, better-paid job opportunities might be plentiful in the face of baby boomer retirements.

Given these blurred lines, the association has two missions: to welcome the specialists into the library fold and to encourage the library graduates who choose another early career path to keep their options open by maintaining their links through the national association. The key to both is to create and communicate a strong and supportive culture by promoting our core values.

Generational Values

Much has been written about the demographics and psychographics of North American society. Characteristic work values have changed significantly with the four "generations" of workers in the LIS sector, what John Izzo and Pam Withers call the "values shift."[3] They list six expectations the new workforce holds: balance and synergy, work as a noble cause, personal growth and development, partnership, community at work, and trust. As Izzo and Withers state, "All their early independence has made them averse to rules and hierarchy, yet they long for mentoring, community, and recognition. They want the benefits of community—belonging—without its bane (rules, procedures, and structure)."[4] While their findings refer to the workplace, the same conclusions are just as appropriate in an association context.

Baby boomers—who historically have dominated the LIS sector—are known for being team players and caring about what others think. They like process, talking about ideas, participation, and consensus. Contrast that with the newer generations.

The LIS sector now includes both Generation X (born between the early 1960s and late 1970s) and Generation Y (born between the late 1970s and mid-1990s). Generation X has been characterized by bluntness, a desire to work alone and take care of themselves, a desire for quick results, a preference for peers rather than authority, a distaste for bureaucracy, and a lack of concern for what others think.

Generation Y prefers collegiality, collaboration, and intellectual challenge. Born into a digital world, members of Generation Y are socially competent, optimistic, and enthusiastic multitaskers who possess a practical morality and thrive on choice.

Following on from X and overlapping Y is the millennial generation, the group now entering universities and part of the LIS sector in the near future. As characterized by Diana Oblinger,[5] millennials "gravitate toward group activity, identify with their parents' values and feel close to their parents; spend more time doing homework and housework and less time watching TV; believe 'it's cool to be smart'; are fascinated by new technologies; are racially and ethnically diverse; and often have at least one immigrant parent." Oblinger adds their learning preferences "tend toward teamwork, experiential activities, structure, and the use of technology. Their strengths include multitasking, goal orientation, positive attitude, and a collaborative style." Thus the positive characteristics of Generation Y are continuing with the millennial generation. Their values bode well for the longevity of the association, as long as they are taken into consideration.

Today's era is all about choice. Just as they expect choice at Starbucks, the young want choice in their career paths. They want support in their job search. They value networking opportunities, not only in a job-related context but also for professional development. They prefer a personal approach—to be treated as an individual, "not just a number." They like internships that provide an opportunity to get grounding in library operations rather than tie them into one defined area. Association membership should provide "professional satisfaction."[6] They want experienced volunteers to introduce them to committees of interest to them.

As multitaskers they are extremely comfortable with technology and expect the association to use it fully for their benefit. They also expect communication to be fast, frequent, and targeted to them, not "one size fits all." "Just in time" is no longer good enough: They want "just for me."

It is also vital to recognize the cultural diversity of our potential membership. While a survey of the seven Canadian library schools shows a predominately white female student populace,[7] the picture seems to change somewhat at the library technology programs. There are more of these programs across the country; the fees are lower and the duration shorter, which makes them a more accessible option for new Canadians. These programs also attract mature students who have been in the workforce already. They might want to gain a new qualification and career, or they may be experienced library assistants who have been encouraged—or even sponsored—to gain a library technology diploma.

Here's an interesting question to consider: As the baby boomers (and male library directors) retire, will there be a shift in the gender balance at senior administrative levels? If so, what effect will it have on association membership, either individual or institutional?

THE CANADIAN LIBRARY ASSOCIATION TODAY

CLA, founded in 1946, is composed of five divisions and has twenty-three interest groups. It is governed by an elected executive council. Membership is open to both individuals and institutions, and as of December 2003, membership stood at 2,085 personal and 450 institutional members.

Unlike the American Library Association (ALA), CLA has no regulatory role in the profession. Library degree programs in Canada are accredited by ALA, and as members of the Association for Library and Information Science Education (ALISE), the library schools have input into accreditation processes.

The Writing the Future commission, appointed to examine CLA's role and future, found the association had little relevance to many in the LIS community.[8] CLA struggled to define a clear role in the face of approximately 150 other library-related associations in Canada. Members felt undervalued and that their needs were not being met.

The commission recommended that CLA concentrate on being the national policy and advocacy voice of the LIS community: promoting the community's value to government, employers, Canadians, and beyond. A second recommendation was to enhance the value of membership through professional development and other services.

Recruitment, Retention, and the Member Gap

The issue the sector faces in recruitment in this new era is echoed in association recruitment. As in the sector as a whole, the majority of association members are baby boomers—more than 50 percent of CLA members are over the age of forty-six—who may be out of step with the generations that follow.

The dearth of permanent positions in the LIS sector in the 1980s and 1990s created a member gap in the association. Many graduates eked out a living from term contract to term contract, worked outside their field at low-status jobs, or emigrated to find work.

This group of graduates—largely from Generation X—grew up in a recession when markets and marriages were collapsing; parents and older siblings were losing jobs and homes; and governments were cutting back services. When the job market improved, it was hard for them to catch up. Others perhaps just gave up and followed other paths.

The larger associations could have played a role at that time as a force for professional support and continuity, but sadly it appears they did not. The small local associations became the focus for the more determined graduates because membership was inexpensive, supporters were close at hand and understood the local job scene, and employers were often present at events. Networks built among peers perhaps contributed to a sense of detachment from the profession's decision makers and the view that the national association was out of touch with their needs, thus the membership gap.

To ensure the viability of the national association, the recruitment of younger members is vital. It is important to recognize not only their predominant traits but also the biases of current baby boomer association leaders, who, due to the level of commitment and support required, are likely to continue to be the source of leadership for some time.

The abundance of positions when baby boomers graduated gave them the luxury of choice from multiple offers. That luxury disappeared in the 1980s and 1990s. As the boomers pass through the system, younger members will come into their own, and choice will reemerge for those who are adaptable. They will bring their own approach to volunteerism and decision making. Not necessarily team players, the manner in which they conduct association business may well change to a more decentralized, incremental approach.

Association agendas will focus not on what matters to the leadership but on what matters to the potential membership. According to Neil Howe and Bill Strauss, the biggest problem millennials see for their generation is "the poor example that adults set for kids."[9] That comment can apply just as well in an association setting.

Many younger workers are employed by library vendors. They have a lot to offer and would learn much from networking with the librarians who use their products. Many have library qualifications and face their own challenges in this era of convergence and takeovers.

THE DIFFERING ROLES OF LIBRARY ASSOCIATIONS

Clearly defined roles for the different levels of library associations maximize their collective effectiveness. While provincial, regional, local, and discipline-specific associations have clear mandates, it is often difficult to put realistic parameters on the national association's mandate. Attempts to cover too many aspects with limited resources weaken the association's effectiveness. Future sustainability will require recognition of how those differing roles can complement each other.

Role of the National Association

The national association exists to provide leadership to the sector and the profession. Its national profile allows access to federal government policy and budget framers, and its national voice can speak on the areas of library education and employment. As the voice of the LIS community, the national association sets the agenda.

CLA's mission is to promote, develop, and support library and information services in Canada and to work in cooperation with all who share our values in order to present a unified voice on issues of mutual concern. Unlike many other national library associations, CLA doesn't specify a role in promoting the profession of librarianship. While it is implicit in its relationship with the library schools, the more general statement recognizes the LIS community as wider than that. The association can serve an important function in promoting paraprofessionals and others, not only to the external community of government, employers, and the general public but also to the professional membership, who may be accused at times of underestimating their contribution.

The national association has a responsibility to build a community of shared values. Because of personal circumstances, many library workers took some library courses but were unable to complete a degree or diploma. Libraries depend on these workers who don't fit neatly into categories but who have much to offer the association as active members. For those working in small or isolated libraries—particularly those new to the field—the association can be viewed as a social and professional hub from which they can be directed toward the people and knowledge they seek. By building the community, the national association develops an identifiable culture.

Associations Provide Value for Membership

The national association looks for a balance between its role as the national advocate for libraries and its relevance to the individual member. Clear linkages are essential to enable each member or prospective member to see exactly how the association's work has personal relevance. Although members of this generation want choice, with so many associations competing for their membership, they need to see a clearly defined role for the national association that offers a vision of what benefits joining will bring.

The LIS community is an information culture. At our best, we consider all pertinent information before reaching a rational decision. At our worst, we can be a hearsay culture, passing on perceptions about our association that may be invalid. Such strong opinions, often based on poor handling of a past issue or lack of appropriate recognition, have the ability to deter potential members. A culture of openness, transparency, and trust is of prime importance.[10]

Recruitment and retention of members are fundamental issues for all associations, and they are essentially services marketing issues. Becoming an association member is in effect the purchase of services. A service is by definition an experience, and experiences are intangible to the purchaser until one has experienced them. Marketing association membership is marketing intangibles.

Marketing literature states that the most powerful advertising medium is word of mouth from peers. Thus the best way to market an association is to provide members with positive experiences, which they will then talk about to their colleagues, members and nonmembers alike. We know that Gen Xers rely on peers rather than authority. Word of mouth carries weight with them.

According to services marketing literature, to overcome the difficulty of determining which service to buy, customers base a large part of their buying decision on their impression of the service provider. Thus the second-best marketing technique is to have face-to-face interaction between the prospective member and the service provider.

In a vast country such as Canada, people understand the challenges of face-to-face meetings, and consequently high value is given to them. Further, meeting people in their own environment shows interest in and commitment to them. Thus the national association strives to maintain a physical presence with members and nonmembers as much as possible, despite the cost of travel.

Another key to association sustainability is recognition of the diverse opinions of what constitutes value to members. Surveys have revealed the following reasons to join library associations: opportunities for networking; promotion or tenure in academic libraries; opportunities to keep abreast of professional issues; continuing education; and opportunities for volunteering, public speaking, and publishing. Those starting out in their careers will focus on networking, mentoring, continuing education, and career advancement. The baby boomers in the last ten years of their career have other priorities: destination conferences, perhaps; consortial issues; and succession planning. The association needs a balance of members so all have something to offer and something to learn from one another. This interaction is what builds culture and strengthens values, which in turn builds the identity of the library of the future.

Particular challenges for new graduates are low entry salaries and large student loans. Canadian students are graduating today with debt the equivalent of a mortgage to graduates of the 1960s and 1970s, and without a house to show for it. They have borrowed to invest in their education, and they want a quick return. Their discretionary funds are meager, so they need to see that what they spend will have a direct benefit. They must be convinced that investing in association membership is an investment in career advancement. Many will choose to join a local association for networking purposes because the cost is often low and the social benefit is high. The challenge for the national association is to convince the graduate the *value* of membership makes it a high priority on a tight budget. A successful association stays alert to perceived changes in the cost/benefit equation, and fine-tunes it accordingly, as trends emerge.

Associations Play an Integral Part in the
Continued Education of the LIS Community

The changing nature of library education and positions means more crossover, flexibility, and movement. With increased competition to fill vacancies, recruitment crosses the traditional boundaries of library type. Associations play a role in helping new appointees learn the culture of their new sectors.

Collaboration with other associations is perhaps the key to maximizing member benefits. In 2003, CLA and ALA held their first joint conference in forty years. CLA members, accustomed to annual attendance of approximately 1,100, found themselves among 17,600 participants, with the benefit of access to over 300 educational sessions and 2,500 different programs, meetings, and social events.

Members desire reasonably priced and convenient continuing education opportunities through their associations. In recognition of the limited market, a collaborative, noncompetitive approach to conferences and workshops makes sense. Distance issues can be addressed by co-offering e-learning, regional, and local sessions of interest to the community. The national association can play a role by developing a system of credit for sessions attended, courses taken, and volunteer positions held.

A strong fund-raising arm is essential to raise scholarships for prospective students and members who want to pursue continuing education opportunities. When students and members see the link between funds and opportunities for advancement, the association's importance in their career paths becomes self-evident. Competition for scholarships becomes a promotional tool in itself. Personal success stories by those who have won scholarships can help perpetuate the importance of association membership.

Associations Must Foster a Wide Range of Volunteers

A study by Independent Sector found young people will give less time to volunteering and prefer shorter, sporadic projects; the tasks they will undertake must be meaningful, not menial.[11] Younger members want wise use of their valuable time, an enjoyable experience, good people to work with, personal reward, and enhanced self-esteem.

Most long-standing associations currently face perceptions of being "old boys' and girls' clubs." The baby boomers are by nature collaborative. Many have worked in the same institutions for a long time. They have built professional networks through their work and their association activities, so they tend to call on people they know they can rely on when looking for fellow volunteers. The Gen Xers, on the other hand, rarely had the luxury of steady employment in one place to enable them to build their professional networks in the same way. They missed out on regular conference attendance and other opportunities to build and reinforce their networks. Thus it appears to them that they are being excluded by a clique, when perhaps the boomers are just co-opting others in their own image because they know them best. The association can counteract this trend by being inclusive and inviting input at all levels. The retirement issue means the volunteer base has to be renewed. Young potential volunteers are interested in the issues facing the community and want to see their opinions welcomed and valued. To make it easy for them to get involved, CLA forms committees with an eye to diversity in experience and background.

Gen Xers hold peer relationships in high regard. Active young members can be champions of the association to their peers. Their generational traits suggest they will respond if the association earns their trust and loyalty and capitalizes on their energy. However, the association's advocacy message is that we value not just libraries but also those who work in them. To reinforce this point, and to emphasize that a dynamic and successful association is member driven, CLA recently redrafted its mission statement: "CLA is my advocate and public voice, educator and network. We build the Canadian library and information community and advance its information professionals."

Before the full brunt of retirements is felt, it is vital to recognize the diversity of the association's entire community of members and potential members now and in the future: the range of ages and experience, ethnic and cultural backgrounds, qualifications and interests, and values and priorities. The association culture must be built while recognizing—and indeed celebrating—this diversity, all within a framework of mutual respect. The synergy that comes from all these sectors being represented is the association's best hope for moving forward.

Many senior professionals are willing to share their expertise and wisdom. As they reach retirement and beyond, they have much to offer the younger sector of the community. They can facilitate volunteer involvement by using their extensive networks to recommend potential volunteers for a specific task group or committee. Mentoring helps both the younger and the older in the partnership. Experience has shown that mentors often become reinvigorated from the experience as they realize they still have something valuable to offer.

The Northern Exposure to Leadership Institute (NELI) identifies potential leaders among young professionals and provides an intense yet supportive learning environment under the mentorship of senior volunteers, often CLA past presidents. This connection often encourages NELI graduates to become active in CLA.

One paradox associations face is that while members expect a strong and transparent underlying organizational structure, few want to be involved in it. Strategic planning is not perceived as valuable or even necessary, and members ask why we don't stop planning and start doing. They want to see results in terms of benefits, services, and incentives. Many will contribute through committee work, but only a few want to work on committees associated with what they see as internal issues. The further paradox is that output can't be achieved without careful strategic input, conducted on a continuous basis and supported by committees. This ongoing strategic work has to be the "white noise" of the association so that it doesn't intrude on interactions with its members. As an analogy, a well-received play gives credit to the actors, with the subtle work of the director largely unnoticed. The best plays happen when everyone knows their roles in creating a successful product.

THE NATIONAL ASSOCIATION: LIGHTING THE WAY

We originally considered "Leading the Charge" as the title for this chapter. We are not convinced, however, that associations will lead the charge in the library's future. Since associations are fundamentally service providers, we consider "Lighting the Way" a better description of the national association's role. The library's future will benefit from a close relationship between the professional schools, the national association, and employers. The national association is well positioned to provide the input the schools need to shape their future direction. We can learn from many countries, particularly developing economies, where the national association was the thrust that drove the development of the library schools.

The Library Schools

The national association is positioned to work closely with the library schools and library technology programs. This function sets it apart from provincial or local associations. Active promotion to these students begins by visiting their campuses, demonstrating the value of association membership, and providing a framework of information about the community they are entering. Such meetings provide an opportunity to outline library values and can emphasize the link between association membership and successful job search and promotion.

The Canadian library school programs will continue to be accredited by ALA and are thus subject to the trends and forces affecting our neighbors to the south. Trained library workers immigrating to Canada can go some way in mitigating the effects of mass retirements. The national association can play a role with the library schools in developing a path for those with foreign credentials to become fully accredited on Canadian terms.

The Employers

A common complaint from library school students is their education is not connected to the working world they are about to enter. Employers must also be part of the equation in building a strong LIS community. Just as for association members, employers also need perceived value for money.

The association must make the case for the integral role association membership and participation plays in their employees' professional development. What the association brings to the table, in both formal continuing education programs and the informal benefits of networking, needs to be tangible.

Employers in turn will contribute by paying at least some of the dues, allowing paid leave for conference and meeting attendance, and paying all or some of the costs provided the association can answer this question: What will employees bring to their work that justifies this financial and other support?

Libraries have been considered under threat from the age of technology for many years, yet those at upper levels in charge of funding them continue for the most part to do so. New library buildings and information commons continue to be built. One could argue then that library advocacy at this level is paying off. However, what is lacking is advocacy from direct employers of library staff, and associations and library schools should work together on an advocacy strategy. A benefit for the schools and the profession would be that in the face of mass retirements, employers might provide support for good staff with experience and partial credentials to become fully qualified. As competition for professional staff becomes fiercer, employers may find their hands tied on salary issues by collective agreements, but the extras they can throw into the mix such as association support may become important bargaining chips. In academic libraries, where professional activities are usually a prerequisite for advancement, it makes sense that librarians at the lower end of the salary scale (often paying off large student loans) should have financial support for these activities.

One side effect of the recruitment crisis libraries are facing is that opportunities for quick advancement for talented young graduates will abound. The national association can play a key role in honing their leadership skills through active participation. An added benefit will come from their exposure through the association to potential employers competing for the brightest and best.

The future of the library and the profession goes hand in hand. A closer, strategic relationship between the national association, the employers, and the schools will bridge the ivory tower and the practical world. This alliance will ensure there is a clear continuum to attract people to the profession—from school age to mature career rethinkers. The profession is known for its organization, orderliness, and rational thinking: The three pillars of the profession should reflect that.

Associations and the Future

Associations are the most effective mechanism for creating the future. The national association can act as the crucible for the recasting of the profession and the library. What has to change is the number of associations fishing from the same membership pond. Alliances and mergers will happen, as was the case with the Library Association and the Institute of Information Scientists in the United Kingdom (now the Chartered Institute of Library and Information Professionals). At the very least, the national association must develop collaborative programs with associations at the local and regional levels, with resources pooled to provide quality experiences for members.

In the advocacy context, working in collaboration with provincial and local associations, the national association can take a mentoring/umbrella role to ensure that a common message is conveyed to government and media. Resources of talent, pooled among associations to address common concerns, also serve the membership at large and reduce perceived competition and divisiveness.

Joining forces with associations across professional boundaries is another trend that will continue to grow as convergence dictates many facets of the information society. Canada's Copyright Forum, for example, is made up of thirteen national library, education, archives, and museum associations.

A unified voice on advocacy issues is a powerful lobby. It has the benefit of being heard locally, regionally, and nationally, at all levels of government. As the national association participates in the International Federation of Library Associations and Institutions (IFLA), that unified voice becomes even stronger. Reviewing policies and positions formed at the international level, and testing and applying them at the national level, creates synergies that build the community far beyond the registered membership of the individual association. That strength in turn motivates nonmembers to join the community. To borrow from W. P. Kinsella, "If you build it, they will come." The value members gain from the association experience will be reflected back in their working life.

The generational profile of those entering the community in the next ten years is very encouraging. Their sense of responsibility, desire for structure, multitasking capabilities, and embrace of new technology are all values that mesh very well with the LIS community. Their expectation of good service coupled with their ethical sense suggests they will recognize the importance of providing good library service. Their civic ideals suggest that the democratic role of the library in society will be assured and well protected. Because the Internet has diminished any sense of distance for them, they tend to be global in their outlook.

It is the association's responsibility to ensure that this generation remains relevant and nimble, to support its members in the pursuit of their career and life goals. The national association, working through its membership in IFLA, can bring the world into their working lives.

Those who argue that technology will soon render physical libraries obsolete might also argue that key elements of association membership—networking, continuing education, and publications—will take place in a virtual environment and thus render a physical association presence unnecessary. The human need for interaction coupled with the fundamental values shared by members of the LIS community means this is unlikely to happen. More likely, given the strengths of the millennial generation, technology will be exploited to break down tasks; minimize time spent on routine, unrewarding activities; and enhance communication by creating e-communities, thus ensuring what remains is productive, inclusive, direct, and vital. Emphasis will therefore be on personal involvement and contribution to a greater good.

Associations provide the professional and social glue that bonds the LIS community. If they are not there to light the way, we will all stumble in the dark. Library workers will be isolated in pockets of activity, with limited frames of reference. Continuing education and professional development will be picked up and shaped by the commercial sector.

Library schools function in academic institutions already perceived by many as invaded by corporatization and commercialism. Directors and collections librarians already worry that aggregation and vendor merges are taking collection decision making away from them. With commercial vendors assuming the collection development role, the medium—to paraphrase Marshall McLuhan—really will become the message.

Without a national association to develop information policy and advocate for the community, policy fragmentation and contradiction will result. Mixed messages will not sit well with government funding agencies. The community's profile will diminish, salaries will stagnate, and an overall weakening of the profession will result.

The national association upholds and promotes the underlying values of our community. In its absence, who will stand up for intellectual freedom when it is challenged? Who will provide a forum for the millennials to exercise their social conscience?

The national association lights and leads the way. Integrating the library schools and the employers, advocating for them in government, and meeting the needs of individual members, the national library association moves the community forward.

NOTES

1. Alvin Schrader, "'More Libraries than Tim Horton's and McDonald's': Capturing the Cultural and Economic Impact of Libraries in Canada," *Feliciter* 49, no. 3 (2003): 142–46.

2. Lynne Howarth, "UpClose," *Information Highways* (May/June 2003), at www.econtentinstitute.org/issues/past_issues.asp (accessed 6 April 2004).

3. John B. Izzo and Pam Withers, *Values Shift: The New Work Ethic & What It Means for Business* (Toronto: Prentice Hall, 2000), 12.

4. Izzo and Withers, *Values Shift*, 36.

5. Diana Oblinger, "Boomers, Gen-Xers and Millennials: Understanding the New Students," *EDUCAUSE Review* 38, no. 4 (July/August 2003): 37–47.

6. Theresa Y. Neely and Khafre K. Abif, *In Our Own Voices: The Changing Face of Librarianship* (Lanham, Md.: Scarecrow, 1996), 368.

7. Jerry D. Saye and Katherine M. Wisser, Students, Table II-3-a, at ils.unc .edu/ALISE/2002/Students/Students01.htm (accessed 5 April 2004).

8. Canadian Library Association, *Writing the Future: Shaping the Canadian Library Association for the 21st Century: Report to the Executive Council of the Canadian Library Association by Its Commission* (Ottawa: CLA, 2001), 1.

9. Neil Howe and Bill Strauss, *Millennials Rising: The Next Great Generation* (New York: Vintage, 2000), 18.

10. Qualities emphasized by Glenn H. Tecker, Jean S. Frankel, and Paul D. Meyer in *The Will to Govern Well: Knowledge, Trust, and Nimbleness* (Washington, D.C.: American Society of Association Executives, 2002), executive summary, 5.

11. Independent Sector, at www.independentsector.org (accessed 21 July 2003).

16

I Don't Wanna Pay If I Can't Play: One New Librarian's Vision of Library Associations

Gillian Byrne

When I was asked to contribute a chapter on the value of professional library associations to young librarians, my first thought was, why me? Associations are not something I think about a whole lot—in fact, associations have meant very little to my career. This naturally led me to my second thought: Why don't associations have any resonance to me? I have been a member of both national and regional associations, attended conferences, and more recently, presented at conferences and even sat on important committees on a regional level. Yet at no point have I ever felt I was truly connected to the aims and purposes of professional library associations. It is something I continue to do because it is expected of me, not because I feel organizations provide me with development opportunities or a platform to advocate for my profession. After many casual conversations with other librarians in my situation, it became clear that I was not the only one who felt this way— many librarians in my peer group have little interest in associations beyond doing what their employers expect of them.

After much musing, I thought it might be helpful to review my experiences with associations to determine why they don't seem to serve my needs as a professional. In doing so, I came up with the title "I Don't Wanna Pay If I Can't Play." What I mean by this is that I associate library associations with organizations to which I pay money but am rarely able to contribute. What I hope this chapter will do is inform those at the decision-making level that membership is not enough to keep associations strong and diverse; rather, the health of the organization should be judged on the *involvement* of its members. If associations want to recruit and maintain young professionals, they must give them the opportunity to make real contributions. A final introductory note—this is intended as a personal account; all opinions, experiences, and errors are mine alone.

SO YOU WANT TO BECOME A LIBRARIAN . . .

Library associations first came on my horizon during library school—in fact, associations place great stress on recruiting members from library school. While I can understand why it is important to introduce the role of associations to the library profession early, my issue with library school recruitment is that I had very little idea of what being a professional librarian meant in library school, much less what direction my career was going to take. Like many other students in MLS programs, I found the structure of the program extremely confining. So despite the great discounts offered on memberships to students, it still didn't seem worth the bother to connect myself with a profession I as yet had little regard for.

Even though I didn't find many appealing aspects of librarian associations, I did think attending a conference would be an exciting prospect. To be sure, it had more to do with traveling than networking or professional development, but conferences do serve as unparalleled exposure to the workings of an organization. Or so I thought. I was lucky enough, fresh out of library school, to obtain a grant to attend a large library conference. However, I was left to choose the sessions I wished to attend on my own. This is extremely difficult when you have yet to choose an area of concentration and, more important, don't have a support network among experienced librarians built up through the job environment. Thus, I didn't get as much out of the sessions as I probably could have. But what disappointed me most while attending the conference was the lack of support and mentoring from the same organization that provided me with the grant to attend.

Ultimately, I left the conference just as mystified about the inner workings of the association as when I started. One could certainly argue that I was not proactive enough, but I really didn't seem to fit in anywhere—I wasn't a library instruction coordinator or a children's librarian, or even working in a specific type of library. The only "interest group" that seemed to fit was new librarians, which at the time seemed to me a case of the blind leading the blind—what I needed was an experienced librarian to show me the ropes, not others in my situation to commiserate with. Perhaps it's not practical to provide individual mentoring to new members, but if associations are using conference grants as recruitment tools, it might be worthwhile to ensure that the experience "sticks." After my conference experience, I certainly didn't think it was worth the money to renew my membership, not when the only benefit seemed to be a monthly newsletter.

I think to make recruitment effective, associations can improve in a couple of areas. First and foremost, provide more support to new librarians as they join. Mentoring should take place not only before and during events but after as well. Following up on an individual basis where possible is one of the most effective ways of avoiding attrition. This is obviously easier to do in small associations, but even larger associations can add personal touches on a smaller scale. Don't underestimate the power of making someone feel they belong. Another possibility is to provide opportunities for new librarians to work with the executive or other important committees. So instead of students winning a conference grant, they could win a chance to sit on the executive and work with that executive for a year. I would argue that the most important facet of effective recruitment is integration. Student chapters and new librarian interest groups are useful as long as the rookies are given the same opportunities to contribute as more experienced members.

MOVING ON UP

As with many new librarians, I started my career on contracts—an important trend for associations to take note of because many contract positions don't have access to professional development funds. This often puts the cost of national associations out of reach. Further, working on contracts often means that people are moving around, taking on different positions in different locations. Thus even regional and/or specialized organizations hold less appeal. I'm not sure there will ever be a perfect membership solution for contract and underemployed librarians, but I was extremely pleased to see that CLA offers a significant discount for those earning less than $40,000 per annum. This is an important development for contract librarians—if organizations continue to recognize trends in the job market and adapt to them, retaining members will be easier.

Now that I have been within the same organization for a couple of years, I've realized another reason I have little to do with library associations: The organization I work for in many ways fulfills many of the roles associations traditionally play. Take for example professional development. The university where I work values professional development tremendously and provides many opportunities for learning within the workplace. There is a culture of team learning, which means that librarians share their expertise in an organized way. Further, the library supports development by bringing in experts to conduct workshops. Associations still play a valuable role in providing professional development within very specific fields of librarianship (e.g., distance learning or competitive intelligence), but for learning opportunities outside one's primary area of expertise, there is less dependence on associations. It is less likely I would spend the money to obtain outside training if my organization is willing to offer it in-house. Thus, I argue that while the specialized associations are able to retain their relevance for professional development, regional and national associations have much less impact in this area than they once did. Of course, this theory is highly dependent on the size, type, and culture of the institution one works for, but I think all organizations, whether small or large, private or public, have an increasing awareness of the value of continuing development. While one hates to base an argument on ignorance, the absence of any role for associations in my professional development indicates to me that associations are not taking advantage of the opportunities provided by the organization shift toward professional development.

Another example of organizations taking on roles conventionally occupied by associations is the mentoring process. At the organization level, mentoring is a far more organic experience. Rather than meet someone, then attempt to develop a professional relationship, you are able to develop mentoring relationships with those people you work well with. In an organization, you are drawn toward those who share your work style and research interests and whose personality is a match for your own. In my experience, my mentors within the workplace have been outstanding in educating me about the profession and helping me make external contacts, two things I perhaps might otherwise look to a library association to do. Many organizations now have formal mentoring processes, which ensures that new librarians obtain career support and guidance without joining associations.

THE RULE BOOK SAYS ...

The organization I work for, and I suspect many others, values association work in its librarians. So despite my personal nonchalance toward associations, I am expected to become involved. In fact, I discovered that one of the most important roles filled by workplace mentors is that they can often get you an "in" (which sadly enough seems to be necessary) to association committees, thus theoretically allowing one to move from membership to involvement.

Despite my earlier disdain for associations, I was actually very excited to be involved in the decision-making process. I hoped it would help me gain a better appreciation for associations and improve their relevancy to my professional life in ways that just belonging had not. What I thought of as "my big chance" came when I was invited to chair a fairly important committee. It didn't take me long to realize that chairing was a rather ceremonial honor—it seemed that anything more than holding the fort was frowned on. It was as if no one wanted anything started that might actually require work beyond basic maintenance. I have since sat on other committees in various associations and have come to the conclusion that this attitude is the norm rather than the exception. The law of bare minimum, as I decided to term it, seems to prevail. Bringing in new people to give fresh perspectives and ideas is absolutely essential for any organization to flourish, but in library associations not only is it needlessly difficult to get involved, but once you are in a position to contribute, it's like pulling teeth!

The other phenomenon I have noted in my brief experience inside associations is the "inner circle." As a neophyte, I thought that if only I could get on a committee, I would get a chance to contribute, a chance to feel a part of something. Now that I've sat on a few committees, I have come to realize there is a further circle to crack—that of the executive. Even with my unfamiliarity with the inner workings of associations, it's hard to ignore my colleagues' grumbling about the "old boys' club" throughout the years. I don't think using such weighted terms is terribly productive, but the fact that even I sensed frustration with the exclusivity of the executive before ever getting involved in an association is quite telling.

I have now seen this characteristic of associations firsthand. In some ways I can see why the decision-making power needs to be centralized—it's simply a matter of practicality within a volunteer association. When you take into account the law of bare minimum, perhaps nothing would get done otherwise. Nevertheless, the level of dissatisfaction this causes among those who want to contribute cannot be discounted. One experience in particular sticks out in my mind: I was chairing an association committee. The executive of that association held a series of meetings, one of which was with the committee I was supposedly chairing. No one informed me! My first thought on hearing about it: Why bother? If the executive wants to do it all, let 'em.

WHAT'S IN A LABEL?

Although hardly scientific, when I told many of my peers I was writing an opinion piece on how library associations affect my professional life, the most common response was a snort of derision and the sentiment, "How about not at all?" Some might explain this attitude by noting that as Generation Xers, my peers and I share characteristics that make us less likely to join associations—we're not team players. Certainly the established thinking about Generation X workers is that they are distrustful of authority and show little tolerance for bureaucracy.

On the other side of the coin, Gen X workers are noted for wanting to be challenged, looking for constant stimulation, and generally desiring much more control over their professional lives. In librarianship, these characteristics are manifested by a willingness to change jobs often, to be less interested in stability and security than in challenging, interesting work. For example, in academic libraries, tenure is no longer the Holy Grail!

As I've noted in my experiences, associations are not the ideal organizations for Generation X workers—the authority is almost totally concentrated in the executive, and the communication between members and committees is almost nonexistent, a certain sign of a bloated bureaucracy. Furthermore, the chances to contribute and to perform challenging activities are nil. Is it any wonder we're not interested? Associations will need to do a lot better at adapting to the needs of the next generations. Maintaining the status quo—somehow assuming that those who follow will develop into the responsible, team-playing librarians of the generations before—will sound the death knell for associations.

AM I IN OR AM I OUT?

It would be very easy to dismiss this chapter as simply one person's opinion—as indeed it is. With that in mind, I think the best way to conclude this essay is to examine one final personal question—when eventually the old guard retires and someone else has to step up to the plate . . . will it be me?

To a certain extent, it is an easy question to answer. My work in the academic profession dictates that I be involved in associations throughout my career, in increasingly responsible positions. It's almost amusing that if I had a job that bored me as much as association work does, I would quit. That's not an option—I can't opt out of associations. Thus I will continue to pay my membership fees, contribute to newsletters, and sit on committees when invited. Yet eventually, I don't doubt I will begin to subscribe to the bare minimum philosophy—doing only what must be done to fulfill my job obligations. I really do dislike the idea of contributing to the mediocrity, but if you don't allow people to contribute, after a while they'll stop wanting to. The fact is, unless associations show they can adapt to the changing needs and attitudes of new professionals rather than wait for them to conform to association norms, I'm out. I'm simply not interested if I can't contribute.

Epilogue

Waynn Pearson

The river of the twenty-first-century library runs through users' experiences.

In 1996, my colleagues in Cerritos, California, and I began a journey of discovery in pursuit of the library of the future. I had just finished reading *The Experience Economy*. Authors Joseph Pine and James Gilmore argue that the service economy of the last twenty-five years is being replaced by an "experience economy."[1] In this new economic era, every business is a stage; to be competitive, companies must design memorable experiences by using goods as props and services as the performance. This approach made sense to me as a model not only for the commercial sector but for public institutions as well. We decided that our primary focus for the design of the facility, collections, programs, and services at the Cerritos Library would be the library visitor's *experience*.

Our goal is not to create experiences for experiences' sake. We believe that positive library experiences provide a creative spark, something that can trigger users' imaginations in a way that is memorable, a way that transforms their thinking. That transformation process is the key to learning. We refer to our new library in various ways: We are an "experience library," a "learning destination," and a "learning organization." I like to think of the Cerritos Library as a "Club Med for the mind," designed to engage our guests in the many pleasures of learning.

Apparently our users agree with our approach. Library use was ex-
cellent before the switch, but since we moved to this new service
model, it's gone through the roof. Circulation is up 63 percent, gate
count is up 94 percent, program attendance is up 120 percent, registration is up 67 percent, website (home page and Clio Institute) traffic
is up 76 percent, and intranet (My Clio) traffic is up 2.18 percent. We
ask everyone who applies for a new library card to answer a few brief
marketing questions, one of which is "When was the last time you used
a library?" More than 26 percent of the people who sign up to use our
library check "10 or more years." Clearly we've tapped into a previously unserved audience.

Not everyone's circumstances are like ours at Cerritos, and your
users' needs may certainly vary. But based on what we learned while
conceptualizing, designing, and building our "library of the future,"
here's some advice on how to create your own version of a vibrant library for the twenty-first century.

DESIGN FOR THE COMMON USER

It's not always easy for trained library professionals to understand the
desires and needs of the average person. We need to look beyond the
customers we already see in the library to the needs and preferences
of the common user. When you do this, you are doing true library
marketing. The point is not to get a small subset of the most scholarly
people to conform to the library's way of doing business. It's just the
opposite—librarians need to understand how regular people prefer
to do business and then plan their services accordingly. We should
strive to understand our prospective users without boring them, talking down to them, or assuming they know what we know or think as
we think.

LOOK OUTSIDE THE LIBRARY FOR IDEAS

Human nature, Fortune 500 company marketing approaches, trends in
the entertainment industry, and research into how different physical
environments affect people all played a part in helping us develop effective library service. Librarians need to worry less about how to exe-

cute traditional library tasks and think more about user-related questions such as "What experiences do people want?" and "What will they enjoy?" Our information gathering outside of libraries was most beneficial in this process.

DEVELOP A STORY LINE

Moving to a new user-driven service model means letting go of the familiar. To get through a period of change, it helps to have a clear sense of what you want the library to accomplish. A good story line can organize the flow of people and ideas. In our case, we adopted a potent blend of history and innovation in our first story line, "Honoring the past, imagining the future." A compelling story line provides a planning framework yet lets your imagination soar.

DON'T LIMIT YOURSELF TO PROVIDING INFORMATION

In the library world we tend to focus heavily on information and the process of finding information. To paraphrase Roy Tennant, only librarians like to search—users like to find. Users want to integrate information into the fabric of their own lives, their own experiences— our job is to inspire and support them in that process. The Cerritos Library does not view itself as the "information place." Instead, we connect imagination with information through users' learning experiences. Our mantra is Albert Einstein's "Imagination is more important than knowledge."

COMMUNICATE WITH MORE THAN WORDS

Learning comes in many forms, and the best learning environments engage the mind, the senses, and the spirit. To reach a broad audience, libraries need to make good use of nonprint and nonverbal ways of getting ideas across. At Cerritos we've integrated print with technology and expanded the definition of collections to include live music, commissioned art works, digital images, story telling, motion pictures . . . and flowers in the restrooms!

GET OUT FROM BEHIND THE DESK

Barriers between staff and users need to be eliminated wherever possible. Instead of sitting behind a desk staring at a computer screen, staff at the Cerritos Library keep their eyes on the users, anticipating their needs and desires. Initiating conversation is strongly encouraged. Roving staff wear wireless two-way radio headsets that allow them to communicate with other staff members and to provide quick responses to user questions on the spot. They also carry PDAs that provide a wealth of information and policies.

CREATE GATHERING PLACES

Our many visits to various civic and entertainment venues gave us a sense of what people are looking for in the design of public spaces. One of my favorite memories revolves around an incident that occurred a few days after the Cerritos Library opened. I was riding up in the elevator with three teenage girls. One of them said to the other two, "Gee, this is such a cool place." Another one said, "It's just like the mall." I was standing in back of the elevator, thinking, "She used the word 'place' to describe our library," and then it hit me that the other girl compared us to a mall. I thought to myself, "You cannot receive higher praise from a teenager." The popularity of the space was reinforced on another occasion when a group of staff overheard a young, enthusiastic library user comment, "All this and books, too!"

ROMANCE YOUR USERS

People want to feel good. At Cerritos we purposefully "romance" our users from the time they enter the public space surrounding the library. They walk from the street or the parking lot past landscaping, fountains, a Refreshment Experience, and sculptures. As they enter the library or wait for it to open, they are entertained by video clips on a large plasma screen. In the morning we want people to feel happiness and energy. To evoke these "planned emotions" we might present, among other things, a movie clip from Rodgers and Hammerstein's *Oklahoma!*: "Oh! What a Beautiful Morning." We might also play a clip from *Rocky*. The alarm goes off, Rocky rolls out of bed, and soon he is running through the streets of Philadelphia with that marvelous sound-track making your blood flow. "I can do it, I can do it!" Visitors enter our library with a very positive attitude, and they love us for making them feel good.

In the evening, we screen other images and movie clips on a spectacular nine-screen video wall to say goodbye to our guests. The last scene from *Casablanca* is popular, but "So Long, Farewell" from *The Sound of Music* is the hands-down favorite. The crowd starts to gather and everyone's eyes are glued to the big screen. Our users sing along with the actors and often perform the dance steps, too. They leave the library smiling.

PLAY YOUR PART

All Cerritos staff are "on stage" when assisting users. They have learned that "emotional leakage" needs to be left behind the scenes. Unless you leave your own troubles at the back door when you come into work, you won't be able to provide a positive environment for your users' experiences. The person you are helping really doesn't care if you had a sleepless night, forgot your lunch, or are having a bad hair day. It is important to create a positive environment for your staff, too. All staff are treated equally—no "professionalitis." Real effort needs to go into promoting your learning organization approach.

MAKE IT FUN

My friend Marty Sklar, vice chairman of Walt Disney Imagineering, advises, "For every ounce of treatment, provide a ton of fun."[2] Give people plenty of opportunities to enjoy themselves by emphasizing services that let them participate rather than just observe or respond. It helps to make your learning environment rich and appealing to all the senses. Fun enhances learning. Making the library a fun place does not mean selling out, dumbing down, or sacrificing quality.

Finally, to create a truly memorable library experience for your visitors, you need to forget everything you have experienced and learned in regard to libraries . . . at least in the beginning. Change isn't just about doing the same things in new ways; it's about doing entirely new things. As Charles Darwin said, "It is not the strongest of the species that survives, nor the most intelligent, but the ones most responsive to change.[3] What you already know is almost certainly based on the "inside out" point of view. What you and your colleagues and the profession have to say about customer service is beside the point. Instead, take an "outside in" approach. Let the users—and prospective users—take center stage and be the driving influence. Walk in their shoes for a while. I guarantee it will change how you understand libraries and library service.

For more details about the Cerritos Library, check out our website: cml.ci.cerritos.ca.us.

NOTES

1. Joseph Pine and James Gilmore, *The Experience Economy* (Boston: Harvard Business School Press, 1999).

2. Mark Sklar, *Mickey's Ten Commandments*, at www.themedattraction .com/mickeys10commandments.htm (accessed 8 October 2004).

3. *The Quotations Page*, at www.quotationspage.com (accessed 8 October 2004).

About the Editors and Contributors

Barry M. Bishop has degrees from the University of Texas at Austin and the University of Houston. He has been an elementary school librarian and a high school librarian, as well as a district level supervisor for two school districts. Bishop has been active in the profession, teaching library courses at the University of Houston–Clear Lake and Sam Houston State University as well as developing standards for Texas State school libraries and the Texas State Library Program. He has been a member of the Texas Library Association since 1979. In his spare time, he, his wife of thirty-two years, and their four daughters enjoy backpacking in the Rocky Mountains. Bishop also loves to read.

Melody Burton is a reference librarian in the humanities and social sciences at Queen's University. She has also worked at the University of Alberta, York University, and the University of Windsor. Her current interests include creating a learning commons, assessment of electronic resources, and jazz.

Don Butcher has been executive director of the Canadian Library Association since 2002. He has worked in the not-for-profit field for eighteen years, the last ten in professional associations. He holds a BA in sociology and urban studies from York, a bachelor of journalism from Carleton University, and a master of business administration in not-for-profit management and marketing from York. Butcher is a certified association executive.

Gillian Byrne graduated from Dalhousie University's MLIS program in 2000. She has worked for Memorial University of Newfoundland's libraries ever since, most recently accepting a permanent position as information services librarian in the QEII Library. Despite her reservations, Byrne is a member of both national and regional library associations and hopes to never subscribe to the "law of bare minimum."

Roch Carrier received a bachelor of arts degree (1957) from the Université Saint-Louis in Edmundston, New Brunswick; a master of arts degree (1964) from the Université de Montréal; and a doctoratès lettres degree (1970) from the Université de Paris. He has also received a number of honorary degrees from both Canadian and American universities. Carrier is a fellow of the Royal Society of Canada, an officer of the Order of Canada, and a recipient of the Stephen Leacock Medal for Humour. In addition to teaching, administrative responsibilities, and writing, Carrier has been active in such prestigious cultural organizations as the Canada Council for the Arts and the Théâtre du Nouveau Monde, where he served on the board of directors, in various capacities, over a period of twelve years. He also acted as a consultant to the Canadian Film Development Corporation for six years. He was the director of Québec 10/10, a collection of Quebec literature published in paperback by Stanké, and was adviser to the Quebec minister of cultural affairs. Carrier became Canada's fourth national librarian on October 1, 1999.

Susan E. Cleyle has a BA from Mount Allison University and an MLIS from Dalhousie University. She is the associate university librarian at Memorial University of Newfoundland. Prior to this, she was involved with library systems. Here she learned that technology has a human factor that needs to be nurtured for any library to have a successful automated service structure. Cleyle has written and spoken on a variety of topics throughout her career, including staff development and staff renewal.

Mary Ellen K. Davis has been the executive director of the Association of College and Research Libraries (ACRL), a nonprofit library association, since 2001, and serves on its board of directors. ACRL is the largest individual membership academic and research library association in North America, with more than 12,200 personal and organizational members. She has worked at ACRL since 1985, serving as chief operating officer for ACRL, editor of *C&RL News*, and manager of the professional development program (including national conferences, preconferences, institutes, and seminars). She has an MS in library and information science from the University of Illinois at Urbana–Champaign and an MA in education from Central Michigan University.

Amanda Etches-Johnson is a reference librarian at McMaster University in Hamilton, Ontario. She has a keen interest in the production and delivery of information, an interest that runs the gamut from language to the Internet and everything in between. Her research interests include the role of the library in a social justice context, the use of content management systems in online information delivery, and educational web design. Etches-Johnson is active in the American and Canadian Library Associations and maintains three blogs regularly, including blogwithoutalibrary.net, which grew out of her contribution to this collection and is devoted to discussion of what libraries are doing with weblogs.

Stephen Good is from Kingston, Ontario, and loved that the public library piled books on the windowsills. He went to library school in Halifax, Nova Scotia, and did reference assignments in the public library. He returned to Kingston for law school and went, as often as possible, to the Isobel Turner and Calvin Park branches of the public library. Now working at the Texas Tech Law School Library in Lubbock, he checks out books by the yard for his four children at the Groves Branch public library. Good is married to the most beautiful woman in the world and has never actually worked in a public library.

Ernie Ingles is associate vice president (learning systems) and chief librarian at the University of Alberta. Along with an MLS from the University of British Columbia, he holds a BA and an MA in history. Ingles has served on over 120 professional associations and related committees and has held numerous executive positions, including the presidencies of the Canadian Library Association, the Bibliographic Society of Canada, the Council of Prairie and Pacific University Libraries, and the Saskatchewan Library Association. A key contribution to the Canadian library community was his founding of the Northern Exposure to

Leadership Institute. Ingles has received many scholarly and professional awards and honors.

Patricia Jobb, associate director (public services) at the Edmonton Public Library (Edmonton, Alberta), is responsible for the operations of the library's sixteen locations. In that capacity she has led many library branch construction, renovation, and expansion projects, along with a broad range of initiatives to revitalize and reorganize aspects of public service provision. Having an extensive record of participation in professional associations and initiatives, she sits on the executive council of the Canadian Library Association.

Ruth E. Kifer is associate university librarian for Distributed Libraries (Johnson Center, Arlington campus, and Prince William campus libraries) at George Mason University in Fairfax, Virginia. Kifer has been responsible for the management of the University's Johnson Center Library since 1996. She has an MLS from the University of Pittsburgh Graduate School of Information and Library Science, a JD from the University of Baltimore School of Law, and a BS in education from Slippery Rock State University (Pennsylvania).

Madeleine Lefebvre was president of the Canadian Library Association in 2003–2004. She has been university librarian at Saint Mary's University in Halifax, Nova Scotia, since 1999. She holds master's degrees in classics from the University of Edinburgh and the University of Alberta and an MLS from the University of Alberta. Lefebvre is a fellow of the Chartered Institute of Library and Information Professionals and an associate of the Australian Library and Information Association. She is also a professional actor, which can come in handy in budget meetings.

Irene E. McDermott is a reference librarian and the systems manager at the San Marino Public Library in California. Her column, Internet Express, appears monthly in *Searcher* magazine. She is author of the book *The Librarians' Internet Survival Guide*, published in 2002. McDermott lives in Pasadena with her husband and son.

Louise M. McGillis has a BA from McGill University and an MLS from the University of Toronto. She began her career in libraries at the age of fourteen, working as a page at the Pointe Claire Public Library. McGillis is a public services librarian at Sir Wilfred Grenfell College, the

Corner Brook campus of Memorial University of Newfoundland. Her research interests include web usability and training. When not at work, McGillis can be found at the local public library enjoying story time with her husband and two daughters, Sarah and Jane.

Alison Nussbaumer, a first-career-choice librarian who delights in her profession, has been a librarian for eighteen years. Nussbaumer received her MLS from the University of Alberta. She has always been committed to learning and investing in herself through further formal and informal education. A commitment to developing and applying her leadership skills began when she participated in the Northern Exposure to Leadership Institute and continues today. Nussbaumer has held executive and leadership roles in three provincial library associations and is the president of British Columbia Library Association. She is the university librarian at University of Northern British Columbia. With twenty-plus years left in her career, Nussbaumer wants to accept more challenges and contribute to the ongoing development of librarianship.

In 1975 **Waynn Pearson** received his master's degree in library science from California State University, Fullerton; his bachelor of arts is in public administration/political science from California State Polytechnic University, Pomona, California. For the past twenty-one years, Pearson has worked for the city of Cerritos as library director. He has acted as a library-building consultant, technology consultant, and project manager on several projects. Most recently, he spent six years in a collaborative effort conceptualizing, designing, and constructing the first "experience library"—the new Cerritos Library, where the focus has moved from books, services, programming, and so on to the user's experience, particularly the user's learning experience, as the library's primary product.

Allison Sivak received her MLIS from the University of Alberta and participated in the academic library intern program at the University of Alberta, specializing in data librarianship. She holds an undergraduate degree in writing from the University of Victoria.

Helen H. Spalding was 2002–2003 president of the Association of College and Research Libraries (ACRL). She has been associate director of libraries at the University of Missouri–Kansas City (UMKC) since 1985. As ACRL president, she initiated the campaign for academic and research libraries, encouraged cross-border relationships, and established the ACRL/E. J. Josey Spectrum Scholar Mentor Program. She was elected Online Computer Library Center Users Council vice president, 1982–1983, and has served on the editorial boards of the *Journal of Academic Librarianship* and *portal: Libraries and the Academy*. Her publications have focused on professional development, implementation of automated systems, and academic library advocacy. Spalding earned a master's degree in library science from the University of Iowa and a master of public administration degree from UMKC.

Barbara K. Stripling has been a classroom teacher, K–12 library media specialist, Library Power director, and school district director of instructional services and is director of library programs at New Visions for Public Schools, a local education fund in New York City. She has written or edited numerous books and articles, including *Brainstorms and Blueprints: Teaching Library Research as a Thinking Process* (coauthored with Judy Pitts) and *Curriculum Connections through the Library: Principles and Practice* (coedited with Sandra Hughes-Hassell). Stripling is a former president of the American Association of School Librarians, served as chair of the certification task force for the American Library Association–Allied Professional Association, and serves on the executive board of the American Library Association.

Roy Tennant is user services architect for the California Digital Library. He is the owner of the Web4Lib (sunsite.berkeley.edu/Web4Lib) and XML4Lib (sunsite.berkeley.edu/XML4Lib) electronic discussions and the creator and editor of *Current Cites* (sunsite.berkeley.edu/CurrentCites), a current awareness newsletter published every month since 1990. His books include *Managing the Digital Library* (2004) and *XML in Libraries* (2002). Tennant has written a monthly column on digital libraries for *Library Journal* since 1997 and has written numerous articles in other professional journals. In 2003, he received the American Library Association's LITA/Library Hi Tech Award for excellence in communication for continuing education.

John Teskey is a graduate of the University of Guelph (BA) and the University of Western Ontario (MLS). He has been director of libraries at the University of New Brunswick since 1991, having held positions at both the University of Saskatchewan and the University of Alberta. Teskey has also lectured at the University of Alberta Faculty of Library

Science and Grant MacEwan College library technician program and the University of New Brunswick continuing education library assistant program. A member of ALA, CLA, and the Atlantic Provinces Library Association (serving as president in 1997–1998), he has also served on numerous boards and associations. His conference presentations, largely on topics relating to electronic licensing, networking, and standards, have taken him across the country and overseas.

Paul Whitney came to the Vancouver Public Library on June 2, 2003, from the Burnaby Public Library, where he was chief librarian since 1989. He has been involved in various professional activities since 1989, including serving as president of the Canadian Library Association and the British Columbia Library Association. He is an active member of many councils and commissions, including chair of the National Library of Canada Council on Access to Information for Print-Disabled Canadians and a member of the International Federation of Library Associations' Copyright and Other Legal Matters committee. Whitney has received a number of awards recognizing his contribution to librarianship, including the Canadian Library Association's Outstanding Service to Librarianship Award (2002) and the University of British Columbia's School of Library, Archival and Information Studies Alumni Service and Leadership Award (2001). Whitney graduated with a BA from the University of Saskatchewan in 1969, and in 1974 he received his MLS from the University of British Columbia.